Torah and Constitution

Modern Jewish History
Henry L. Feingold, *Series Editor*

Torah and Constitution

Essays in American Jewish Thought

Milton R. Konvitz

Syracuse University Press

First Edition 1998
99 00 01 02 03   6 5 4 3 2

The paper used in this publication meets the minimum requirements of
American National Standard for Information Sciences—Permanence of Paper
for Printed Library Materials, ANSI Z39.48-1984. ☺™

Permission to reprint from the following sources is gratefully acknowledged:

Judaism and the American Jewish Congress for "What Is Jewish Living?" "Many Are Called and Many Are Chosen," "Zionism: Homecoming or Homelessness?" and "Natural Law and Judaism: The Case of Maimonides."

Commentary and the American Jewish Committee for "Tradition and Change in American Judaism: A Letter to David Daiches," and the American Jewish Committee for "The Jewish Quest for Equality and The American Experience," which appeared as a chapter in *Jewish Life in America*, edited by Gladys Rosen.

Midstream and the Theodor Herzl Foundation for "Chaim Grade's Quarrel" and "Herman Melville Makes a Pilgrimage to the Holy Land."

Conservative Judaism, the Rabbinical Assembly of America, and the American Jewish Archives for "The Confluence of Torah and Constitution," and *Conservative Judaism* 1and the Rabbinical Assembly of America for "Law and Morals in the Bible, Plato, and Aristotle."

Library of Congress Cataloging-in-Publication Data

Konvitz, Milton Ridvas, 1908–
Torah and Constitution : essays in American Jewish thought /
Milton R. Konvitz.
p. cm. — (Modern Jewish history)
Includes index.
ISBN 0-8156-2755-6 (cloth : alk. paper). — ISBN 0-8156-2762-9
(pbk. : alk. paper)
1. Law—United States—Jewish influences. 2. Law—Religious
aspects—Judaism. 3. Jews—Legal status, laws, etc.—United States.
4. Judaism and state. I. Title. II. Series.
KF358.K66 1997
296.3'8—dc21   97-30230

This book, this portion of myself,
is my gift to my grandsons Eli and Ezra
and my brother Philip

By means of [this book] I only intend to impart a single thought. Yet, notwithstanding all my endeavors, I could find no shorter way of imparting it than the whole book.

—Arthur Schopenhauer
The World as Will and Idea

Milton R. Konvitz, professor emeritus of industrial and labor relations and of law at Cornell University, is the author of ten books, including *The Constitution and Civil Rights, A Century of Civil Rights, Religious Liberty and Conscience,* and *Judaism and the American Idea,* and he has edited thirteen other books, including *First Amendment Freedoms, The Recognition of Ralph Waldo Emerson, Judaism and Human Rights,* and *Bill of Rights Reader.*

Contents

PART THREE

Zionism and Homelessness

Preface

The essays in this book are additional explorations and applications of the concepts, principles, and beliefs that I dealt with in my *Judaism and the American Idea* (1978). These essays were written over a span of years but are not, I believe, "dated." They deal with subjects and problems that are perennial. Some of the essays were originally lectures delivered in celebration of the constitutional bicentennial and other commemorative occasions. I have left them in their original fluid style.

I am very grateful to Professor Henry L. Feingold—who welcomed this book into the Modern Jewish History Series, of which he is general editor and which is published by Syracuse University Press—and to Professor Abraham J. Karp for their careful reading of the manuscript and their helpful suggestions. They have confirmed the fact that friendship is a sheltering tree. I also wish to thank Steve Holmes for his careful and helpful copyediting of the manuscript.

Introduction

Maimonides, who is almost universally regarded and revered as the greatest Jewish sage since the fifth century, studied the writings of Alfarabi, Ghazali, and other Muslim philosophers and theologians as well as those of ancient Greek philosophers, but above all he recognized Aristotle as the master thinker. "His knowledge," wrote Maimonides, "is the most perfect that a human being can possess, aside from those who, through divine illumination, have reached the level of prophecy, the most sublime level that exists."

About a millenium before Maimonides, Philo of Alexandria interpreted Judaism in a way that also manifested his familiarity with the works of early Greek philosophers, but it was to Plato to whom he was chiefly indebted. In modern times, Moses Mendelssohn may justly be characterized as a disciple of Leibniz and of Christian Wolff. Hermann Cohen was certainly a Kantian in his philosophy of Judaism. In our own time, Rabbi Joseph B. Soloveitchik was a profound student of philosophy; in his remarkable study *The Halakhic Mind: an Essay on Jewish Tradition and Modern Thought* (1986), there are numerous references to Jewish thinkers but there are also sixteen references to Aristotle, seven to Plato, thirteen to Hegel, fifteen to William James, six to Bertrand Russell, eleven to Newton, and many more to philosophers and scientists too numerous to mention.

If Judaism can assimilate Aristotle, Plato, Kant, Leibniz, and other thinkers, why cannot Judaism take in the best of the Declaration of Independence, the best of the United States Constitution? Why should I not write about Torah and Constitution? I am a Jew who was brought up not in a wilderness but in the United States, where I have been influenced by Torah but also by American philosophers, American culture, American political institutions and political and constitutional theory. I am, in a sense, more Jew than American, because (as several essays in this book will explain) I can see myself exiled from the United States—as Jews were exiled from Spain and Portugal, and as Jews, in our own tragic time, were exiled from their countries in Western Europe—but I could never be exiled from my Judaism. My Judaism is inherent, inalienable. Happily I can claim to be an American Jew, a person who sees his Judaism with American eyes, even as I see my Americanism with my Jewish eyes.

The ancient rabbis said of the Torah, "Turn it over, turn it over, for everything is in it." There are ultra-Orthodox rabbis and lay persons who maintain that one should study only Torah, for it contains all the knowlege and wisdom that one needs to have. There are others, however, like Maimonides, Mendelssohn, and Soloveitchik, who have taught by their example that Torah is open to admit into itself knowledge and wisdom from countless sources, from grammarians and linguists, from historians and philosophers, from art and science, from novels and poems. According to a passage in the Talmud, Torah can be interpreted in seventy different ways. Well, why not the American way, by way of Jefferson, Emerson, and William James, by way of the Constitution and the Bill of Rights?

There are many who fear that hyphenation separates people and cultures; they fail to see that the hyphen can serve as a coupling. Multiple loyalties can be multiple enrichments. A single loyalty can be a form of crippling monomania.

In the famous flag salute case of 1943, Justice Jackson wrote that Americans have the right to differ: "But freedom to differ is not limited to things that do not matter much. That would be a mere shadow of freedom. The test of its substance is the right to differ as to things that touch the heart of the existing order. If there is any fixed star in our constitutional constellation, it is that no official, high or petty, can prescribe what shall be orthodox in politics, nationalism, religion, or other matters of opinion." There must be, Justice Jackson wrote, "no fear that freedom to be intellectually and spiritually diverse or even contrary will disintegrate the social organization."

It is in the spirit of this philosophy, this faith, that the essays in this book were written and in which they find shelter under the rubric *Torah and Constitution.* The union of Torah and Constitution, I like to think, is an enlargement of Japhet and letting him dwell in the tents of Shem (Genesis 9:27).

Oakhurst, New Jersey   Milton R. Konvitz
June 18, 1997

PART ONE

Jewish, Constitutional, and Natural Law

1

The Confluence of Torah and Constitution

This essay was originally the featured American Bicentennial Address at the Seventy-sixth Annual Convention of the Rabbinical Assembly of America. The essay looks at the Torah with the eyes of an American constitutional lawyer or jurist and at the Constitution with the eyes of a Jewish scholar, and each finds himself on familiar, congenial ground. The essay was published in the Rabbinical Assembly Proceedings *for 1976, and in a pamphlet entitled* Jews, Judaism, and the American Constitution *(1982) by the American Jewish Archives.*

1

When we speak or think of Torah, usually the reference is to *Sefer Torah,* the scroll comprising the first five books of the Bible; that is, we refer to a written document. For millenia, however, there has been in normative Judaism the firm belief that just as there is the written Torah; that just as there was at Sinai the revelation of the written Torah, so too there was the revelation of the oral Torah *(Torah she bal-peh).* Indeed, Samson Raphael Hirsch contended that the revelation of the oral Torah preceded in time the giving of the written Torah to Moses, for, he argued, the written Torah would be incomprehensible without a knowledge of the oral teaching. For example, the written Torah states: "Six days you shall labor, and do all your work; but the seventh day is a sabbath to the Lord your God; in it you shall not do any work."[1] But when does the sabbath "day" begin and when does it end? Is it from sunrise to sunrise, or from sunrise to sunset, or from sunset to sunset? The text does not say. And what is "work"? The text does not say. Just as you must know the English language before you can read a book in English, so you must know the oral Torah before you can understand the written Torah.

This, as I have said, has been the belief in normative Judaism. Two thousand years ago the Sadducees, and in the eighth century the Karaites, rejected the oral Torah, the teachings and traditions of the rabbis, in favor of the written Torah as the single authoritative source of Jewish law and practice; these sects were rejected by mainstream Judaism, however, and one thinks of them as having been only historical aberrations.

Although the Bible is the primary source of authority in Judaism, the oral teachings are to be found in the great library of sources comprised of the Mishnah, the Babylonian and the Jerusalem Talmuds, the great collections of writings of the post-Talmudic period, the various codes and other texts, and the responsa (the legal decisions on specific questions that were presented to the rabbis and scholars from day to day, estimated to be a total of three hundred thousand judgments and decisions).[2] This staggering legal structure was made possible by the fact that the rabbis were not literalists, not fundamentalists. According to the Babylonian Talmud, the school of Rabbi Ishmael taught that the word of God in the written Torah is like a hammer that breaks a rock into many pieces. Just as a hammer striking a rock sends forth countless sparks, so too, the rabbis said, every word emanating from God divides into seventy interpretations.[3] The words of the written Torah contain countless meanings that move in different, sometimes even contradictory, interpretations.

The Talmud relates that when Moses ascended to heaven, where he was to be taught the Torah, he saw God placing small crowns on top of the letters in the Torah. He asked why the crowns were necessary, and he was told that one day a great scholar named Akiba would live, and he would be a great, creative legal genius who would derive mounds and mounds of laws from each crown. Moses was astounded that this would be possible, that any man could be so creative, so he asked God if he could not have a prevision of Akiba. "Show me Akiba," he said. God complied, and Moses was placed in Akiba's yeshiva, where he sat down in the eighteenth row of students. Moses did not understand what was said, he could not follow the line of argument, and he grew weak in spirit from a sense of inferiority and frustration. However, when the class reached a conclusion and acknowledged the legal decision, they turned to Akiba and asked him how he knew that this was the law. "Master, how do you know this?" they asked. He said to them, "It is a law transmitted to Moses at Sinai." When Moses heard this explanation, he felt at ease again.[4]

This charming legend points up the proposition that there is a creative principle at work in Halakha, in the development of Jewish law; that although the whole Torah, both oral and written, was revealed to Moses, paradoxically Rabbi Akiba's judgments and decisions had in them a newness that would have surprised Moses himself had he been present in Akiba's classroom—at the same time as they were of such a quality that Moses would have accepted them as integral parts of the Torah that he knew. The legend attempts to express the paradox of the legal process, which is (in the words of Roscoe Pound) that the law must be stable, but it must not stand still.[5] Thus the Talmudic legend says: The Torah is stable; it was all revealed at Sinai; yet it must not stand still. Just as there was a place for Moses, so too was there a place for Akiba—and for Hillel and Shammai, for Maimonides, for Saadye Gaon, and for Rashi.

Emergence of law is possible because man has been given intelligence to meet the challenges of life, not mechanically or instinctively, like the ant or the bee, but creatively, through the work of his rational powers. Akiba was great because he had a great mind, given to him as a gift by his Creator. Judgments and decisions must be reached, then, by the use of logic, knowledge, inquiry, intelligence. By the powers of his mind, Akiba, as it were, transcended the confines of his classroom, reached Moses at Sinai, and heard what the judgment should be, and thus Akiba's decision was "a law transmitted to Moses at Sinai." Thus was the law stable and yet had not stood still.

Another legend in the Talmud gives further expression to this paradoxical process. The Talmud relates that one day there was a dispute between Rabbi Eliezer and his colleagues. Eliezer tried by every argument to win them over to his side, but without success. Then he said to them that if he was right, a certain miracle would occur. The miracle occurred; the sages, however, were not convinced. He resorted to two other miracles, but still the sages were not convinced. Then Eliezer said that if he was right, heaven itself would prove it, and then a heavenly voice cried out that the law always is as Rabbi Eliezer states it to be. At this point Rabbi Joshua rose to his feet and cried out that the decision of the law does not rest in heaven!

The Talmud then asks, what did Rabbi Joshua mean by this? And the Talmud proceeds to give the answer in the words of Rabbi Jeremiah: "That the Torah had already been given at Mount Sinai; we therefore pay no attention to a voice out of heaven, because Thou hast long since written in the Torah at Mount Sinai[6] that one must be bound by the vote of the majority."

Had the Talmud ended the story at this point, the story would have been amazing enough, but there is an addendum that intensifies the astonishing wonderfulness of the legend. The Talmud adds that Rabbi Nathan met Elijah the prophet, who, it was believed, had never died, and Rabbi Nathan asked him: "What did the Holy One, blessed be He, do in that hour?" Elijah answered: "He laughed, saying, 'My sons have defeated me, My sons have defeated me.'"[7]

The point of this extravagant legend is, of course, that the power of the law rests not on miracles, not on supernatural events, but on the intelligence, on the God-given powers of the mind. The charming legend can be read as another way of stating what is said in Psalm 115:

> The heavens are the heavens of the Lord;
> But the earth He has given to mankind.

By making man in His image, by giving man a mind, an intelligence, the Creator limited His own power, His own jurisdiction, and has allowed Adam and Eve and their progeny to be subcreators. It is with their God-given intelligence that human beings work in the garden in which they have been placed, till it and keep it; and it is with the same God-given intelligence—this is what the Talmudic legend tells us—that human beings cultivate the law, by which they subdue the social wilderness and make of it a farm and a garden.

Given this principle, it is not surprising that the traditional prayer book contains the passage from the Sifra that sets forth thirteen principles of logic by which the written Torah is to be expounded, so that by their application to the text new judgments and decisions may be reached. I am sure that the prayer book of no other religion contains statements that so definitively underscore the rule of reason in the daily, ordinary affairs of men and women; for the thirteen principles of logic, attributed to Rabbi Ishmael, contemporary and colleague of Rabbi Akiba, serve more than a summary of exegetical principles; they symbolize the dignity and power of the human intelligence and its transcendent role in the development of Jewish law, and thereby in the order of Jewish values.[8]

As Solomon B. Freehof has noted,

> If in the Bible God speaks through man's conscience, in the Talmud He speaks through man's intelligence. If the prophetic idea that God is to be worhsiped through righteousness is a flash of light in human history, then the Talmudic ideal that God is to be worshiped through the active intelligence is an equally brilliant illumination. In fact, the mood of the Talmud and the later legal studies constitutes a great novelty in the history of religion. It is not the simple-hearted ignoramus, lovable as he may be, who is deemed to be the true wor-

shiper of God, but the man who uses all his mind to search out the meaning of God's law. Judaism is the first religion, and it seems still to be the only one that demands that God be worshiped through the exercise of the intelligence.[9]

2

Most often when one speaks of the United States Constitution, or when journalists editorialize about the Constitution, the reference is to a specific document, adopted in 1789, supplemented by relatively few amendments. Often even so sophisticated and brilliant a person as Justice Hugo Black meant by "the Constitution" that document, which, he said, he always had with him. This simplistic notion of what the Constitution is can be exemplified by the following passage from the majority opinion by Justice Owen Roberts in which, in 1936, the Supreme Court held the Agricultural Adjustment Act to be unconstitutional. The Constitution, he said,

> is the supreme law of the land ordained and established by the people. All legislation must conform to the principles it lays down. When an act of Congress is appropriately challenged in the courts as not conforming to the constitutional mandate the judicial branch of the government has only one duty,—to lay the article of the Constitution which is invoked beside the statute which is challenged and to decide whether the latter squares with the former. All the court does, or can do, is to announce its considered judgment upon the question.[10]

If this "yardstick theory" of the Constitution were true, the work of a justice of the Supreme Court would be simple and easy. The fact is, however, that by 1994 there were over 500 massive published volumes of the opinions and decisions of the Court. Although many of these cases did not involve constitutional questions, many thousands of them did involve constitutional issues—questions of constitutional interpretation and construction. In many cases there are multiple opinions, concurring and dissenting, and this is especially true in cases of constitutional law that have wide and deep significance for the American people.

The plain fact is that the Constitution under which Americans live encompasses a great deal more than the written document—precisely as the Torah is infinitely more than the scroll that is in the ark of the temple or synagogue. The United States Constitution includes the opinions and decisions in the hundreds of volumes of the Supreme Court reports. It includes the ideals and values towards which the Supreme Court decisions reach out and only sometimes grasp. "It is an inadmissible narrow conception of American constitutional law," wrote Justice Felix Frankfurter, "to confine it to the words of the Constitution and to disregard the gloss which life has written upon them."[11] One may venture the statement that just as there is a written Constitution, so too is there an oral Constitution. To maintain that there is only a written Constitution is to be a political Karaite.

In theory, the oral Constitution of the United States was, in a manner of speaking, implicitly or potentially in the minds of the framers of the written Constitution, in the way in which the judgments and reasoning of Rabbi Akiba were in the mind of Moses as he received both the written and the oral Torah at Sinai. In cases involving constitutional interpretation, the justices of the Supreme Court frequently quote from the writings and speeches of the framers of the Constitution, and base their conclusions on intentions attributed to the framers. For example, in his opinion for the Court in a New Jersey case involving bus fares for pupils attending parochial schools, Justice Black said: "In the words of Jefferson, the clause against the establishment of religion by law [the First Amendment] was intended to erect 'a wall of separation between Church and State.'"[12] The theory was definitively stated by Chief Justice Taney. The Constitution, he said, "speaks not only in the same words, but with the same meaning and intent with which it spoke when it came from the hands of its framers, and was voted on and adopted by the people of the United States."[13] This theory or doctrine has never been attacked or abrogated by the Court. Although it often has been attacked by critics— realists and cynics, scholars and journalists—no substitute theory or doctrine has achieved a measure of acceptance or respectability. To be sure, Charles Evans Hughes is often quoted as having said that "We are under a Constitution, but the Constitution is what the judges say it is." However, those who quote Hughes fail to disclose the facts that Hughes made this statement not when he was a justice of the Supreme Court but while he was governor of the state of New York and that the statement was made in a speech. Furthermore, the quoted statement is only part of what Hughes said. The full statement conveys quite a different meaning and spirit. "We are under a Constitution, but the Constitution is what the judges say it is," said Hughes, who then went on to say, "and the judiciary is the safeguard of our liberty and of our property under the Constitution." That is, the judges do not speak with their own voices and words but with the voice and words of the Constitution; the security of our liberty and property rests on the Constitution, of which the judges are our guardians. Charles Evans Hughes was no legal cynic when in 1930 he was appointed chief justice by President Herbert Hoover.

Thus it is maintained that (again in the words of Roscoe Pound) our constitutional law is stable; but it is also an article of faith that it does not stand still. The strongest force that motivates constitutional development is the Court's insistence on the rule of reason. In the exercise of its great power of judicial review of acts of Congress under the Fifth Amendment or of the acts of the state legislatures under the Fourteenth Amendment, the Court has consistently demanded that the laws be shown to meet the test of reasonableness. In the sphere of economic or social regulation, the Court will uphold the constitutionality of the legislation if the regulation is based upon a state of facts "that reasonably can be conceived" to constitute a distinction or difference in governmental policy.[14] Thus, for example, the Court upheld the constitutionality of an Oklahoma statute that regulated opticians but not a business establishment that sold ready-to-wear glasses. "Evils in the same field," said the Court, "may be of different dimensions and proportions, requiring different remedies. Or so the legislature may think." The point that I wish to make is that the Court upholds the ideal of the rule of reason in legislation. Under the Constitution, the will of Congress or of a state legislature is not ultimate. The constitutionality of what it does will be tested by a standard of reasonableness. "I regard it as a salutary doctrine," wrote Justice Robert H. Jackson, "that cities, States and the Federal Government must exercise their powers so as not to discriminate between their inhabitants except upon some reasonable differentiation fairly related to the object of regulation."[15] In certain areas affecting fundamental rights or disadvantaged minorities, the test of reasonableness is much more stringent; the government is required to meet a "compelling state interest" test that imposes a burden that is heavier than the minimum rationality test.[16] However, whether the scrutiny of legislation be relatively light or strict, the scrutiny is on the scale of reasonableness, and so repeatedly the rule of reason is vindicated as the motive force that, in theory, keeps the Constitution stable and yet keeps it from standing still.

One should enter a caveat at this point, however. Laymen often have the idea that ordinary intelligence can pass judgment on the reasonableness or unreasonableness of a law. Thus thousands of newspaper editorials sit in judgment on the Supreme Court's decisions, as do countless letters to the editors. Such challenges to courts have a long history. A dramatic example is the confrontation between James I and Sir Edward Coke, chief justice of common pleas, in 1608.

Coke and all the other judges of the realm met with the king at Hampton Court to confute the notion (instilled in the king by Archbishop Bancroft) that, since the judges were only the king's agents or delegates, the king had the right and the power himself to decide cases. The judges informed the king that since the Conquest no king had assumed the judicial power. To this the king answered that "he thought the law was founded on reason, and that he and others had reason, as well as the Judges." Coke countered this argument with the following statement:

> True it was, that God had endowed his Majesty with excellent science, and great endowments of nature; but his Majesty was not learned in the laws of his realm of England, and causes which concern the life, or inheritance, or goods, or fortunes of his subjects, are not to be decided by natural reason, but by the artificial reason and judgment of the law, which law is an act which requires long study and experience, before that a man can attain to the cognizance of it.[17]

Justice Benjamin Cardozo has given a more elegant and definitive answer to James I and his followers. In *The Nature of the Judicial Process,* Cardozo wrote that a judge

> is not a knight-errant, roaming at will in pursuit of his own ideal of beauty or of goodness. He is to draw his inspiration from consecrated principles. He is not to yield to spasmodic sentiment, to vague and unregulated benevolence. He is to exercise a discretion informed by tradition, methodized by analogy, disciplined by system, and subordinated to the primordial necessity of order in the social life.[18]

I submit that Chief Justice Coke and Hughes and Rabbis Akiba and Ishmael would approve this statement by Justice Cardozo as fully applicable to the jurisprudential process in the Anglo-American and in the Judaic legal orders. Coke and Hughes would say that law must follow reason. Akiba and Ishmael would say that law must follow God. Plutarch, however, has said that to follow reason and to follow God is the same thing. I think that the justices of the Supreme Court and the rabbis who sat in the Halakhic court would agree with Plutarch.

3

There is, as we have seen, a common pool of ideas that are shared, in varying degrees, by the Torah and by American constitutional law. Of these ideas, perhaps the most basic and most significant is that of the covenant. It is one of the most pervasive ideas of the Bible, and is one that has cut deeply into American political thought and institutions.

In the Bible, the word for covenant is *berit*, which is probably derived from the word meaning "binding." Various types of covenant can be found in the Bible. There is, for instance, the unilateral covenant that the Creator made immediately after the Flood, symbolized by the rainbow: "I establish," said God to Noah and his children, "my covenant with you, that never again shall all flesh be cut off by the waters of a flood, never again shall there be a flood to destroy the earth."[19] Chapter 15 of Genesis relates how God made a covenant with Abraham, promising him a son, from whom shall come a multitude of descendants. For Judaism, the central covenant is that of Sinai, which is bilateral and conditional: " 'Now therefore, if you will obey my voice and keep my covenant, you shall be my own possession among all peoples; for all the earth is mine, and you shall be to me a kingdom of priests and a holy nation. . . .' And all the people answered together and said, 'All that the Lord has spoken we will do.' "[20]

At the heart of the idea of covenant is the desire to find a way to impose limits both on God and on man. For each may be limitlessly arbitrary, God because He is omnipotent and man because he has freedom of the will. Arbitrariness on the part of either God or man was a frightening danger. Each had to be hemmed in; each could have only limited freedom of action if the earth was to be a habitable place for Adam and Eve and their progeny. The idea of limiting God may seem a blasphemous conception, but blasphemous or not, the idea is found in many places in the Bible. When Abraham argued with God about God's intention to destroy Sodom and Gemorrah, underlying that argument was certainly the though that God would not act arbitrarily and violate the demands of justice. The same thought is the foundation for Job's outcries against God. Many of the Psalms call upon God to carry out *His* part of the bargain. We ask, in Psalm 115, "Why should the nations say, 'Where is their God?'" At the end of Psalm 118, we cry out: "Arise, O God, and judge all the earth, for your dominion is over all nations." Even God may be nudged to act as befits God, for He has obligations as well as rights, and in all times even pious persons have wondered why God is at times so slow in performing His part of the covenant. The inscription by Albert Einstein in Fine Hall at Princeton University states that "The Lord God is subtle, but malicious He is not." This is another way of saying that God will not again send a flood to destroy mankind; that He will not make two plus two equal five; that He will not commit injustice; that He will not break the covenants that He has made; that God will not transgress His self-imposed limitations.

Now, this daring idea of a covenant between a deity and a people is a special aspect of the religion of Israel. It was taken over by Christianity and adapted to the latter's own theological needs, and it became especially prominent as a feature of Protestant thought, for the Reformation placed the Bible at the center of Christian theology. The Puritans, and particularly the Pilgrims, placed special stress on the idea of covenant, and one of the most interesting aspects of colonial thought was the "covenant theology" developed by Richard Baxter, William Perkins, John Preston, William Ames, and other colonial theologians. Sometimes they were known as the "federal" theologians, from the Latin word *foedus,* covenant or compact—from which derives the sense of "federal" as implying a league or an association, an organization that flows out of a covenant. Covenant or federal theology was based on an effort to establish a ground for the moral and political obedience of citizens as well as a basis for the possibility of salvation. The Puritan theologians found the essence of covenant in the idea of a voluntary engagement, such as an agreement made between businessmen like a bond or a mortgage, an agreement binding two parties. The covenant in the Bible brought God and man together within a single order. As Perry Miller has put the matter:

> The Covenant was a gift of God, yet it entailed responsibility on Him as well as upon men. . . . In Himself He remains an unknowable transcendence, but in His Covenant He freely takes upon Himself a local habitation and a name; outside the pale He is wholly irresponsible, but within it He has placed Himself under a yoke. In His nature, He remains above all law, outside all morality, beyond all reason, but in the Covenant He is ruled by a law, constrained to be moral, committed to sweet reasonableness.[21]

Several significant consequences followed from this emphasis on covenant. One was the nature of church organization. Just as Jews have always considered the synagogue a voluntary association and not part of a hierarchical order, so too Puritans developed congregationalism as their expression of a covenant among Christians who would be fellow congregants. The church in New England thus became a voluntary society of Christians who shared common beliefs and practices. The basic fact about congregationalism, Daniel Boorstin has written, "was its emphasis on the ongoing relationship among men. Each church was not a part of a hierarchy, nor a branch of a perfected institution, but a kind of club composed of individual Christians searching for a godly way of life. . . . What held them together was no unified administrative structure, but a common quest, a common way of living."[22]

A second and even more important consequence of the idea of covenant was its obvious relevance to political life. Just as the church is created by covenanters, so too the political order comes into existence as the voluntary creation of covenanting members of society. Thus in 1620, the Pilgrims aboard their sailing vessel on their way to Plymouth entered into a covenant, known as the Mayflower Compact, in which they stated: "We whose names are underwritten . . . Do by these Presents, solemnly and mutually in the Presence of God and one another, covenant and combine ourselves together into a civil Body Politick." It is an extraordinary statement, without precedent in history, but it was also the most natural thing for the Pilgrims to do, for it was a direct and an unavoidable consequence of their invincible belief in their covenant theology. For how else can human beings limit their own freedom of action but by freely entering into a covenant among themselves?

Another remarkable example of this covenanting force is the covenant made in 1639 by the inhabitants of three towns in Connecticut. In the Fundamental Orders of Connecticut, the inhabitants declared that, in keeping with the words of the Bible, they associated and conjoined themselves to be "as one Public State or Commonwealth" and that they entered into "combination and confederation together" to maintain and preserve the purity of their religion and to make civil laws for their governance. Thus was created a written constitution that established a government.

Thus, by various charters and compacts, the American colonists developed the habit of writing constitutions. The civil or political compact or covenant followed quite naturally from the church covenant, precisely the way the church covenant had come out of covenant theology. The movement was from biblical covenant to congregationalism to constitution. In belief and thought, the steps were easy, though in life the developments were often blocked by strife, and even revolution and civil war.

In the history of American political thought, the roots of constitutionalism are to be found in biblical ideas: That man is born free but is limited by laws ordained by God and by the terms of covenants made between God and men; that men can and should further limit themselves by covenants made among themselves for their own civil governance and by covenants between themselves and the governments that they institute. Thus the United States Constitution is only the Mayflower Compact written large.

No man was more responsible for the success of the Puritan political order in New England than John Winthrop, governor of the Massachusetts Bay colony and one of the most remarkable men in our colonial history. In 1630, while aboard the *Arbella* as it made its way across the Atlantic, Winthrop wrote and probably delivered to his fellow passengers a sermon in which he tried to tell his fellow passengers what it was that they were trying to accomplish. Using biblical language and figures of speech, Winthrop said that just as God had entered into a marriage covenant with the people of Israel in the Sinai wilderness, so too God has made a covenant with those who are on their way to the American wilderness. The articles of the covenant must be strictly observed. Quoting the prophet Amos, Winthrop said that God speaks to those aboard the sail-ship and says: "You only have I known of all the families of the earth, therefore will I punish you for your transgressions." Winthrop went on:

> Thus stands the cause between God and us. We are entered into a covenant with him for this work. We have taken out a commission. The Lord hath given us leave to draw our own articles. . . . Now if the Lord shall please to hear us and bring us in peace to the place we desire, then hath he ratified this covenant and sealed our commission and will expect a strict performance of the articles contained in it. . . . We shall find that the God of Israel is among us when ten of us shall be able to resist a thousand of our enemies, when he shall make us a praise and glory that men shall say of succeeding plantations: "The Lord make it like that of New England." For we must consider that we shall be as a city upon a hill. The eyes of all people are upon us.

The covenant, Winthrop went on to explain, is conditional, like the covenant at Sinai. The people of the colony have the option to choose the blessing or the curse. "Therefore," he concluded in the famous, moving words of Deuteronomy, "let us choose life, that wee and our Seede, may live; by obeying his voyce, and cleaving to him, for he is our life, and our prosperity."[23]

4

In 1730, to mark the centennial of the arrival of the Puritans at Massachusetts Bay, Thomas Prince—New England's leading minister, successor to Cotton Mather, and recognized as the most learned man of his time—was given the honor to deliver the election sermon, in which he was to pay tribute to Governor Winthrop and the other pioneers on the *Arbella* and the other ten sailing vessels, incorporating by reference the Pilgrim Fathers who came on the *Mayflower*, together making up a goodly company of about a thousand persons. In his very notable sermon, Prince in effect reaffirmed the covenantal message that Winthrop had addressed to the Puritans aboard the *Arbella*.

God, said Prince, could have brought Israel out of Egypt and put them in possession of Canaan by His operation of the course of nature instead of by a train of miracles; and in the case of the Puritans, God in fact did bring them to their promised land simply by His operation of the course of nature. According to Prince, there never had been any people on earth who were so parallel in their general history to that of the ancient Israelites as the people of "this New England." One would think, he said, that "the greater part of the Old Testament were written about us." The people of the American colonies, he said, are "a covenant people of God," for they had united to "publicly and solemnly enter into covenant with him, and to love and obey him, to make his doctrines the only rule of faith and his institutions the only rule of worship."

Now, what was the covenant between God and the people of the colonies? The substance of this covenant, said Prince,

> is that he will deal with us and we will carry to him according to his inspired Word. The sacred Scriptures, the promises and the threatenings exhibited in them, are the declared rule of his dispensations to us; and the same divine writings, the doctrines and injunctions represented in them, are the professed rule of our carriage to him. . . . We hold to nothing but what we apprehend to be revealed, taught, and required in them. . . . By our sacred covenant we are therefore under the most solemn obligations to preserve an entire and strict adherence to this divine standard, both in belief and practice, both in life and worship. . . . We also [are] to look on all his past dealings . . . as his righteous and faithful acts according to his wise and well-ordered covenant; they are nothing else but his first and faithful performance of it [his covenant], and by the terms of this sacred indenture we are to expect his treatment of us for the future.[24]

Starting with Winthrop's sermon in 1630, the covenant idea became an obsessive preoccupation of New England's clergy and laymen. Israel became their typological model; New England had become the New Israel; the Bible, particularly the Hebrew Scriptures, became God's covenant with New England. Christian theology had become, as it came to be known, covenant theology.

Soon after 1730, there was a notable shift in New England ideology. The writings of John Locke and the works of Montesquieu and of other political thinkers of the Enlightenment often displaced the Bible as the center of interest. The covenant idea was by no means lost or discarded, but it was given a secular name. Just as God had guided the Puritans to their haven not by miracles but by His operation of the laws of nature, so now the Americans had begun to think that men must be guided by their own rational powers, which were God's gift to them, and to consider their legislative enactments and judicial judgments as an expression of providential rule. *Covenant had become constitution,* God's covenant was translated and extended into charters, compacts, patents, legal enactments; God's rule became the rule of law as administered by courts and legislatures. Theology had become politics.[25]

By 1776 about one hundred fifty years had passed since the Puritans had come to Salem and Boston, but that was not such a long time. The men who signed the Declaration of Independence and the fifty-five men who drafted the Constitution were great-grandsons— and some perhaps were only grandsons—of the generation of Winthrop and Prince. The elements and spirit of the covenant theology were deeply imbedded in their minds. When the colonists revolted against England, they were like the people of Israel who had revolted against the Egyptian tyrants. The American Revolution was first and foremost a struggle of the colonists to preserve their identity as a covenanted people. The Declaration of Independence rejected the claim of King George III that they had the duty of "unlimited submission" in "all cases whatsoever." The English king had tried to displace God as the ultimate sovereign, and this was tyranny—it had to be resisted. From this perspective, resistance to England was first of all a reaffirmation of God's covenant with the New Israel. Further, when the time came to consider a constitution, the people did not think of following the English pattern of an unwritten constitution; they followed the biblical idea of a written compact. Again, the Puritan ministers had shown the way; in a 1729 sermon Thomas Buckingham had stressed the necessity of a *written constitution:* "This is absolutely needful for the well Ordering and Governing of any People. . . . There should be some fixed Rules of Government, and these duely Published, that the subject might know what Terms he stands upon, and how to escape the last of the Laws."[26]

When a legislature proposes to have a statute on murder or theft, no one proposes that the statute name God or the Ten Commandments as the basis for the enactment. So, too, when the framers of the Constitution met in Philadelphia, no one proposed that God or the covenant theology be mentioned in the Preamble. The greatest tribute to religion is the translation of religion into morality, the substitution of constitution for covenant—the conversion of the sacred into the secular.

2

Religious Liberty

The Congruence of Thomas Jefferson and Moses Mendelssohn

To celebrate the bicentennial of Thomas Jefferson's famous 1786 Bill for Establishing Religious Freedom in Virginia, the Jewish Community Federation of Richmond, the Valentine Museum of the Life and History of Richmond, and the Thomas Jefferson Memorial Foundation published this article in Jewish Social Studies *in 1987. The essay also takes note of two other documents that ought to have been celebrated for their contribution to religious liberty, namely, Moses Mendelssohn's* Jerusalem *(1783) and John Locke's* Letter on Toleration *(1689). Mendelssohn knew of Jefferson's bill while it was pending in the legislature of Virginia, and Jefferson had read Locke's* Letter; *thus it seemed fitting that in marking the bicentennial of Jefferson's bill, recognition also be given to the bicentennial of Mendelssohn's book and to the tricentennial of Locke's* Letter.

1

"Take care of me when [I am] dead."[1] This was the cry from the heart of Thomas Jefferson to his old friend and coworker James Madison, less than five months before Jefferson's death. It is a cry that has reverberated through over a century and a half.

What did Jefferson mean by asking Madison to take care of him when he is dead? A large part of the long letter in which the sentence appears is devoted to matters relating to the University of Virginia: the ten boxes of books he had ordered from Paris for the university, seven boxes from London, the room for them and their shelving, the selection of a law professor, and other details. Soon, he wrote, he will not be able to give further attention to the University; and when he be

17

removed "beyond the bourne of life itself, as I soon must," it is, Jefferson told his friend (eight years his junior), "a comfort to leave that institution under your care." By crying out to Madison "Take care of me when [I am] dead," Jefferson of course meant keeping an eye on the institutions and ideals to which both friends were deeply devoted.

At the age of fifty-seven, when he had twenty-six more years to live, Jefferson wrote a memorandum, the first sentence of which reads as follows: "I have sometimes asked myself whether my country is the better for my having lived at all?"[2] He then proceeded to list the things he had done that would account for his days and years, an *apologia pro vita sua*, a procedure familiar in Hebrew literature as a *heshben anefesh*. Jefferson listed the following actions:

1. His first act of constructive public service was making the North Branch of the James River, known as the Rivanna, navigable. This happened when he had just reached his majority. He learned that it was not possible to transport tobacco down the Rivanna to where it met the James. He took a canoe and went downstream and saw that it could be made navigable to loaded boats merely by the removal of loose rock. He raised two hundred pounds by subscription and interested a neighbor who was a member of the House of Burgesses, and who introduced a bill that was passed in 1765 to clear the Rivanna by private expense.[3] Thirty-five years later Jefferson still took pride in this accomplishment—and who could blame him?

2. Next Jefferson listed the Declaration of Independence.

3. He proposed "the demolition of the church establishment, and the freedom of religion." He went on to add that this could be accomplished only by degrees. First, in 1776, was the Virginia act that exempted dissenters from the Episcopal Church from contributing to that church, which was then the established church. This left the support of the Anglican clergy to voluntary contributions by members of the church. In the following year, 1777, he drafted the Statute for Religious Freedom as part of his revision of the laws of Virginia, but the bill was not reported to the Assembly until 1779, and then, with the support of James Madison, it was enacted in 1785 and became law January 16, 1786. (It is the bicentennial of this law that we are celebrating, and we shall have a closer look at it in due course.)

4. He drafted a revision of the criminal and penal laws to make them more humane. His revision eliminated the death penalty except for treason and murder and in general relaxed the severity of punishments and made the criminal law more rational. Jefferson's bill (with some further revisions) was adopted in 1796.[4]

5. He led the movement in the Virginia legislature to liberalize and democratize the land and inheritance laws by the abolition of

entails and primogeniture. These changes in the law had the effect of loosening up the aristocratic, land-holding society by broadening the economic base of society.[5]

6. In 1776 he introduced a bill to discontinue the slave trade, and this measure was adopted two years later.[6]

7. His bill to liberalize naturalization asserted the natural right of a person to expatriate himself voluntarily. All persons, the bill asserted, have the natural right "of relinquishing the country in which birth or other accident may have thrown them, and seeking subsistence and happiness wheresoever they may be able or may hope to find them."[7]

8. One of the bills Jefferson drafted as part of his revision of the laws of the Commonwealth was an act for the diffusion of knowledge. The measure proposed the establishment of primary and what we today call secondary schools; the most promising graduates would be given free tuition at the College of William and Mary, which was to become, by the law that he drafted, a state university. In 1796 the section in the bill providing for primary schools was adopted, but the legislators refused to enact the other provisions because they would be too costly. Jefferson later said that the wealthy Virginians did not want to assume the financial burden of educating the children of the poor. Even though in his own day Jefferson did not see the success of his act for the diffusion of knowledge, its underlying principles were ultimately vindicated, and Jefferson has been recognized as "the chief prophet of public education."[8]

9. In 1789 and 1790 Jefferson imported a great number of olive plants from France, which were planted in South Carolina and Georgia, and in 1790 he managed to get a cask of heavy upland rice from Africa, which was planted in Georgia and which, he hoped, would also be planted in South Carolina, Tennessee, and Kentucky. He expected this species of rice to supplant the wet rice that rendered some of the Southern states "pestilential through the summer." "The greatest service which can be rendered any country," Jefferson wrote, "is to add an useful plant to its culture; especially, a bread grain [like rice]; next in value to bread is oil."[9]

In 1800, when Jefferson asked himself whether his country was better for his having lived, it was by these nine actions that he judged himself. Any one of these would have made a person's honor and reputation. Jefferson might have added a tenth item, namely, his bill to establish a public library in Richmond. His bill was not enacted,[10] but it was a window into Jefferson's mind, and posterity should honor him for it. He probably did not include this bill in his memorandum that we have been considering because the idea of a public library was not a novel one. A public library had been opened in Boston as early as 1653; today the Boston Public Library is the oldest free public city library supported by taxation in the world. Benjamin Franklin had established a circulating library in Philadelphia in 1732, and Jefferson knew of these precedents. However, in 1800, probably soon after he had written the memorandum on his services to his country, while serving as vice president in the administration of John Adams, Jefferson became the prime mover for the establishment of the Library of Congress, which he strongly supported during his presidency; in 1814 his own fine library became the basis for the collection of books of the Library of Congress. Today it is one of the world's great libraries and is, I think it fair to say, one of the monuments to Jefferson's greatness, one that speaks much more eloquently of Jefferson's character and spirit than does the marble building that was dedicated to his memory in 1943.

While only a few Americans are familiar with Jefferson's memorandum of 1800, the provision he made for his epitaph shortly before his death in 1826 is famous. From the nine items he had previously listed, he selected to mention only two, namely, "Author of the Declaration of American Independence and of the Statute of Virginia for religious freedom." He also added a third item, "Father of the University of Virginia," which had been chartered in 1819 and opened in 1825 with Jefferson as its rector—the country's first state university.

The memorandum of 1800 and the epitaph are significant not only for what they include but also for what they do not mention. There is no mention of the important offices that Jefferson had filled. He had been governor of Virginia and a member of the Continental Congress; he had prepared a measure for the Continental Congress in 1784 that was the basis for the important Ordinance of 1787; he had been minister to France, secretary of state in President Washington's first term, and vice president under President John Adams; he had helped plan the city of Washington; he had served two terms as president of the United States; and in 1803, he had arranged and effected the Louisiana Purchase, which doubled the national domain, increasing it by over eight hundred thousand square miles.

Yet Jefferson was quite right to exclude from his memorandum and epitaph the public offices. A person ought to take credit only for his own actions. Jefferson did not elect himself governor or president; he was the recipient of offices to which citizens had elected him. He would not take the credit. By contrast, it was Jefferson himself who drafted the Declaration of Independence and the Statute for Religious Freedom. It was Jefferson himself who planned the University of Virginia. It was he who imported special breeds of olives and rice; it was he who made the river Rivanna navigable. Only these and other such actions could he rightly consider when he asked himself whether his country was better for his having lived. In the draft of his epitaph, he said that "because of these, as testimonials that I have lived, I wish most to be remembered."[11] Jefferson did not need to write to Madison "Take care of me when [I am] dead." The testimonials that he had lived take care of him.

In a letter to Victor Hugo, Flaubert made a distinction between grandeur inherent in a person and grandeur that is conferred by circumstances. Jefferson, in reflecting upon his life in 1800 and again in 1826, removed from his reckoning the conferred grandeur, and we too follow his example and pay honor to him for his inherent grandeur, which he had in the fullest possible measure as the Creator's gift to him—and to us.

2

Just as Jefferson, when he came to prepare his epitaph, chose only three of his actions from a much larger number, so we can choose the Statute for Religious Freedom as the most significant and the most consequential of all of Jefferson's most famous works and contributions. If he had to choose only one act to memorialize him on his tombstone, I think that he would have said simply, "Thomas Jefferson, Author of the Statute for Religious Freedom." That alone would have sufficed to mark Jefferson as a man who had left his country the better for his having lived. By enacting Jefferson's Bill 82, as the measure was known while it was being debated, Virginia became the first state to end by law all forms of religious discrimination and persecution. Jefferson's statute became a model for other states to follow, and its essence became enshrined in the religion clauses of the First Amendment to the United States Constitution.

Jefferson's bill was known in intellectual and liberal circles in Europe, and its career through Virginia's legislative mill was followed with interest. The bill was reproduced in Diderot's *Encyclopédie* in 1780.[12] The statute deserves a place among the most celebrated defenses of intellectual and religious liberty in history. In the eighteenth century the bill had been translated into French and Italian, and today it probably can be found in all major languages throughout the world. By this statute alone Jefferson can be said to have left not only his country but the world a better place for his having lived.

The enacting part of the statute is brief.[13] It provides that no one shall be compelled to support or to attend any religious worship, religious place, or religious ministry, nor shall any person be burdened or molested or in any way suffer on account of his religious beliefs or opinions; that all persons shall be free to profess and to argue their religious opinions; and that such acts shall in no way enlarge, diminish, or affect the person's civil rights.

The enactment thus, in a few words, prohibited any form of religious establishment. It placed religion outside the sphere of the government and the laws of the state. It not only prohibited the establishment of any single church but of all religions, denominations, and sects. The statute denied the power of taxation to the state for any religious purpose. These provisions of the statute became the foundation for the judicial interpretation of the establishment clause of the First Amendment.

The enactment had force in another direction as well: it guaranteed full religious liberty to every person. No person may be discriminated against, or be made to suffer in any way, by reason of his or her religious beliefs or opinions; and all persons shall be free to maintain his or her religion, without prejudice to his or her civil rights. These provisions of the statute became the foundation for the judicial interpretation of the free exercise clause of the First Amendment.

The statute also is important for its preamble. This part of the statute expresses the philosophy, the intellectual and moral convictions, on which the enactment is based. Jefferson's bill is one of the few statutes in American jurisprudence in which the preamble plays an important role for judicial interpretation. The preamble was quoted and given weight in the Supreme Court's opinion in the famous New Jersey bus fare case,[14] the first case that spelled out the doctrine of the separation of church and state and held that the establishment clause of the First Amendment was intended to erect, in Jefferson's words, "a wall of separation between Church and State."[15]

The preamble starts by asserting that God created the mind free. Because God is the Lord of both body and mind, He could have fashioned man's mind to have certain fixed beliefs, but He did not do this, He left the mind free and made it insusceptible to constraint. Attempts to influence the mind by punishments, burdens, or civil incapacitations tend only to beget hypocrisy or meanness. God intended that we should propagate our religion by influence of the reason alone, so that it is an impious imposition when rulers (civil or ecclesiastical) who are themselves fallible assume dominion over the faith of others, claim that their opinions alone are true and infallible, and presume to impose those opinions on others and to establish religions, as has been done throughout the world and through all time.

The preamble goes on to state that to compel a person to contribute money for the propagation of opinions that he disbelieves and abhors is sinful and tyrannical; that even forcing a person to support a minister or religious teacher of his own religious persuasion is wrong. Further, a person's civil rights should not be dependent on his or her religious opinions, any more than on his or her opinions relating to physics or geometry; in particular, depriving a person of public office because of his religious beliefs is to deprive him of privileges and advantages to which he has a natural right. Conversely, a religion becomes corrupt when honors and benefits are linked with external profession of and conformance to that religion.

These propositions that relate to religious liberty and to the separation of church and state are then followed by certain broad statements concerning intellectual freedom and free speech. The opinions of persons are not the object of civil government; government has no jurisdiction to intrude into men's opinions on the claim of their ill tendency. The concluding sentences are a passionate, grand, and moving statement in defense of freedom of thought and of speech, asserting

> that it is time enough for the rightful purposes of civil government for its officers to interfere when principles break out into overt acts against peace and good order; and finally, that truth is great and will prevail if left to herself; that she is the proper and sufficient antagonist to error, and has nothing to fear from the conflict unless by human interposition disarmed of her natural weapons, free argument and debate; errors ceasing to be dangerous when it is permitted freely to contradict them.

Is it any wonder that Jefferson's Statute for Religious Freedom has withstood the ravages of time and that it is one of the few documents that have been kept from falling into obsolescence and obscurity? A few other thinkers before Jefferson had pleaded for religious and intellectual toleration; e.g., John Locke, whom Jefferson considered one of the three greatest men of all time (the other two being Francis Bacon and Isaac Newton).[16] However, Locke called not for religious liberty but for toleration for those who would not share the beliefs of the established church, and he excluded from toleration Roman Catholics and atheists. Jefferson went beyond Locke. Sometime in 1776, when he was taking notes on Locke's *Letter on Toleration*, Jefferson wrote: "It was a great thing [for Locke] to go so far [in his plea for toleration] but where he stopped short, we may go on."[17] He did go on, drafting a statute that has become a landmark in the history of religious freedom. Interpreting Jefferson's language and reading it into the First Amendment, the United States Supreme Court has held that:

> Neither a state nor the Federal Government can set up a church.
> Neither can pass laws which aid one religion, aid all religions, or
> prefer one religion over another. Neither can force nor influence a
> person to go to or to remain away from church against his will or
> force him to profess a belief or disbelief in any religion. No person
> can be punished for entertaining or professing religious beliefs or
> disbeliefs, for church attendance or non-attendance. No tax in any
> amount, large or small, can be levied to support any religious activ-
> ities or institutions, whatever they may be called, or whatever form
> they may adopt to teach or practice religion. Neither a state nor the
> Federal Government can, openly or secretly, participate in the affairs
> of any religious organizations or groups and vice versa. In the words
> of Jefferson, the clause against establishment of religion by law was
> intended to erect "a wall of separation between Church and State."[18]

At this point I want to call attention to a paradox. In interpreting
the meaning of the establishment clause of the First Amendment, the
Supreme Court has gone back to the intention of the framers, Jefferson and Madison; and here we are paying tribute to Jefferson for
what he drafted as a law that was enacted by Virginia two centuries
ago. Yet Jefferson himself was not a man who looked back in time.
Ten years before his death, Jefferson believed that the dead have no
rights. "They are nothing," he wrote. A generation that is dead has no
right to hold to obedience to their will future generations. This earth,
he wrote, and everything upon it, belongs to its present occupants:
"They alone have a right to direct what is the concern of themselves
alone."[19] One might argue from these premises that it is foolish and
idolatrous to pay tribute to Jefferson for a document that he wrote in
the 1770s and to honor a statute that was adopted two hundred years
ago.

However, we are persuaded by a countervailing line of thought.
Jefferson was a firm believer in natural law and in natural rights; that
certain rights are inherent and inalienable, and they constitute essential aspects of what makes a human being; that government is not the
source of these rights; that these rights existed before governments
were instituted; that no person can be deprived of his natural rights;
that no government can be given the legitimate power to curtail these
rights. These propositions are the foundation for the Statute of Religious Freedom. The truth and force of these propositions did not
cease with the death of the persons who formulated them. They are
as meaningful and pertinent today as they were in 1786. By looking
back in such instances to the intention of the founders, we are not
engaged in worship of the dead; we adopt their thoughts and words
as our own; we ourselves become the framers and founders. It is like

the commandment to believe that it is we ourselves (and not only our ancestors) who are standing at the foot of Mount Sinai, that we ourselves are among those who experienced the Exodus from Egypt, the march from slavery into freedom.

It is not fashionable today to speak of natural law or of natural rights. But no matter, for it is quite permissible to speak of human rights. Indeed, when the heads of governments meet, human rights are on the agenda for discussion and negotiation. There is a Universal Declaration of Human Rights, adopted by the General Assembly of the United Nations; the European Convention for the Protection of Human Rights and Fundamental Freedoms, adopted in 1953; the Helsinki Agreement of 1975—all of these and other charters and conventions translate natural rights into human rights, affirming and vindicating the natural law and natural rights philosophy of Thomas Jefferson. They are all based on the beliefs that there are rights inherent in the human being, that these rights are inalienable, and that a government that denies them is a tyranny.

Yes, we have a right and even a duty to look backward, even as we have a right and even a duty to look forward. There is a useless past, but there is also a usable past, a pastness that is congenially present. The pastness of Jefferson is part of our present—and will be part of the future. Jefferson himself assimilated into his presentness John Locke, Francis Bacon, and Isaac Newton; in the same way we assimilate Thomas Jefferson. He wrote, as we have noted, that the dead are nothing, but obviously that was a rhetorical overstatement, due, I believe, to his exaggerated belief in progress. He condemned what he called "the Gothic idea" "that we are to look backwards instead of forwards for the improvement of the human mind, and to recur to the annals of our ancestors for what is most perfect in government, in religion & in learning."[20] People who have this Gothic idea he called "bigots." If Jefferson were alive today, would he think that he was justified in his radical disparagement of the past and in his belief in the inevitability of progress? I doubt it. Jefferson believed that farmers are "the most virtuous and independent citizens," while "artificers"—that is, artisans and industrial workers—are "the panders of vice & the instruments by which the liberties of a country are generally overturned."[21] Today there are only two million farms in the United States, only one-third of the number we had fifty years ago. Instead of the agricultural society that Jefferson hoped for, we have the military-industrial complex that President Eisenhower bewailed. Instead of a society in which swords are beaten into ploughshares, we are members of a society in which ploughshares are quite literally beaten into swords.

Still, there has been progress in a paradoxical way: everywhere in the civilized world there is a firm belief in human rights, a belief that each and every human being, regardless of race, religion, nationality, or sex, has rights that are inherent and inalienable. Thus we have made the past part of our present, and we read Jefferson's Statute for Religious Freedom as if it were written for us no less than for his own generation.

3

As we have noted, Jefferson's Bill 82, probably drafted in 1777 and not enacted until 1786, attracted interest in Europe and was reproduced by Diderot in his *Encyclopédie* while the bill was pending. Among those who were keenly interested in what was happening in Virginia and in Jefferson's bill was Moses Mendelssohn. Mendelssohn was also quite familiar with the *Toleranzpatent*, the edict of toleration that was issued by Emperor Joseph II in 1782, originally applicable only to Vienna and Lower Austria but later made applicable to other provinces. Although this edict continued existing restrictions against an increase in the number of tolerated Jews, some economic restrictions were lifted and Jews were encouraged to establish schools and enter universities. The main thrust of the edict was to encourage upperclass Jews to integrate socially. The edict was certainly important as a milestone on the way to emancipation. Moses Mendelssohn, however, had misgivings, for he feared that it was offered as an enticement to assimilation.[22] Coincident with the developments in Virginia and in the Holy Roman Empire, there was the publication of Christian Wilhelm von Dohm's book *Ueber die buergerliche Verbesserung der Juden* (on the civil improvement of the Jews), which essentially was an elaboration of the policies on which the *Toleranzpatent* was based.

It was these events that motivated Mendelssohn to write his *Jerusalem*, which was published in 1783, directly following the issuance of the edict by Joseph II and the publication of Dohm's book and while there was a great deal of public agitation over religious freedom in Virginia. *Jerusalem* deserves recognition both by non-Jews and by Jews as one of the most eloquent and reasoned pleas for intellectual liberty and religious freedom. Mendelssohn knew the works of Locke, but like Jefferson he took the argument beyond Locke and formulated a reasoned philosophy of total religious liberty and separation of church and state. I submit that it would have been altogether appropriate, as we marked the bicentenary of Jefferson's Statute for Religious Freedom, had we also honored *Jerusalem* on its bicentennial and recalled with reverence the grandfather of these monumental achievements, John Locke's *Letter on Toleration,* the tricentennial of which should have been celebrated in 1985.

Mendelssohn shared Locke's and Jefferson's belief in natural law and in natural rights. The human being, as created by God, possesses the ability to reason and to have moral principles. These are God-given qualities and are not dependent on the state or any other institution. Nor does natural man, or man in society, need supernatural revelation to teach him that God exists, that there is providential governance, and that the soul is immortal. Merely by the use of his natural reason every person can reach these three fundamental beliefs, which are the basis for his bliss or salvation. Mendelssohn took quite literally the message of Psalm 19: It is the heavens that declare the glory of God; it is day and night that give instruction; no words are spoken, yet their message goes to the ends of the earth.[23] True religious beliefs and the principles of virtue are not, therefore, dependent on any special supernatural revelation. They are not dependent on any religion's holy scriptures. Why, he asked rhetorically, must human beings in remote parts of the earth such as India wait until it pleases some persons in Europe to come to them with the message or gospel without which they would remain abandoned by God without virtue or happiness?[24]

By entering into civil society, man does not surrender the natural rights that he theretofore enjoyed, and among these rights is the right to determine his own thoughts and his own beliefs. This right is inherent in him as a human being, and is inalienable. A person cannot give up this right, and it is tyranny to deprive him of it. It follows, wrote Mendelssohn, that "neither church nor state has a right to subject men's principles and convictions to any coercion whatsoever. Neither church nor state is authorized to connect privileges and rights . . . with principles and convictions. . . . Not even the social contract could grant such a right to either state or church."[25] No honors or emoluments and no penalties may be connected with opinions or beliefs.[26]

By their belief in inherent and inalienable human rights, Jefferson and Mendelssohn affirmed that the essential liberty is not a civil liberty but one that transcends any civil or social order, a liberty that is absolute, a liberty that is an essential part of the definition of man—not merely of man as citizen but of man as man. Inherent in that liberty is the essence of one's religion, for it is there that man knows himself or herself as one who is made in the image of God. It is there that man's alienation is overcome; it is there that he or she discovers one's true essence under the aspect of eternity and divinity, that is, under the aspect of one's true humanity.

———

I want to close with Mendelssohn's own concluding words. In a foot-note, he referred to the contemporary agitation over religious free-dom in Virginia:

> Reward and punish no doctrine, tempt and bribe no one to adopt any religious opinion! Let everyone be permitted to speak as he thinks, to invoke God after his own manner or that of his fathers, and to seek eternal salvation where he thinks he may find it, as long as he does not disturb public felicity and acts honestly toward the civil laws. . . . Let no one . . . be a searcher of hearts and a judge of thoughts; let no one assume a right that the Omniscient has reserved to Himself alone! If we render unto Caesar what is Caesar's, then do you yourselves render unto God what is God's! Love truth! Love peace![27]

Although Mendelssohn knew of Jefferson's Statute for Religious Freedom, it is too bad that Jefferson did not know of Mendelssohn's *Jerusalem;* for they were kindred spirits. There are those who are de-voted exclusively to religion; there are those who are devoted exclu-sively to liberty. The genius of Jefferson and Mendelssohn was that they saw that liberty was inextricably linked with religion, for, where there is no liberty, religion can be only hypocrisy, superstition, or an instrument of cruelty, tyranny, and corruption. We pay tribute to Jefferson and to Mendelssohn because they were pioneers in estab-lishing the link between religion and liberty.

3

The Jewish Quest for Equality and the American Experience

This essay was written for the American Jewish Committee's celebration of the Bicentennial of American independence and was delivered as a lecture in 1976 at the Baltimore Hebrew University, sponsored by the American Jewish Committee's Jacob Blaustein Institute for the Advancement of Human Rights. The essay appeared in Jewish Life in America: Historical Perspectives, *edited by Gladys Rosen and published for the Committee by Ktav Publishing House in 1978.*

In a letter to the editor of the *New York Times,* the administrator of the American Revolution Bicentennial Administration wrote: "I have met with many blacks, Mexican Americans and other minorities who sometimes ask with not a little heat, 'What have we got to celebrate?'"[1] I think it is safe to assert that he met with no American Jews who asked that question.

America, however, is the great exception in Jewish history. Not so many years ago, when the *New York Times* reported the death of the celebrated cellist Gregor Piatigorsky, the obituary mentioned the fact that before he was fourteen years of age Piatigorsky had lived through a pogrom in Russia.[2] Indeed, I myself recall my parents discussing a pogrom that they had lived through. For almost two thousand years persecution and discrimination were part of the common life of the Jewish people almost everywhere in the world. The Talmud records that early in the second century, when a non-Jew asked to be converted, the rabbis said to him: "What reason have you for seeking conversion? Do you not know that Israelites today are in travail, that they are persecuted, that they are driven from place to place, that they are harassed and full of suffering?"[3] It is precisely in these terms—ceaseless persecution, trouble, expulsion, harassment, and

29

suffering—that the history of the Jews of almost every country in the world, not excepting even England or France, can be written.

As we celebrated the American Bicentennial, we could not help but think and cry out how different, how radically different the American Jewish experience has been.

1

In the late 1960s, when militant blacks staged demonstrations in various churches demanding a half-billion dollars in "reparations" for three hundred years of subjugation and discrimination, a writer in an Anglo-Jewish journal formulated a demand for "reparations" from various nations on behalf of the Jewish people, including demands on the Vatican for the harm done by teaching that the Jewish people were guilty of deicide and for promotion of the blood libel; on Spain for the Inquisition and for the expulsion of Jews in 1492; on Germany, France, Austria, and Italy, as successors of the Holy Roman Empire, for imprisoning Jews in ghettos; on Arab governments for oppression of the Jews for hundreds of years; on Russia for forcing Jews to live in the Pale of Settlement, for prohibiting them from owning land, for imposing on Jews a quota system that severely restricted their admission to high school and to the universities, and for the forgery of the notorious *Protocols of the Elders of Zion*.[4] These are only some of the claims that could be made against governments and nations. No Jewish writer, however, would for a moment think that America owes the Jews anything, that American Jewry would be warranted in demanding "reparations" from the United States government for any wrongs or outrages against the Jewish people.

Indeed, historians, in searching and sifting the facts of American history, claim that they have found only a single instance of a governmental action against the Jewish people. This refers to General Order no. 11, issued in December 1862 by order of Maj. Gen. Ulysses S. Grant, which provided for the expulsion of "the Jews, as a class," from the Department of the Tennessee, "within twenty-four hours" of receipt of the order. Post commanders were instructed by the order to see that "all of this class of people" be furnished passes and be required to leave.[5] The general order was issued in the midst of a scandal of widespread illegal cotton speculation and illegal trading in which thousands of people were implicated, including federal agents, army officers, and even General Grant's father.

However, the Jews who were directly affected by the expulsion order did not accept the affront and injustice supinely. Three Jewish citizens of Paducah, Kentucky, at once sent a telegram to President

Lincoln protesting "this inhuman order, the carrying out of which would be the grossest violation of the Constitution and our rights as citizens under it, [and] which will place us . . . as outlaws before the whole world." Receiving no reply (it is not known that Lincoln was ever shown the telegram), one of the Paducah expellees alerted the press and especially Jewish community leaders and hastened to Washington, where he induced a friendly member of Congress to arrange for an immediate appointment with the President, to which he was accompanied by the congressman. The report of the meeting in the White House shows that Lincoln had known nothing about the order. As soon as he heard the facts, Lincoln instructed the General-in-Chief to send a telegram cancelling General Grant's order. Three days later Rabbi Isaac Mayer Wise, Rabbi Max Lilienthal, and delegations of Jews from Cincinnati and from Louisville arrived in Washington and were taken at once by two Ohio congressmen to the White House, where they expressed to Lincoln their gratitude for his prompt and firm cancellation of the odious General Order no. 11.

In fairness to Grant it should be noted that apart from this incident, there is no proof that he ever revealed any antipathy towards Jews. During his two terms as president, Grant appointed many Jews to major and minor offices; he appointed a Jew as governor of the Washington Territory and he offered the position of secretary of the treasury to Joseph Seligman (who declined); and when pogroms broke out in Romania in 1870, he appointed the Grand Master of B'nai B'rith as American consul at Bucharest, as part of the government's effort to exert pressure on the Romanian government to desist from its anti-Semitic actions.

The case of General Order no. 11 is deserving of our attention for three reasons: First, as we have noted, historians point to it as "the only instance of collective punishment of Jews in American history"[6] or as the "first instance of something approaching explicit ideological anti-Semitism."[7] I think that one can accept the judgment that "American antisemitism has almost never been official or governmental";[8] but the exceptions to the rule must include, I think, besides General Grant's order, the restrictive immigration laws that were in effect until 1965.[9] Second, the case of General Grant's order is significant for the Jewish reaction it caused. Jews of Kentucky who were personally affected, along with other Jewish community leaders, rabbis, and laymen, reacted to the order with vigor, expedition, self-regard, and dignity. After all, this was not the Old World, this was America, and no one, not even General Grant, and not even in a time of civil war, could be allowed to unjustly abuse Jews and to use them as scapegoats. Third, the telegram sent by Jewish citizens of Kentucky protested the violation of their constitutional rights. There was nothing cringing in their words, no plea for mere toleration or compassion; the Jews took their stand on their legal, civil rights, on their rights as American citizens.

Although it is admittedly hazardous (if not worse) to formulate laws of history, I submit that the course of American Jewish history over the two centuries marked by the Bicentennial celebration demonstrates the following two generalizations: whenever American Jews felt themselves to be unjustly treated, they did not suffer the injustice or wrongdoing passively, insensibly, or obsequiously but reacted with forthright courage, with head erect, and with proud-minded steps; and furthermore, when they felt themselves discriminated against, their resistance was placed on the high ground of constitutional principle and of legal rights. In these important respects American Jews have always acted as a civil rights movement.

Indeed, one can go back to the earliest days of our colonial history for the original precedent of this principled Jewish response to a threatened deprivation. Soon after the first Jews—twenty-three of them—settled in New Amsterdam in 1654, Governor Peter Stuyvesant prohibited them from trading with Indians on the Delaware and the Hudson. On November 29, 1655, three of the Jewish settlers wrote a petition to the governor and to his council in which they respectfully but firmly protested against his action and called attention to the fact that the lords director of the West India Company had given them permission and consent, "like the other inhabitants, to travel, reside, and trade here, and enjoy the same liberties."[10] Also in 1655 Stuyvesant denied Jews the right to keep "watch and ward" and imposed on them a special tax in lieu of the military service from which he had barred them. Two of the settlers, Asser Levy and Jacob Barsimson, petitioned the governor and council for either the right to bear arms or exemption from the onerous Jews' tax. Although the petition was not granted, the records show that by spring 1657 Asser Levy was in fact serving in the guard.

When they were denied recognition as burghers, they brought a court action; and when they lost in court, they appealed to the governor and council, and in their petition the Jews of New Amsterdam said: "Further, that our nation enjoys in the city of Amsterdam in Holland the burgher right . . . as appears by the burgher certificate hereto annexed; also that our nation, as long as they have been here, have, with others, borne and paid and still bear, all burgher burdens."[11] In reply, on April 20, 1657, the authorities acted to admit the Jews of their town to the rights of burghership. As the Jewish refugees from Brazil won their rights to trade with Indians, to stand guard, and to claim their status as burghers, their successes in their struggles for civil and political rights "obtained benefits not only for themselves but also opened the door for other disenfranchised groups. The intolerant Stuyvesant, writing to the Directors in Amsterdam in October, 1655, had thought of this too: 'Giving them liberty, we cannot refuse the Lutherans and Papists.' "[12]

2

According to Maimonides, a proselyte, as he is received into the people of Israel, is forewarned and comforted in these words:

> [A]nd though you see Israel in distress in this world, good is in store for them [in the world to come], for they cannot receive overmuch good in this world like the other nations, lest their heart become proud and go astray and lose the reward of the world to come, as it is said, "But Jeshurun waxed fat, and kicked"; and the Holy One, blessed be He, does not inflict too much punishment upon them in order that they should not perish.[13]

Maimonides, having witnessed at the age of thirteen religious persecution in his native Cordoba and having wandered with his parents for eight or nine years from place to place, settling in Morocco (where he found life for a Jew intolerable) before fleeing to the Holy Land and then to Egypt, could still thank God for not inflicting "too much punishment" on the people of Israel, for they had not altogether perished; and certainly he could thank God for not having bestowed on Israel "overmuch good in this world," such as other nations enjoyed. As an Aristotelian, Maimonides was reconciled to the idea that happiness is attained through following the mean, through avoidance of extremes, which he probably thought the history of the Jews providentially manifested: persecution falling short of extinction, prosperity falling short of absolute security.

At long last, however, after several thousand years, Jewish history can now cite an instance of a Jewish community that, Maimonides might say, has in fact received "overmuch good in this world like the other nations," perhaps even surpassing those "other nations."

For according to the best available evidence and the judgment of the most knowledgeable scholars, American Jewry constitute "a relatively prosperous" people, "in which in its income and occupational profile compares favorably with the nation's high-status Protestant founding groups."[14] This is a relatively conservative or moderate judgment. Another reputable scholar puts the matter as follows: "[T]he Jews have become in every measure one could care to choose the most successful group in American society," adding that this is "a fact which no one at this point would presume to deny."[15] What do the facts show?

A survey taken in 1972 by the Census Bureau showed that of the eight ethnic groups surveyed, comprising 102 million Americans, the Jews had the highest median family income.[16] The Jews had the highest percentage of high school and college graduates: 26 percent of the Jewish population, twenty-five years of age and over, were college graduates; the next ethnic group was the English with 18 percent, and after them the Germans with 12 percent. With respect to occupational distribution, 77.8 percent of the Jews were white-collar workers, only 17.2 percent were blue-collar workers. The next ethnic group was again the English, with 49.2 percent white-collar and 39.4 percent blue-collar workers.

Using a religious rather than an ethnic identification approach, Andrew M. Greeley of the National Opinion Research Center at Chicago finds that the Jews are the best educated Americans, with fourteen as the average years of education. Next come Episcopalians with 13.5, Presbyterians with 12.7, Methodists with 11.9, and Catholics with 11.5. Although the spread between Jews and Episcopalians may not be substantial, that between Jews and Catholics is certainly notable.[17] Looking at educational mobility, that is, given where they started educationally, the Greeley study concludes that although Catholics are catching up with Episcopalians, "Jews are leaving the rest of the American population far behind."[18]

Looking at the occupational pattern, "Jews and Episcopalians and Presbyterians represent the elite of non-Spanish white Americans, Methodists and Catholics and Lutherans, the middle class, and Baptists the less successful."[19] With respect to income, the Greeley study says that "Jewish income success seems to have kept pace with and benefited by Jewish educational success." The average Jewish family income was $13,340. Next followed Catholics with $11,374 and Episcopalians with $11,032; Baptists were in seventh place with $8,693. With a national average of $9,953 in 1974, the Jewish family's income was above average by $3,387—around $2,300 more than the family income of Episcopalians and around $4,600 more than that of Baptists.[20]

During the years of the Vietnam War, 88 percent of young Jews attended college; the next groups, with 65 percent each, were Episcopalians and Presbyterians; then came Methodists and Catholics, with 45 percent each, Lutherans with 43 percent, and lowest of all, Baptists with 28 percent. Today, "the odds of a young Jew attending college are better than seven to one." At the turn of the century, the order of rank among denominations attending college was quite different: Presbyterians were first with 48 percent, while Jews were fourth with 17 percent, which was then the national average. The rise of the percentage of Jews attending college has been steady and substantial since then, from 17 to 88.[21] If the trend should continue, the time will come when every American Jew will be a college graduate.

Based on seven surveys by the National Opinion Research Center, Jews rate first with respect to years of education, prestige of occupation, percentage of white-collar jobs, and family income.[22] This holds true among ethnic as well as among religious groups. The Jews, says Greeley, "are America's most impressive success story."[23]

These surveys and studies are substantiated by others made since World War II, although some scholars tend to put their conclusions in more guarded terms than those of Greeley. Thus, e.g., Nathan Glazer puts the matter this way: American Jews have become "an extremely prosperous group, probably as prosperous as some of the oldest and longest-established elements of the population of the United States."[24] However, Glazer has noted that the relative prosperity and success of Jews could be seen even at the turn of the century. Reviewing the data for that time, Glazer concluded that "there is no question that the Jews earned more than did non-Jews," even though the average Jewish immigrant at that time landed with only $9 in his pocket.[25] Although the immigrant Jews tended to settle in ghetto areas in large urban centers, they also tended to leave these ghettos as quickly as possible, indeed more rapidly than did other immigrant groups.[26] Writing in 1954, in connection with the American Jewish tercentenary celebration, Glazer concluded that the statistics "demonstrate that the rise in the social and economic position of the Jews has been extremely rapid, far surpassing that which can be shown for any other immigrant group, and indeed surpassing, for the period, changes in the socio-economic position of long-settled groups."[27] In a study prepared for the American Jewish Committee in 1970 in which he surveyed and summarized the extensive literature, Sidney Goldstein concluded that the "fact remains that, on the whole, both the average income of Jews and the proportion of Jews in high income groups are well above those of most of the population."[28]

The success of Jewish academicians has deservedly received special attention, for the facts are impressive. A study conducted by the Carnegie Commission on Higher Education in 1969 showed that 9 percent of those teaching in colleges and universities identified themselves as Jews. In the elite colleges and universities, the percentage of Jewish professors was 19. In the Ivy League schools, of the professors under fifty years of age—which would mean those who were hired since the end of World War II—a quarter were Jews. When the schools in the Carnegie study are rank ordered according to academic quality, 32 percent of the Jewish professors are at schools that are in the highest quality category, while only 9 percent of Christian professors are teaching at such schools; conversely, over 40 percent of the Christian professors are at the lowest quality category schools as compared to 13.5 percent of the Jews.[29] Jews have been named presidents of leading universities and deans of leading colleges and professional schools. These developments have been especially dramatic and impressive because they have taken place in the lifetime of many who remember when it was possible to name only a total of five or six Jews who had the honor to hold professorships.[30]

3

Just as Americans in general tended to forget that there were millions of poor among them until Michael Harrington's *The Other America* (1962) forcefully propelled the facts to front-page space, so too American Jews have only belatedly recognized the fact that success and affluence have bypassed hundreds of thousands of their own people. It was not until 1971 that the existence of "the other Jews" came to be talked about. At about the same time the so-called Black Panthers of Israel attracted international attention by their demonstrations against the existence of poverty especially among the Jews who had emigrated from North Africa and Yemen.[31]

Just how many Jewish poor there are in the United States is uncertain; the estimates run from 350,000 to 700,000. A 1972 report of the Federation of Jewish Philanthropies of New York showed 272,000, or 15.1 percent of the Jewish population of New York, as poor or near-poor. In addition, there were 423,000 persons, or 25 percent of the Jewish population, who were between the near-poverty level and the moderate level of living as fixed by the Bureau of Labor Statistics standards.[32]

Who are these poor among American Jews? They can be divided into two classes: (a) As many as two-thirds are old Jews, sixty years of age or older. The proportion of aged among Jews is far larger than among America's poor generally—in the early seventies the proportion of persons 65 or over within the Jewish population was 14, and was expected to rise. Writing about this class of Jewish poor, Bertram H. Gold, executive vice president of the American Jewish Committee, noted: "Many of the aged poor are in ill health. For the most part, they do not live close to hospital care. . . . They live in wretchedly neglected houses, in neighborhoods no longer Jewish. Many are so afraid of crime in the street—with good reason—that they rarely venture out even to shop or see the doctor and do not visit with friends at all."[33] (b) The other one-third are young and middle-aged, and are poor because they are Jews:

> [T]he Hasidic and other strictly Orthodox Jews, whose beliefs obligate them to raise large families, use only *glat* kosher foods and send their children to cheder and yeshiva rather than public school [i.e., to schools where they are required to pay tuition and fees]. The Hasidim are additionally held down in their earning capacity by their deep-rooted tradition of limiting secular education, of excluding certain aspects of the modern world from their society and their children's schooling.[34]

These people, both the old and the young among the Jewish poor, were neglected by the Jewish community and overlooked by the federal and local antipoverty programs. These programs were directed toward neighborhoods occupied by blacks or by Puerto Ricans—of the twenty-six community operations in New York, only five had Jewish representatives; furthermore, the poverty programs made no provision for the special cultural and economic needs of the Jewish poor.[35] It perhaps was not because of purposeful discrimination that the poverty programs simply overlooked the Jewish poor; the fact is that American society no longer sees the Jews as a "minority." In his speech accepting the Democratic Party nomination for president of the United States, Jimmy Carter said: "It is time to guarantee an end to discrimination because of race or sex"; he made no reference to discrimination because of religion, creed, or national origin. This was not an oversight, nor was it intended as an expression of indifference or animosity towards Jews—not at all. It was simply that the Jews are no longer thought of as belonging to the class of Americans who need special attention, special laws, and special massive appropriations of funds to help them in their various needs.

4

However, this poverty that afflicts from five to ten percent of American Jews is hardly more than an aberration—like the twelve percent of the American people who are classified as poor.[36] It is the wart on the face. Jewish poverty only tarnishes but does not belie the fact that American Jews constitute the most successful and affluent ethnic group or religious denomination in the wealthiest country in the world.[37] What accounts for this Jewish success, for this dramatic movement from rags to riches? A variety of theories have been offered, but generally only timidly, mostly by way of suggestion.

Andrew Greeley, reviewing the findings of the various studies (especially those of the National Opinion Research Center), notes that while the most wealthy American group are the Jews, the ethnic Catholic groups—the Irish Catholics, the Italian Catholics, the German and Polish Catholics—follow right after the Jews in a rank order of family income, ranging from $13,340 for Jews to $11,298 for Poles, and that the latter are followed by Episcopalians and Presbyterians. At the bottom of the ladder are other Protestant groups.[38] Can it be, Greeley asks, that the so-called Protestant ethic has been not merely refuted but reversed? The question, he says, is a good one, but there is no obvious answer to it. Greeley has, however, less trouble explaining the specifically Jewish success: "The Jewish immigrants were the product of two millenia of ancestors who had to live by their wits. Many of them were craftsmen, tradesmen, inhabitants of small towns or even cities. They were people of the Book, believing firmly in education and practical learning. It is not difficult to see why they would be successful in the United States."[39] At the end of his report to the Ford Foundation, facing the success of the Jews and of other ethnic groups, Greeley ventures to suggest a psychological theory:

> Might we be seeing a phenomenon for which I can find no other name but "overthrust" (though you might also want to try overcompensation)? Could it be that the first stage cohort of a population group that "makes it" in American society does so with such tremendous energy and such tremendous "need for achievement," that they not only do as well as everyone else, but better, because of the sheer, raw power of their elemental drive for respectability and success? May it be that in another generation or two, the effect may wear off, and the Catholic and Protestant and Jewish ethnic groups will have relatively similar levels of achievement—while the blacks and the Spanish-speaking profit from the "overthrust" phenomenon?[40]

This point is similar to one that has frequently been made about the nations of the world: the Western industrial nations are bound to lose their nerve and vigor, and their primacy will be lost to nations of the third world. "Overthrust," however, is hardly an explanation; it is a pejorative label placed on a phenomenon; it leaves unanswered why there was a "thrust" by one group and not by another, why one group had such an "elemental drive for respectability and success" while other groups lacked it.

Greeley projects also the theory that achievement can be explained by a group's culture. "There are, it turns out," he says, "strong relationships between culture and achievement."[41] However, what precise aspects of Jewish culture, different from the components of other groups' cultures, can explain the attainments of American Jews? As we have seen, Greeley mentions some well-known facts: that for some two thousand years Jews have had to live by their wits; that Jewish immigrants brought with them to American shores certain skills or aptitudes that prepared them to become craftsmen and traders; that they came ready for urban life; and that they had been prepared to seek education and practical knowledge.[42]

Other scholars have also pointed to these and related cultural factors as being somehow causally related to Jewish achievement. Nathan Glazer, in his Jewish tercentenary article,[43] explains Jewish success in America by pointing to the following facts:

> The Jews for generations were engaged in middle-class occupations, in the professions, in buying and selling.
>
> The middle-class occupations are associated with certain characteristic habits—habits of care and foresight. The Jew was trained to save money so that with the capital, and with intelligence and ability, he may be able to advance himself. He was taught generally to postpone his pleasures—to save himself and his money for enjoyment later.
>
> Judaism, for at least fifteen hundred years before Calvinism, has emphasized the traits that businessmen and intellectuals require; and so it is no wonder that it is in a modern society like America that the Jews, who have been stamped with the values that make for good businessmen and intellectuals, should flourish. Long before Calvinism, Judaism placed emphasis on study and learning, on habits of foresight, care and moderation. The bent given to them by religion and culture was strengthened by their economic experience.
>
> While Jews were traders, businessmen, and scholars, a large group of them were artisans; but unlike Christian artisans, they were not members of guilds and corporations [from which they were excluded], consequently Jewish artisans were actually or potentially tradesmen, with middle-class habits, psychology and ambitions. The Jewish artisans carried with them the values conducive to middle-class success, and so, under proper circumstances, they easily turned to trade and study. The Jewish artisans were the sons and grandsons of traders and scholars, and could readily turn their minds to ways and means of improving themselves that were quite beyond the imagination of their fellow workers. Business and education were therefore not remote but familiar and attainable possibilities. With the prospect of success beckoning, it became worthwhile for the Jewish immigrants to work harder and save more than other immigrant groups.

Unlike other scholars, Glazer does not consider the urban experience of Jewish immigrants important, for large numbers who came from Germany and Eastern European countries were from small towns and villages that were scarcely "urban." I think that Glazer is right about this, for the experience of the shtetl could hardly be thought a preparation for what the immigrant faced in New York, Chicago, Kansas City, or Rochester. If not the experience of the shtetl, the experience of the Jew did, in subtle and complex ways, prepare the Jewish immigrant for the challenges and opportunities that America offered people with intelligence, imagination, enterprise, courage, and habits of prudence and moderation. In any case, as Glazer says,

> the pattern of foresight and sobriety so essential for middle-class success was so well established in Jewish life that it was maintained even where there was no prospect of going into business. The Jews did not drink; the Jewish students were docile, accepting—as lower-class children rarely do today—today's restraints for tomorrow's rewards; the Jewish workers stayed out of jail. When we look at the working-class Jewish neighborhoods of the great American cities of the 1920's and 1930's, it is clear we are not dealing with ordinary workers. It was not dangerous to walk through the New York slums at night when they were inhabited by Jews.[44]

Significantly, Jewish workers tended to join more organizations than did Christian workers, and even more than did Jewish white-collar workers, and they wrote more frequently to their congressmen than did even high-income Catholics or Protestants.[45] As Glazer wrote a few years later in his book *American Judaism:*

> The Jewish working class had a broader horizon than the working class of other groups. They tended to form powerful unions, which helped improve their conditions. And they made sure their children would not also be workers. As early as 1900, so authoritative a historian of the American working classes as John R. Commons observed that "Jewish women are employed [in factories] to a much less extent than the women of other nationalities, and their children are kept in school until 15 or 16 years of age. It is quite unusual for Jewish tailors to teach their children their own trade." With the Jewish mother at home, the Jewish child received a better education and better care, as shown in lower delinquency and death rates. . . . Never were teachers in slum schools happier than when they had Jewish pupils; never were settlement-house workers more delighted with the results of their work than when the Jews filled the slums of the large cities.[46]

Joseph L. Blau, in his book *Judaism in America* (1976), lists substantially the same characteristics that account for or have contributed to the success of the Jewish immigrant: that is, the ethos of hard work, thrift, the readiness to defer satisfaction for the sake of goals to be achieved later, an intense desire for respectability, and the secular application of the traditional conception of study and scholastic achievement. However, Blau adds another characteristic that is significant: "a strong sense of family that produced innumerable instances of mutual assistance." In part, Blau explains, this characteristic

> may derive from the age-old Jewish tradition that it would be a scandal if any one of their number was forced to ask and accept assistance from the non-Jewish public. It was a matter of pride to the Jewish community that it took care of its own. . . . The family was a source of mutual aid for its members not only in times of adversity, but even in times of prosperity. Any Jew who moved ahead saw to it that he carried others with him, as far as it was possible for him to do so.[47]
> Every family of whatever background envisions a brighter future for the new generation. What is outstanding is the sacrifice that all members of the Jewish immigrant family were willing to make to advance those who showed potential for fulfilling the vision. Noteworthy is the extent to which those who did scale the heights—having benefitted from their family's sacrifice—used their achievements and prominence to ease the lives of those who supported and encouraged them.[48]

5

There is no doubt that the Jewish immigrants from Germany, Russia, Romania, the Austro-Hungarian empire, and other parts of Europe brought with them energies, talents, and gifts that greatly contributed to their usefulness, enterprise, and success. There are scholars who would reduce all the Jewish aptitudes to the simple fact that the Jewish immigrants came with an urban background and that they were equipped thereby to engage in types of activities that went with urban status and life;[49] but I believe that this oversimplifies a complex cultural, historical event.

In any case, the great talents and gifts that the Jews possessed cannot alone explain their success, for they had the *same gifts* before they emigrated from the Old Country, and there they had been only paupers, failures—the poor, the "huddled masses," the "wretched refuse" of whom Emma Lazarus wrote. It is obvious that America provided certain ingredients without which the Jewish adventure in the

United States would have turned out quite differently. The American Jewish success story is a story of a partnership. To this partnership, America—to use terms made familiar by Toynbee—provided the Challenge, and the immigrant Jews provided the Response. America provided challenges that fortunately were of a "salutary severity" that stimulated these immigrants and their children to an ordeal that was, as the results have shown, "a creative response."[50] To see only what the Jews brought with them is to see only a part, which is not fully understandable in isolation from the whole. A complex social, historical phenomenon can be studied only by the holistic approach, which sees causes as part of a complex web rather than in a simple chain-link relationship.

First of all there was the great bounty that nature and a rapidly-developing industrial society provided. As Greeley graphically put it:

> How has a society of such diverse components as the United States survived? The country's richness of natural resources and its resultant economic prosperity have had something to do with the success of pluralism. People seem less inclined to go after their neighbors with a rock, club, or knife when they have just consumed a succulent steak from the backyard barbecue.[51]

Secondly, the social order put relatively few obstacles in the way of economic and social progress. There were no kings and royal retinue; there was no aristocracy by birth. The original church establishments in the colonies were feeble institutions and were not even memories when mass Jewish immigration took place. There were no guilds to dominate the crafts and the lives of artisans and workers. The economic and social structure was such as to encourage fluidity. The movement from peddling to store-keeping encountered no artificial obstacles. It was often relatively easy for a man who had himself worked at tailoring to open a small shop and set other tailors to work for him. Thus Jewish jobs became transformed into middle-class businesses in a social order that needed to value a man for his function and for the quality of his performance. As Macaulay noted in 1831 when the civil disabilities of the Jews of Britain were under consideration, it was certainly better to have one's shoes mended by a heretical cobbler who knew his work well than by a person who had subscribed to the Thirty-nine Articles but had never handled an awl.[52] This proposition needed to be debated in Great Britain, where religious and class lines were still prominent and effective, but Americans did not need to have the obvious demonstrated to them.

The late Chief Rabbi Isaac Herzog once wrote: "We are apt to speak of Jews and Gentiles as if the human race consisted of one half Jews and the other half non-Jews."[53] We are apt to forget that of the forty-six million immigrants who have settled America, only less than three million were Jews. The non-Jews who came here also brought with them various energies, talents, gifts, attitudes, and prejudices, some of which they, sooner or later, discarded and replaced with others; and it was the new and old elements in their mental and spiritual baggage that made the secure settlement of the Jews possible and that became the basis for the ultimate achievement of equality by the Jewish settlers and their children and grandchildren.[54] The host nation brought as much to the success of the Jews as the immigrant Jews themselves did.

What the Jewish immigrants found when they came here by the tens of thousands was not only a country superlatively rich in natural endowment but also one in which the social environment was receptive and hospitable to the immigrants' qualities of character.[55] America's institutional conditions welcomed individual initiative; it offered strong incentives for risk-taking, for industrial and commercial pioneering, for self-reliant action, for newness, for creativity, for ingenuity, for productivity, for enterprise—for, indeed, every form and aspect of human endeavor.

Thirdly, it is important to see the ineluctable connection that existed between America's opulence and the ideal of equality, both of which features of American life and promise loomed large in the dreams, hopes, and lives of the Jewish immigrants. David M. Potter has cogently described that connection:

Abundance has influenced American life in many ways, but there is perhaps no respect in which this influence has been more profound than in the forming and strengthening of the American ideal and practice of equality, with all that the ideal has implied for the individual in the way of opportunity to make his own place in society and emancipation from a system of status.

The very meaning of the term "equality" reflects this influence, for the connotations to an American are quite unlike what they might be to a European. A European, advocating equality, might very well mean that all men should occupy positions that are on roughly the same level in wealth, power, or enviability. But the American, with his emphasis upon equality of opportunity, has never conceived of it in this sense. He has traditionally expected to find a gamut ranging from rags to riches, from tramps to millionaires. To call this "equality" may seem a contradiction in terms, but the paradox has been resolved in two ways: first by declaring that all men are equal in the eyes of the law . . . and, second, by

assuming that no man is restricted or confined by his status to any
one station, or even to any maximum station. . . . At one end of the
scale might stand a log cabin [or shall we say, a peddler's pack], at
the other the White House [or shall we say, a department store]; but
equality meant that anyone might run the entire scale. This emphasis
upon unrestricted latitude as the essence of equality in turn involved
a heavy emphasis upon liberty as an essential means for keeping the
scale open and hence making equality a reality.[56]

Equality, for the American, carried the connotation of upward
mobility, without the need to overcome legal impediments or deeply
rooted vested and institutionalized interests. However—and this is of
crucial importance—unless objectively there was a large measure of
abundance, created by nature intermixed with the energy and ingenuity of man, equality of opportunity would have been a mere fan-
tasy. Given abundance in fact, equality of opportunity meant the
fulfillment of the promise of success. The result has been that "America has had a greater measure of social equality and social mobility
than any [other] highly developed society in human history."[57]

Moreover, although questions have been raised about the degree
of actual mobility or advancement from status to status shown by
Americans generally (quite apart from the problem of blacks, American Indians, and Hispanic Americans), no such questions have been
raised about American Jews. Indeed, the facts show that while other
immigrant groups have also left their ghettos or first places of settlement, the Jews left them more rapidly and in greater numbers, and in
general their rate of social-economic mobility was greater than that of
other groups.[58]

6

The Jewish masses came to America from countries where they had
been hated and persecuted because of their religion. Although there
were, without doubt, other factors that contributed to the drive to
hate and to destroy Jews—economic competition and envy, hatred of
the stranger—religious difference was felt to be an intolerable afflic-
tion on the body politic, for a people's religion was conceived of as
the single spiritual tie that held them together and that kept them
from devouring one another. Religion had to be homogeneous, single;
religious difference was heresy or treason or both; religious persecution was, therefore, altogether legitimate, necessary, and even honorable and meritorious.

The Jews who came to the United States found this country to be
indeed a New World. For the first time in their lives they did not

need to apologize for their religious difference. The United States Constitution guaranteed religious liberty and banned any religious establishment. The Constitution prohibited oaths that tested a person's religious beliefs. No official stigma could attach to a man because he was a Jew.

More than that, in the Old World, even within the Jewish community itself, a Jew was not as free as he may have wanted to be. The Jewish communities in Germany and in Russia were organized on the principle that Jews were defined by their religion—they were not a nation, a nationality, or an ethnic group but a religious society; and the Jewish religion was Judaism—a single religion, without inner divisions into denominations or sects. When, e.g., Rabbi Samson Raphael Hirsch wanted to organize an Orthodox Jewish community in Frankfurt-on-the-Main, separate from the Reform community (which alone had official recognition), it took him years until he was able to induce the Prussian Parliament to enact a law that permitted him and his followers to withdraw from the official Jewish community and to establish their own religious association. The "Law of Secession," the *Austrittsgesetz* (passed in July 1876), permitted a Jew to leave his local congregation without leaving Judaism, and this law was considered in its day a significant victory for religious conscience and for Judaism.[59] By contrast, the Jewish immigrants to the United States had no need to petition the government for permission to perform any religious function or for permission to be free from any religious prohibitions or restrictions. Synagogues and temples were organized on the congregational model and were wholly voluntary associations, in which membership was altogether voluntary.[60] Joseph Blau is quite right in stressing the fact that this principle of voluntaryism, "the idea that a man's religious affiliations are his own concern and not the business of the community," was "a novelty of the American scene." It was no part of the Jewish or European experience, and it was an element of the American environment that was "a novelty to practically all Jews at the time of their arrival in America."[61]

Jews were not only freed form disabilities and restrictions because of their religion but in time even won recognition precisely because of their religion. Instead of speaking of Christian civilization or Christian ideals, Americans learned to speak of the Judeo-Christian tradition, thus making Judaism an equal partner with Christianity when pointing to America's living ideas. Although Jews constitute less than three percent of the population, Judaism is looked upon as the third faith and given equal status with Protestantism and Catholicism. Thus, even nonreligious Jews have become identified as Jews-by-religion—not, however, for the imposition of disabilities but rather for the recognition of their equality with Christians.[62] Whatever may be the case with regard to other ethnic groups, Jewish ethnic concerns are filtered mainly through Jewish religious institutions, symbols, communities, and ideals.

Once again, however, we want to stress that these developments serve as sources of strength for American Jews, who can look to their status as a religious community for a guarantee of freedom from discrimination and a guarantee of equality of treatment and dignity with Protestants and with Catholics. American Jews thus have the best of both worlds; they can be as religious or as secular as they please and in either case enjoy the benefit of the religion clauses of the First Amendment. And this is consistent with the Halakhic principle that one remains a Jew even if he strays: "Even if he has sinned, he remains an Israelite."[63]

Possibly one factor contributing to this result—admittedly impossible to measure—is that Christianity shares with Judaism passionate devotion to the Hebrew Scriptures. Whatever vilification the Jewish people suffer from some writers of the New Testament, the impact of the Hebrew Scriptures—of Genesis, Deuteronomy, the Psalms, Job, Ecclesiastes, the Song of Songs, Micah, Amos, Jeremiah—could not be totally lost. Because of the pervasive Protestant (especially Puritan) influence, American culture perhaps has been more strongly influenced by the Hebrew Scriptures than has English culture—and the influence has, at least until recent years, assimilated itself into the very substance and basic fabric of the American mind. What Shakespeare has been to English literature and thought, the Bible—especially the Hebrew Scriptures, and the large elements of them that are absorbed into the New Testament—has been to American language and thought. This thought and language link Christians and Jews with a common past, a common set of ideals, a common set of sentiments, which together make up the essence of a common tradition.[64]

Jews are differentiated, even sharply, among themselves. They are attached to different Judaisms—Orthodox, Conservative, Reform, each broken down into various shadings; Hasidim, rationalists, and just nondescript Jews; Hebraists and Yiddishists; pious Jews and secularists; Zionists and anti-Zionists. However, just as in the dark (as Hegel noted) all cows are black, so to the Christian all Jews are defined by their religion, which is to the outsider a single, undifferentiated Judaism. They are identified not ethnically but denominationally, and they thus, providentially, find themselves—even against the wishes of some of them—under the beneficent shelter of the First Amendment. This has been, and continues to be, a boon, the extent of which is beyond our capacity to measure.

Moreover, when we think of American Jews as defined by their religion, which differentiates them from Catholics and Protestants, and compare them with British or Israeli Jews, one of the great differences that strikes us is the fact that it is largely only American Jews who are differentiated *among themselves* denominationally as Reform, Conservative, and Orthodox, and that each of these groupings is made up of a variety of subgroups. This is a distinctively American, not Jewish, phenomenon, for e.g. the Israeli Jews have no such divisions. In Israel the Jews are either Orthodox or nonreligious; the Reform (or Progressive) and Conservative congregations in Israel are very few, and their congregations are made up largely of American and other English-speaking Jews (often those who attend their services are mainly American tourists). Although Reform Judaism had its origin and early development in Germany, it made relatively little headway there and became largely an American development; and Conservative Judaism is almost exclusively an American phenomenon. Similarly, Reform had an early start (1840) in England but developed along conservative lines and made so little headway that in 1901 a new movement appeared under the name of Liberal Judaism with a more radical position respecting beliefs and practices and in 1910 established in London the Liberal Jewish Synagogue; neither of these movements, however, has ever attracted more than small numbers of Jews. The masses of British Jews are either members of Orthodox congregations that are affiliated with the United Synagogue or with the Federation of Synagogues or belong to no religious organization.

This phenomenon—the pluralistic character of American Judaism and Jewry—is, as we have said, an American contribution to Jewish historical development. It is rooted in the voluntaryism that is characteristic of American civilization, and especially of the history of religion in America. Once it became clear that the state has no power in any matter affecting religious belief or worship, ecclesiastical organization, or religious association, it followed that no other agency could assert such power; that every man was absolutely free to choose, change, or deny his religion; that there can be no official compulsion in any matter relating to religion; and that no government official has power to declare what is orthodox or heretical. The result is a great proliferation of religions, denominations, and sects, such as is not to be seen anywhere else in the world, and among them is the variety of Judaisms that one finds in the United States today—variations on a common core of tradition that compete with each other and yet feel themselves united by a common history and a common destiny. There are those who bemoan this as fragmentation, and there are those who see in the phenomenon a flowering of the Jewish religious spirit that is an enrichment and a blessing. In any case, what we witness is the fact that for the first time in history, Jews are wholly free to make of Judaism whatever they choose it to be, from Hasidism to Jewish humanism, with an infinite variety of stations between. In a unique way American Jews can say, in the words of Moses: "Not with our fathers did the Lord make this covenant, but with us, who are all of us here alive this day."[65]

7

The liberties and rights of Americans have their roots partly in English history. The Bill of Rights of the United States Constitution can hardly be understood when totally separated from its background in Magna Carta, the Petition of Right (1627), and the Bill of Rights of 1688.[66] This is not true, however, of the rights of American Jews. With respect to them, the reverse situation is true: the rights and liberties of American Jews became a model for England. Although English Jews enjoyed a large measure of social and economic freedom, they were under severe civic and political disabilities. It was not until 1835 that they were admitted to the office of sheriff, and ten years later to other but minor offices; and in 1846 the Religious Opinions Relief Bill removed minor disabilities. However, they could not take their place as members of Parliament because they could not take the Christian oath of office that the law required. Lionel de Rothschild, though elected by the City of London as its parliamentary representative time after time from 1847, could not take his seat. It is notable that Macaulay, in his great speech in Parliament in 1829 in support of a bill to remove the civil disabilities of Jews, observed that in the United States "the Jews are already admitted to all the rights of citizens"; and in his second speech on the subject in 1833 Macaulay stated that it is "an undoubted fact that, in the United States of America, Jewish citizens do possess all the privileges possessed by Christian citizens."[67] Although Dissenters and Roman Catholics had been admitted to full civil and political rights in 1828 and 1829, it was not until 1858 that Baron Rothschild was permitted to take his seat in Parliament upon passage of the Jews' Disabilities Bill.

In America, although Jews were subject to some civil and political disabilities in the colonies, and even at times in some of the states, as citizens of the United States they enjoyed full equality with all other citizens.[68] This was the guarantee of the First Amendment, which all branches of the federal government have observed in full measure. However, James Madison's insight is still relevant. "Is a bill of rights a security for religion?" he asked in 1788. If all the people of the United States belonged to one sect, he said, "a bill of rights would be a poor protection for liberty." If the states enjoy freedom of religion, Madison went on to say, this is due to the "multiplicity of sects . . . which is the best and only security for religious liberty in any society."[69] Because at least forty percent of the population of the American colonies was of non-English stock, and followers of the Church of England were in fact a minority,[70] religious liberty and equality were indispensable conditions for the effective operation of government, for the development of the country and its resources, for the encouragement of immigration, and for the enjoyment of civil life in peace and prosperity.

Despite these fortunate conditions, however, Jews often found themselves the victims of prejudice and discrimination. The Constitution of the United States and the constitutions of the various states shielded them from unfriendly or discriminatory official acts, but most constitutional guarantees were not restrictions on the actions of private persons. Special legislative enactments were therefore required to prohibit private discrimination. The movement for such enactments, which came to be known as civil rights laws, began in 1865 when Massachusetts enacted the first such law, banning discrimination based on race or color in places of public accommodation. Today states, and even many municipalities, prohibit discrimination on account of race, color, religion, creed, national origin, sex, age, and disability, in places of public accommodation. There are also fair employment practice acts; fair housing laws; fair education laws. More important than these state or municipal laws are the federal statutes, most notably the Civil Rights Act of 1964.[71]

This network of federal and state laws, providing the most comprehensive protection against racial, ethnic, or religious discrimination by government officials or private persons, implements the ideal of equality and serves as a model for democratic countries throughout the world. Equally important have been decisions of the United States Supreme Court, especially since *Brown v. Board of Education* in 1954.[72] Although the cases have involved racial rather than religious discrimination, there can be no doubt that their spirit serves to protect minorities exposed to persecution on account of religion or creed.

Although Jews share the benefits of these statutes and court decisions with other religious, ethnic, and racial minorities, Jews were among the leading proponents of these developments. In every important civil rights or civil liberties struggle in the twentieth century, American Jews and their organizations—notably the American Jewish Committee, the American Jewish Congress, the Anti-Defamation League of B'nai B'rith, the Jewish Labor Committee, and the Synagogue Council of America—have been in the forefront as lobbyists, propagandists, financial supporters, organizers, and legal activists or defenders. Indeed, often these organizations have pioneered path-breaking legislative and litigation approaches, with a demonstration of courage and determination to fight back, to resist, and to vindicate their rights and liberties. True enough, the Jews had allies, but often the initiative came from Jewish organizations, and often they were *primus inter pares.*

8

The world being what it is, we can hardly expect that the America in which our children and grandchildren will need to live and to make their life will not have its quota of misanthropes, anti-Semites, and men and women whose passions will be fired by envy and by suspicion. In the Talmud it is stated that God speaks to the children of Israel and says: "My children, I created the evil desire *[yezer ha-ra]*, but I also created the Torah as its antidote."[73] So too we must think that though there will be some Americans who will scheme and plot against American Jewry and against Judaism and Jewish life, culture, and aspirations, the Constitution and laws will stand as an antidote.

However, no sooner have we said this then we are confounded by the bitter words of James Madison that bills of rights are only "parchment barriers" against the will of "overbearing majorities." A government, he wrote to Jefferson, will invade private rights when its acts are supported by the people.[74] The record of American history shows, I believe, that Jewish immigrants attained liberty and equality during the scores of years when America was a land of unprecedented opportunity. In his speech accepting the Republican Party nomination for president, Gerald Ford, referring to the pioneer vision of our revolutionary founders and immigrant ancestors, said: "Their vision was of free men and free women enjoying . . . unlimited opportunity."[75] We can well ask, however, whether anyone can speak responsibly of today's or of tomorrow's unlimited opportunity. For what we see are millions of young people with wants unsatisfied and with feelings that their satisfactions may be beyond their reach because for them the promise of opportunity will remain unfulfilled. There is grave danger when millions of young people are led to think that their future is dependent on their education and training but find themselves educated and trained for a world that does not need their skills and knowledge. As David Potter cautioned us, society "must not hold out the promise of opportunity unless there is a reasonable prospect of the opportunity's being fulfilled."[76] When promises and expectations remain frustrated, envy—the sixth of St. Gregory's deadly sins—takes over and breeds suspicion, hate, and violence. A society in which there is widespread disenchantment with the economic race, in which the work ethic is obsolete, in which there is limited opportunity and a diminution of mobility, in which the normal processes and institutions of government are distrusted, in which the voices of morality and of religion tend to be discredited, in which the foundations of family life are shaken—such a society offers fertile soil for the breeding of demagogues and of rabble-rousing racists. American Jews would find life in such a society difficult if not intolerable. We therefore face a future that may be menacing. Fortunately, the menace will be not only to American Jews but to all Americans who, as the American Bicentennial celebration reminded us, stand committed to our nation's basic ideals and values. Although up to the present this country's material conditions were preeminently congenial to the fostering of our ideals and values, in the future we will need to reverse the order: give priority to the ideals but at the same time *compel the material conditions to conform to them.* It will be a case of mind or spirit over matter. We must struggle with the angel until it will bless us. All of us, Jews and non-Jews alike, will need to be guided by the saying of Theodor Herzl, *"Wenn ihr wollt, ist es kein Märchen"*—"If you will it, then it is no fairy-tale."

The uniqueness of the Jewish experience in America probably would not have happened were it not for the pluralistic character of American society from its very origins: we were Jews among Presbyterians, Episcopalians, Baptists, Catholics, Quakers, Mennonites, and scores of other religious denominations and sects. There could be civil peace only if each religious group followed the principle of live and let live. Should religious pluralism disappear through the ultimate success of ecumenism or of secularism, or both, then Jews, marked off as a religious group, would be exposed to grave dangers. Ironically, it is in our self-interest that we should wish to see the Christian denominations and sects continue and flourish, for the life of Christianity will insure the life of Judaism.

Nor would the uniqueness of the Jewish experience in America have happened were it not for ethnic pluralism: we were Jews among Italians, Poles, Irish, Swedes, Germans, and scores of other ethnic or national groups. There could be civil peace only if each ethnic group followed the principle of live and let live. Should assimilation succeed to the point where ethnic consciousness and pride would become too feeble to be reckoned an important aspect of American culture and life, then the Jews, marked off as an ethnic group, would be exposed to grave dangers. It is, therefore, in the self-interest of Jews to do all they can to sustain and to foster the idea of ethnic heritage, ethnic consciousness, and pride for the Irish and the Poles, the Italians and the Hungarians, no less than for themselves; for their ethnic survival will help insure the survival of American Jews as a distinctive people.

The security and prosperity of American Jewry require one other material-social condition, one that we have already noted: America should become again and remain a land of unlimited opportunity. Where there is no opportunity, or equality of opportunity, the have-nots will demand equality of results, equality of actual economic and material conditions. For the twentieth century has aroused colossal expectations, which will not be denied. If there is to be no equality of opportunity—both in law and in fact—then there will be a demand for equality of status. It is, therefore, in the self-interest of American Jews to work for a legal and social order in which the demand for jobs will not exceed the supply, in which reasonable goals of people for a good life will be attainable, in which essential human needs will be met, in which human attainments will be within every American's reach.

The English poet Edward Thomas wrote: "The Past is the only dead thing that smells sweet." To Americans—and especially to American Jews—America's past smells sweet. It is up to us, the living and future generations, to see to it that America's past is not a dead thing but a living, meaningful, continuing presence.

4

Profane Religion and Sacred Law

This essay was the annual Ware Lecture for 1977 at the Sixteenth General Assembly of the Unitarian Universalist Association and was published by the Association in 1977; it also appeared in Go and Study: Essays and Studies in Honor of Alfred Jospe, *edited by Raphael Jospe and Samuel Z. Fishman and published by B'nai B'rith Hillel Foundations in 1980.*

1

Towards the end of the seventh century B.C.E. there reigned in Judah a king who, following the ways of the Egyptian pharaoh, his contemporary, built himself palaces by forced labor. In the book that bears his name, Jeremiah wrote: "Thus says the Lord: 'Go down to the house of the king of Judah, and speak there this word, and say . . .

> Woe to him who builds his house by unrighteousness,
>> and his upper rooms by injustice;
>> who makes his neighbor serve him for nothing,
>> and does not give him his wages; . . .
> Do you think you are a king because you compete in cedar?
> Did not your father eat and drink and do justice and righteousness?
> Then it was well with him.
> He judged the case of the poor and needy;
>> then it was well.
> Is not this to know me?'
>> says the Lord.[1]

Now let us assume something most improbable: that a president of the United States would find a way of conscripting men to build for him a private mansion. What would happen? A team of courageous investigative reporters would uncover the facts and the story

53

would be published in leading newspapers and reported on television and radio, so that within a matter of days or hours there would be a great public scandal, the president would face court actions and impeachment proceedings, and editorials would call for his resignation, indictment, and removal.

In the kingdom of Judah twenty-six hundred years ago there were no newspapers, there were no investigative reporters, there were no congressional investigative committees, there was no radio or television. The technology was different, the institutions were different. Jeremiah stood before the king and, in the name of the Lord, condemned him for injustices and cruelties. We call Jeremiah a prophet, and we think of his words as part of our great religious heritage. No one, however, would think of referring to Sam Ervin as anything but a senator, or to Bob Woodward and Carl Bernstein as anything but journalists, or to Archibald Cox as anything but the Watergate special prosecutor, or to John Sirica as anything but a federal district court judge.

Or take the book of Jonah. It relates that the word of the Lord came to Jonah and instructed him to go to Nineveh and to proclaim judgment upon it, for, said the Lord, "their wickedness has come before Me."[2] Now, Nineveh was a great city in Assyria. Whatever wickedness the Lord had seen in Nineveh, it had nothing to do with the people of Judah. The wickedness of Nineveh was purely, as a Brezhnev would say today, an internal, a domestic affair. What the king of Nineveh did to his people, or what the inhabitants of that city did to one another, need not have distressed the people of Jerusalem. Yet the book relates that the word of the Lord came to Jonah, son of Amittai, and told him to leave his home, go to Nineveh, uncover the wickedness of the place, and tell the people there how the Lord judges them.

Soon after taking office, President Jimmy Carter took actions that clearly showed that the American government and people were very much concerned about the cruel, inhuman ways in which the government of the U.S.S.R. was treating its own dissidents; on March 17, 1977, when he appeared before the United Nations, President Carter gave special emphasis to the American concern with human rights in other countries as well as at home. The president knew, of course, that the Soviet government would strongly resent what it termed interference into internal affairs—matters that did not threaten the peace or security of the United States (just as the wickedness of Nineveh was no threat to the peace or security of Judah). President Carter, however, answered this criticism by saying that all of the states that have signed the U.N. Charter have pledged themselves to observe and to respect human rights, referring also to the U.N.'s Universal Declaration of Human Rights and the Helsinki accords; and he concluded by saying, "Thus, no member of the United Nations can claim that mistreatment of its citizens is solely its own business."[3]

When Jonah appeared in Nineveh,[4] he could not speak of the United Nations documents and the Helsinki Declaration; he could speak only of the Lord. Jimmy Carter, on the other hand, no matter what his private feelings and thoughts may have been at the moment, could not speak in the name of the Lord, but he could speak of the international commitments and agreements, which bind all nations, the U.S.S.R. no less than the U.S.A. We know of Jonah as a prophet and his book as part of our sacred scriptures, as part of our religious heritage; but we identify Jimmy Carter as head of our state and government and think of his speech as a political action. Jeremiah and Jonah each spoke in the name of the Lord; President Carter, speaking to representatives of nearly one hundred fifty member states of the U.N., spoke in the name of American ideals, which, he said, "we are determined fully to maintain as the backbone of our foreign policy."

There are obviously good reasons why the president of the United States cannot say that he speaks in the name of the Lord, and why we must continue to distinguish in our language between the religious and the secular, between the sacred and the profane; however, we must also be prepared to penetrate through words to the realities behind them. When we do that, I submit, we find that there is more similarity than difference between Jonah addressing the king of Nineveh and Carter addressing the United Nations; between Jeremiah addressing the king of Judah and Judge John Sirica issuing an order against the president of the United States.[5]

We make a sharp distinction between the things that are God's and the things that are Caesar's, and for many purposes this is wise and even necessary. Often, however, this language misleads; it cloaks a reality and keeps us from seeing the substance; it prevents us from penetrating to what goes on under the mask of convention, tradition, and habit. Seeing the representation and not the substance, we fail to see that Jeremiah and Jonah acted out their political role as prophets, and that John Sirica and Jimmy Carter acted out their prophetic role as politicians. When we look at the realities and not at what Francis Bacon called "Idols of the Threatre,"[6] we see that often words are interchangeable; nonetheless, for prudential reasons, we stick to the convention, but it is important to bear in mind that there is a deeper wisdom than that which prudence offers.

2

"Whence this worship of the past?" Emerson asked. "The centuries," he went on to say, "are conspirators against the sanity and authority of the soul. . . . Yet see what strong intellects dare not yet hear God himself unless he speak the phraseology of I know not what David, or Jeremiah, or Paul.'"[7] Emerson expressed the hope that the time will come when man will see that "the world is the perennial miracle"; "he will learn that there is no profane history; that all history is sacred."[8]

When Ahab, king of Samaria, and his wife Jezebel contrived the judicial murder of their neighbor Naboth, so that they could add his vineyard to their property, and Elijah the prophet appeared before the king and asked, "Have you killed, and also taken possession?"—we think of the events as sacred history, as we should.[9] When the case of President Nixon came before the Supreme Court in 1974, however, and the Court unanimously ruled that the president must turn over sixty-four tapes of his White House conversations—a decision that precipitated Nixon's resignation about a fortnight later—we do not think of these events as part of sacred history.[10] But why? When Ahab saw Elijah, he cried out: "Have you found me, O my enemy?" The prophet replied: "I have found you, because you have sold yourself to do what is evil in the sight of the Lord."[11] The institutions are different, the style of address is different; but the essence is the same: in each instance the rule of law was affirmed, the principle was vindicated that the head of government, called king or president, is subject to the law and is not above or beyond it. Nixon, too, could have cried out: "Have you found me, O my enemy?" And the Court could have replied: "Yes, we have found you, because you have sold yourself to do what is evil in the sight of the Constitution." With Emerson we could say, There is no profane history, all history is sacred.

The plain fact is that we get out of our thoughts only what we put into them. If we think of religion as only that which goes on in our churches and synagogues and only that which is found in certain books that we call sacred, then it follows that our schools and colleges, our libraries, art museums, and concert halls, our offices, shops, mills, and factories, our legislatures and courts, our parks and forests, even our homes—then it follows, I say, that all the furniture of earth, that everything but the choir of heaven falls into the domain of Caesar, from which God is shut out. To my mind, there can be no greater blasphemy.

Nor, I think, can there be a greater perversion of thought. For what we have done is this: We have taken the principle of separation of church and state, which is of transcendent importance for our political organization and civil life, and made it applicable to all phases of our personal and social life. We have carried it over from the political sphere, wherein its usefulness can hardly be exaggerated, and have applied it to our culture generally, including our ethics and metaphysics. This may be an instance of the logical fallacy of composition, which arises when we affirm something to be true of a whole when it is true only of a part. The result has been a trivialization of religion into a part-time leisure interest—a process that has left much of life absurd, shallow, and inane.

The whole purport and drive of biblical religion was to exclude nothing—absolutely nothing—from the rule and judgment of God. The religious tradition rooted in biblical categories took its stand to repudiate, plainly and forcefully, any dualism that would relegate or confine God to a restricted jurisdiction. Marcionism, Gnosticism, and Manichaeism, all of which taught that a substantial part of the world and of man was ruled not by God but by Satan or by evil archons, inspired some of their votaries toward extreme asceticism and others toward extreme licentiousness, and each of these sects offered a certain logic that sounded convincing. The main streams of Judaism and Christianity, however, denied the premises of these dualistic religions and refused to turn over the world as we know it to the power of Satan.

It is no longer fashionable to avow a belief in Satan or his entourage of evil archons, but the fact is, nonetheless, that we are dualists. We have divided the world between God and ourselves. Part of what we consider our own, we are willing to turn over to Caesar, but—believing in civil liberties—part we retain as our private domain. Some are willing to share part of this domain with God, but some are very jealous of their privacy and exclude Him from it; they divide the world only between themselves and Caesar. The dualist is either a total or partial atheist. If he totally excludes God, then obviously he is an atheist. If he excludes God from a substantial part of the world, then to that degree he is an atheist.

The foundation on which modern man in the West builds his world is not God, not Satan, not Caesar, but himself. This individualism is the inheritance from the Cartesian philosophy, which starts with oneself—*Cogito, ergo sum;* from the Protestant Reformation, and especially the notion of the duty of the private judgment—*Hier steh' ich, ich kann nicht anders;* and from the Renaissance, which glorified the integrity and dignity of the individual mind. It is man, then, who assigns a place to everything, even to God. It is just as it is related in Genesis: every creature passes before Adam, and he gives to everything a name; but there is a significant difference, for even God, too, passes before him, and it is not God who names man, but man who names God.

Although many good and some even sublime values can be attributed to this development, it is necessary to say that some consequences have been highly detrimental and even odious, because of the tendency to absolutize the individual and to make individualism into an all-encompassing ideology—like the tendency to make the scientific method and the spirit of science into scientism, or to make the secularizing process into secularism. Individualism was carried to the extreme where it was forgotten that the self is always the social self; to the extreme where it was forgotten that, as John Macmurray wrote, "The self is one term in a relation between two selves . . . . The self exists only in the communion of selves."[12] The individual man may have all the grandeur and greatness that was spoken of him by Giannozzo Manetti in his treatise *On the Excellency and Dignity of Man* and by Pico della Mirandola in his *Oration on the Dignity of Man* and that is assigned to him by the Bible when it says that God made man in His own image, and that He made him only a little less than Himself.[13] This can be true, however, only if we recognize the fact that man is not man if he exists in isolation, alone. "Imagine yourself alone in the midst of nothingness," said A. S. Eddington, "and then you try to tell me how large you are." We tend constantly to forget that God did not create the solitary man but man-in-relation, or mankind.

> Then God said, "Let us make man in our image, after our likeness; and let *them* have dominion over the fish of the sea, and over the birds of the air, and over the cattle, and over all the earth, and over every creeping thing that creeps upon the earth." So God created man in his own image, in the image of God he created him; male and female he created *them*.[14]

Before there were two there was no one, for there is no male when there is no female; and when there are male and female, then, and only then, is there the genus man, which the Hebrew word *adam* means, and only then is there mankind. The self, as Macmurray has said, can exist only in relation to the other; he exists as a person only as he is in relation to others.[15]

In biblical contemplation, a man fulfills himself as person chiefly insofar as he fulfills his role as neighbor; in other words, he realizes himself mainly in his relations with others, or as and when he *sees himself as the other*.

3

This, I think, is the way it was intended that the parable of the good Samaritan be understood. The lawyer who stood up to test Jesus asked, in effect, the following question: "The Torah commands me, as you say, to love my neighbor as myself. What I want to know is, who is my neighbor?" In answer Jesus told of a man who was robbed and beaten while on the highway. A priest and a Levite saw the helpless man but looked the other way. Then along came a Samaritan, who stopped and took care of him. Now, asked Jesus, "Which of these three, do you think, proved neighbor to the man who fell among the robbers?" The lawyer said, "The one who showed mercy on him." Jesus said to him, "Go and do likewise."[16] One of the two significant elements in the parable is the way Jesus handled the word "neighbor." We ordinarily think of the other man being the neighbor, but Jesus turned the relationship around: "Which of the three, do you think, proved *neighbor to the man* who fell among the robbers?" That is, it was only the Samaritan, himself a stranger, who showed *himself to be a neighbor* to the man in need of a neighbor.

The essence of man is to be a neighbor. Each of us is born a neighbor. "To be a man," Leo Baeck wrote in *The Essence of Judaism,* "means to be a fellow man."[17] Kierkegaard, commenting on the parable of the good Samaritan in *Works of Love,* wrote:

> He towards whom I have a duty is my neighbor, and when I fulfill my duty I prove that I am a neighbor. Christ does not speak about recognizing one's neighbor but about being a neighbor oneself, about proving oneself to be a neighbor, something the Samaritan showed by his compassion. By this he did not prove that the assaulted man was his neighbor but that he was a neighbor of the one assaulted.[18]

The neo-Kantian philosopher Hermann Cohen, in his *Religion of Reason Out of the Sources of Judaism,* has argued—I believe convincingly—that before one can think of man, one must think, first of all, of *fellowman*—not *Mensch* but *Mitmensch.*[19] This is so not only for psychological, sociological, and philosophical reasons but even more for religious, ethical, and even metaphysical reasons. Ethics and religion depend, according to Cohen, on the concept of fellowman.[20] For if, he wrote, "the correlation between God and man is the fundamental equation of religion, then *man* in this correlation must first of all be thought of as fellowman."[21]

That the correlation between God and man is the fundamental

equation of religion—at least of the biblical religions—we can readily see as we go back to the parable of the good Samaritan. The gospel according to Luke relates that a lawyer stood up and asked Jesus, "Teacher [Rabbi], what shall I do to inherit eternal life?" Jesus said to him: "What is written in the law [Torah]?" The lawyer answered: "You shall love the Lord your God with all your heart, and with all your soul, and with all your strength, and with all your mind; and your neighbor as yourself." Jesus said to him, "You have answered right; do this, and you will live [i.e., inherit eternal life]."[22] Then the lawyer, feeling a bit argumentative, went on to ask Jesus, "And who is my neighbor?"—a question that provoked the exegesis so wonderfully concretized in the parable of the good Samaritan.

In the version given in Matthew, it is not the lawyer but Jesus himself who combines the sayings from Deuteronomy and from Leviticus. "Teacher," said the lawyer, "which is the great commandment in the law?" Jesus answered with the texts from the Torah: "You shall love the Lord your God with all your heart, and with all your soul, and with all your mind. This is the great and first commandment. And a second is like it. You shall love your neighbor as yourself. On these two commandments depend all the law and the prophets."[23]

But how does one love God? Judaism and Christianity never left one in doubt on the answer to this question, for one can love God chiefly through the love of man, by being a neighbor, by being a fellowman. There are, indeed, not two commandments but only one: *You shall love the Lord your God by loving your neighbor as yourself.*

I shall not go so far as to say that this love commandment exhausts the nature of Judaism or of Christianity. The religions rooted in the Bible have been conditioned by history, by culture, and by the nature of man, and they reflect and express men's frustrations and aspirations. As William Ernest Hocking wrote:

> Religion has fostered everything valuable to man and has obstructed everything: it has welded states and disintegrated them; it has rescued races and it has oppressed them, destroyed them, condemned them to perpetual wandering and outlawry. It has raised the value of human life, and it has depressed the esteem of that life almost to the point of vanishing; it has honored womanhood, it has slandered marriage. Here is an energy of huge potency but of ambiguous character.[24]

It was precisely because religions have so much potentiality for evil as well as for good, for enslavement as well as for liberation of the human spirit—it was because of their ambiguous character that Theodore Parker drew a distinction between their transient and their permanent qualities.[25] What, then, is fundamental or permanent in Judaism and in Christianity if it is not the love commandment?

The prophets drew a distinction between the transient and the permanent, between the essential and the accidental. Jeremiah, for example, has God saying to Israel: "[I]n the day that I brought them out of the land of Egypt, I did not speak to your fathers or command them concerning burnt offerings and sacrifices. But this command I gave them, 'Obey my voice, and I will be your God, and you shall be my people; and walk in the way that I command you.'"[26] What is the way that God commanded? Jeremiah left no doubt as to its meaning:

> Thus says the Lord: "Let not the wise man glory in his wisdom, let not the mighty man glory in his might, let not the rich man glory in his riches; but let him who glories glory in this, that he understands and knows me, that I am the Lord who practices steadfast love, justice, and righteousness in the earth; for in these things I delight, says the Lord."[27]

Walking in His ways means to live a life in imitation of God, that is, a life that manifests the practice of steadfast love, justice, and righteousness: "You shall be holy, for I the Lord your God am holy";[28] "You, therefore, must be perfect, as your heavenly Father is perfect."[29] Examine, said Theodore Parker, the duties enjoined by a life in the imitation of God, and what do we find? "[H]umility, reverence, sobriety, gentleness, charity, forgiveness, fortitude, resignation, faith, and active love"; and all these duties are summed up in the command, "Thou shalt love the Lord thy God . . . thou shalt love thy neighbor as thyself."[30]

The true love of God, said William Ellery Channing, "perfectly coincides, and is in fact the same thing, with the love of virtue, rectitude, and goodness." We esteem as a pious man, wrote Channing, only him "who practically conforms to God's moral perfections and government; who shows his delight in God's benevolence, by loving and serving his neighbor; his delight in God's justice, by being resolutely upright."[31]

To say that this is the whole of religion, that Judaism and Christianity teach only this, would be to overlook, at one's peril, a great deal that is of vital importance and to falsify the record. First things should come first, however, and one has a moral as well as an intellectual duty to distinguish between the permanent and the transient, between the fundamental or intrinsic and the accessory, derivative, adventitious, and historically-conditioned aspects of religions. When we look for this differentiation in Judaism and in Christianity, there can be no doubt as to what we will uncover. Let me cite but one other instance out of many. It is the stirring passage in which Job portrays the model biblical man of righteousness and lovingkindness:

> because I delivered the poor who cried,
>   and the fatherless who had none to help him.
> The blessing of him who was about to perish came upon me,
>   and I caused the widow's heart to sing for joy.
> I put on righteousness, and it clothed me;
>   my justice was like a robe and a turban.
> I was eyes to the blind,
>   and feet to the lame.
> I was a father to the poor,
>   and I searched out the cause of him whom I did not know.
> I broke the fangs of the unrighteous,
>   and made him drop his prey from his teeth.[32]

The differences between the essential and the accessory or adventitious is put in a dramatic and paradoxical way in *Lamentations Rabbah*, where God is made to exclaim: "If only they were to forsake Me but observe My teachings!" The rabbis felt safe in saying this because they knew that the evil man consciously or implicitly denies, forsakes, or forgets God but that the man who observes God's teachings—whether he knows it or not—has faith in God, for he hates what God hates and he loves what God loves. With Jeremiah we can ask, Is this not to know Him?[33]

4

If we are correct in this analysis, then it follows that the sharp differentiation that we make between the this-worldly and the other-wordly, between the immanent and the transcendent, between the profane or secular and the religious or sacred, falls away—because these polarities come together in the nature of God and in the nature of man. God, being infinite, is found in all spheres and in all levels of existence. Because God is the Creator and His essence is definable in ethical terms (inadequate as such terms may be), and because man is made in His image, it follows that there is no separate realm that can be denoted as the "religious"—except for some specific purposes, in order to achieve certain ends—and that to exclude God from the realm of Caesar is a supreme blasphemy and heresy. It is easy enough to find God in the hushed, awesome candlelight of the temple or of the church, or in the stillness of the forest, or in a storm on the high seas; our great need, however, is to look for Him where Caesar wields his power: to look for Him in the marketplace, in our teeming cities and towns, in our shops and factories; to find Him in our sciences and technologies, in our clinics and hospitals, in our constitutions and bills of rights.

It is only a perverse blindness that makes it possible for us to see the law of God in the Bible but only the law of Caesar in the statutes enacted by Congress or by the state legislatures or in the decisions and opinions of our courts.

There can be no question but that this-worldliness opens the door to staggering corruptions, but who that knows the history of religions will care to say that other-worldliness is totally exempt from its own kinds of perversion and corruption?

The Bible provides: "Thou shalt not have in thy bag divers weights, a great and a small. . . . A perfect and just weight shalt thou have; a perfect and just measure shalt thou have."[34] When we read this in Deuteronomy, we think of it as an example of what God ordained as a moral principle of honest, fair, and just dealing; but why do we consider our legislative enactments on just weights and measures as something of lesser worth and dignity? Why does one belong in the realm of God and the other in the realm of Caesar? A law in Deuteronomy provides that when a war is waged against a city, its trees (at least its fruit-bearing trees) shall not be cut down: "Are the trees in the field men that they should be besieged by you?"[35] From this passage the ancient rabbis derived the general principle that no natural or manmade object may be wasted or needlessly destroyed.[36] We think of these laws as divinely ordained, for they are based on the principles that "[t]he earth is the Lord's and the fulness thereof"[37] and that man is only a temporary tenant and a steward. However, Congress and our state legislatures have enacted laws for the protection of the environment and for the conservation of resources that seek to achieve the same ends. In 1964, for example, Congress set up a National Wilderness Preservation System. The statute defines a wilderness as "an area where the earth and its community of life are untrammeled by man, where man himself is a visitor who does not remain" and which offers "outstanding opportunities for solitude."[38] I submit that it is only dullness of sensibility and a perverse kind of spirituality that refuses or fails to see that our own enactments are no less religious, no less sacred. The religious man who has not turned over governance of this world to Satan must see in man's intelligence a manifestation of God's governance of the world, for how shall God govern this nation but through the intelligence of its citizens and of the officers of government whom they have chosen? The Federal Rehabilitation Act of 1973 prohibits discrimination against a qualified handicapped individual in federally-funded programs. Is such a law not "sacred"?

If there is any principle that is distinctively biblical it is the bias of righteousness in favor of the poor and helpless. Time and again the Bible singles them out for special concern. But if God is so deeply concerned with the poor, why does He not save them? Why do the prophets call upon us to practice righteousness toward the poor and needy?

Martin Buber relates that Rabbi Moshe Leib of Sasov taught his disciples that no human quality or power was created by God to no purpose and that even base qualities can be uplifted to serve God. A disciple asked him what purpose can atheism serve in God's world. This, too, said the rabbi, can be uplifted. For if someone should come to you and ask your help—someone who needs bread to eat, or shelter, or clothing—you might be inclined to say to the poor man, "You believe in God, as I do. Well, take your needs to God and pray that He may help you." Only an evil man, said the rabbi, can give this response. For when the poor man comes to you, you must act *as if there were no God* and as if there were only one person in the whole world who could help him—only yourself.[39]

Heaven knows how far short of perfection are the antipoverty programs that we have evolved since President Johnson in 1964 declared "unconditional war on poverty." In his State of the Union message, Johnson said that the goal of the war on poverty was "total victory." We know how far we are from this goal. No personal or social ideal is ever fully realized, however; what is important is that we have committed ourselves to an ideal that had never before been so fully articulated and projected by a nation and its government. No one who knows the record can accuse us of being callous, indifferent, or miserly. Why is the biblical law on leaving gleanings for the poor to gather a sacred text but the Economic Opportunity Act of 1964 a mere profane piece of congressional legislation? "Bread for myself," wrote Berdyaev, "is a material question: bread for my neighbor is a spiritual question."[40] Insofar as we devote our time, thought, and resources to the question of bread for our neighbors, we concern ourselves with a central religious duty, and it is a gross corruption of thought and of language to assign our efforts a place in the realm of Caesar as if the light of God does not penetrate that place of total spiritual darkness. We continually forget that it is in His light that we see light; that it is only through His infinite wisdom that we have ideals, thoughts, and plans.[41]

It is, I believe, important for us never for a moment to forget that there is no word for "religion" in the whole of the Hebrew Scriptures and that the word appears only very few times (five, to be exact) in the New Testament.[42] Judaism and Christianity were conceived of as "teachings" or as "ways of life." To be a Jew or a Christian did not mean to be "religious" only on certain days of the week or year or to perform only certain acts. It meant to spiritualize, to sanctify everything that one does, to elevate all that one touches. It meant that religion must pervade all of one's work, that it should blend into all one's actions, so that there would be no separation between the sacred and the secular but only between the sacred and the sacred.

5

The way our lives and our society are organized, however, we feel compelled to fragmentize and to compartmentize our thoughts and our actions. In the interest of a greater liberty, we must believe that the United States Constitution provides for a strict separation between church and state and that the realm of God and the realm of Caesar must not be allowed to intermingle. However, we must recognize the fact that these terms are arbitrary signs, constructed and imposed for practical and concrete purposes, and were intended to contribute to the safeguarding of our lives and liberties. They are semantic and institutional inventions. Used appropriately, they are superb conventions, but these concepts have no legitimate place outside the political arena. Our innermost thoughts and our lives as we live them ought to know no such artificial divisions, which we have arbitrarily yet rationally imposed upon ourselves and upon our institutions.

Maimonides, commenting on the statement in the Talmud "Let all thy deeds be for the sake of God,"[43] wrote that a man must seek his physical health and vigor, for he cannot pursue intellectual work and think properly if he is hungry, sick, or in pain. Whoever, he wrote,

> throughout his life follows this course will be continually serving God, even while engaged in business, and even during cohabitation, because his purpose in all that he does will be to . . . serve God. Even when he sleeps and seeks repose, to calm his mind and rest his body, so as not to fall sick and be incapacitated . . . his sleep is service of the Almighty.[44]

How ridiculous, Maimonides thought, is the veil that men have imposed between the transcendent and the immanent and between themselves and God. All natural forces are, so to speak, "angels":

How great is the blindness of ignorance and how harmful. If you told a man who is one of those who deemed themselves "the Sages of Israel" that the Deity sends an angel, who enters the womb of a woman and forms the fetus there, he would be pleased with this assertion and would accept it and would regard it as a manifestation of greatness and power on the part of the Deity. . . . But if you tell him that God has placed in the sperm a formative force shaping the limbs and giving them their configuration and that this force is the "angel" . . . the man would shrink from this opinion. For he does not understand the notion of the true greatness and power that consists in the bringing into existence of forces active in a thing.[45]

When, in 1962, the Supreme Court held that the prayer formulated by the New York Board of Regents and authorized by them to be recited in the public schools of that state was unconstitutional,[46] there was a great outcry that the Court had taken God out of the schools and had "deconsecrated the nation."[47] What a shocking corruption of religion these charges were! God is in a school, and that school is consecrated, when the teachers—supported by the parents in their homes—feel themselves dedicated to a high and noble vocation and bring to bear on their work and in all their relations with their students the best of their thoughts and energies. Whether the children do or do not hurry through the mumbo-jumbo of a twenty-two-word officially-drafted so-called prayer, if the teachers, administrators, and parents perform their services with purity of motives and with singleness of heart, that school will be no less sacred than any synagogue or church. "Would that all the Lord's people were prophets, that the Lord would put His spirit upon them!"[48]

We must remember, wrote Jeremy Taylor in the seventeenth century,

that the life of every man may be so ordered (and indeed must) that it may be a perpetual serving of God: the greatest trouble and most busy trade and worldly encumbrances, when they are necessary, or charitable, or profitable in order to any of those ends which we are bound to serve, whether public or private, being a doing [of] God's work. For God provides the good things of the world to serve the needs of nature, by the labors of the ploughman, the skill and pains of the artisan, and the dangers and traffic of the merchant; these men are, in their calling, the ministers of the Divine Providence, and the stewards of the creation, and servants of a great family of God . . . So that no man can complain that his calling takes him off from religion; his calling itself, and his very worldly employment . . . is a serving of God. . . . Blessed be that goodness and grace of God, which, out of infinite desire to glorify and save mankind, would make the very works of nature capable of becoming acts of virtue, that all our life-time we may do Him service.[49]

We conclude, then, where we began: that the God whom we worship wants not sacerdotalism but religions that see the sacred in the secular, the holy in the profane, so that in the end the distinction will be not between the sacred and the secular but between the sacred and the sacred.

5

Law and Morals in the Bible, Plato, and Aristotle

This essay was written for the volume Social Responsibility in an Age of Revolution, *edited by Louis Finkelstein, president of the Jewish Theological Seminary, and published by the Seminary in 1971. It also appeared in* Conservative Judaism *in 1969.*

The tension between enacted or positive law and morals or a higher law is one that has become, in the twentieth century, visible to everyone familiar with the Nüremberg trials and the Eichmann trial; the Universal Declaration of Human Rights, adopted by the General Assembly of the United Nations; the International Covenants on Human Rights, approved by the United Nations; the European Convention for the Protection of Human Rights and Fundamental Freedoms, adopted by the Council of Europe; the American Declaration of the Rights and Duties of Man, adopted by the Organization of American States; the Helsinki document; the widespread resort to civil disobedience; the renewed dignity given to conscience by the Second Vatican Council; the resistance to the war in Vietnam, especially by church and synagogue groups, in the name of conscience; the expansion in the meaning and reach of the Bill of Rights of the United States Constitution that has been effected by the Supreme Court since 1954; the enlarged and deepened interest in the plight of the poor; the pressure on legislatures and on courts to adapt the law to moral changes brought about by technological advances—e.g., artificial insemination, the use of contraceptive devices, the transplanting of organs. This is only a partial bill of particulars that show the reasons for the deepening stress and strain between law and morals.

One the one hand, there are those who cry for "law and order." Among them are men who are simply for the *status quo*, or really for the *status quo ante,* who want a restoration of "the good old days." Among them are also men who want to see the "law and order" changed, but only as the result of peaceful dissent and of intelligent discussion. On the other hand, there are those who have their eyes on a new law and a new order and who relegate existing law to the gross, material, valueless world, which they want to see subverted. They take their stand for morality and against the law.

Years ago Ahad Ha-am portrayed the essentials of this conflict in his essay on "Priest and Prophet." The priest is the man who seeks not "what *ought* to be, but what *can* be": his battle is not against actuality—he fights in the name of actuality against its enemies. The prophet, on the other hand, is carried away by his idea; he is "essentially a one-sided man," for

> A certain moral idea fills his whole being, masters his every feeling and sensation, engrosses his whole attention. He can only see the world through the mirror of his idea; he desires nothing, strives for nothing, except to make every phase of the life around him an embodiment of that idea in its perfect form . . . regardless of the conditions of life and the demands of the general harmony.[1]

The tension between law and morals and the complexity of relations between them are part of our intellectual and institutional history. They are perhaps ineradicable. There is even lacking a vocabulary adequate to describe the complexity of the problem. Our contemporary experience of the problem is rooted in ancient Hebraic and Greek categories, and we probably will come no nearer to its resolution than did ancient Israel with its priests and prophets or the ancient Greeks with their Plato and Aristotle.

1

In the Hebrew Scriptures, the distinction between law and morals does not exist; the least one can say is that it is not articulated. Nor is there a difference between religion and morals, or between religion and law. There is a single order of values that makes a total claim on the people of Israel. By covenant, they became God's people. Their rights are all subordinated to God's rights; their duties are all subordinated to their duties to Him; and these duties are all commanded by God, who made the law and whose will and nature fixed what is good and what is evil—what is allowed or commanded and what is prohibited. The same code provides what shall be the duties and the dues of the priests, the distinctions between clean and unclean animals, the procedures for the purification of women, the test for and treatment of leprosy, the definition and prohibition of incest, the duty to treat the stranger as an equal, and the requirement to have just balances and just weights. All duties, to whomsoever owed, are placed under the all-embracing commandment: "You shall therefore keep my statutes and my ordinances, by doing which a man shall live: I am the Lord. . . . You shall be holy; for I the Lord your God am holy."[2]

Implicit in this single order of values, however, is the need to differentiate, to classify, to establish an order of priorities, and above all to transcend the existing system into some higher sphere.

An example of transcendence is the dedication of the boy Samuel to abide "for ever" in the presence of the Lord at the temple at Shiloh. The Nazirites generally, with their lifelong obligations to abstain from wine or strong drink and to have untrimmed hair—to symbolize their complete separation from the ways of the original peoples of Canaan and from the worship of the nature gods—are an example of the drive to transcend the socially accepted order and to reach more nearly what is assumed to be the spirit behind it, an example of the compulsion to absolutize values.

A more normal instance of transcendence is found in the story of Ruth. When Boaz observed Ruth gleaning in his field after the reapers, he instructed his young men to pull out some of the barley from the sheaves for her to glean. This was going beyond what the law required. It is an instance of what the Talmud later referred to as the principle of *lifnim mi-shurat ha-din*, interpreted as the duty not to insist on the strict law but to go beyond the line of the law.[3] The example and the principle point to an awareness of the existence of a moral law that is higher than the existing law and that makes greater demands on the conscience. The law only required that Boaz was not to pick up the ears of corn that fell from the hand of the reaper and was not to gather up the grapes that dropped in the gathering—these belonged to the poor and not to Boaz.[4] When Boaz contrived that Ruth was to have as gleanings what the law held were his own, however, he certainly felt that there was a distinction between law and morals.

The great prophets, with their shrill emphasis on what we would today call moral conduct, were feeling their way to an order of priorities among legal duties and to a distinction between law and morals. Thus Micah cried out:

> He has showed you, O man, what is good;
>> and what does the Lord require of you
> but to do justice, and to love kindness,
>> and to walk humbly with your God?[5]

Isaiah, as well, felt that holiness meant to "seek judgment, relieve the oppressed, judge the fatherless, plead for the widow."[6] The rationale is an inarticulate feeling that somehow man must put first things first, just as God does when He says: "For I desire mercy, and not sacrifice; and the knowledge of God more than burnt offerings."[7] Implicit in these judgments is the differentiation of law and morals, though the prophets would have denied vehemently that these spheres could ever be completely separated, even only conceptually, one from the other.

Perhaps the strongest ground for a differentiation between law and morals lay in the fact that the Hebraic mind seemed to work with two sets of categories.

The first category is that of the pure moral commandment: "You shall love your neighbor as yourself."[8] The love commandment is often expressed in terms that point specifically to certain classes of persons as one's neighbors in a special sense: the widow, the fatherless child, the stranger, the poor and needy. These commandments were given a religious provenance by the commandment to live a life in the imitation of God, to be holy as God is holy: "For the Lord your God is God of gods and Lord of lords, the great, the mighty, and the terrible God, who is not partial and takes no bribe. He executes justice for the fatherless and the widow, and loves the stranger, giving him food and clothing. Love the stranger, therefore, for you were strangers in the land of Egypt."[9] These commandments are so sweepingly broad and so deeply moral that they cannot be confined to any legal enactments; they speak to the law in the heart,[10] the law written on the tablets of the heart.[11]

At the same time and equally pervasive is the second category, that of positive law: e.g., the sabbath day as a day of rest, for "in it you shall not do any work, you, or your son, or your daughter, or your man-servant, or your maid-servant, or your ox, or your ass, or any of your cattle, or the stranger who is within your gates, that your manservant and your maidservant may rest as well as you."[12] So too the year of release, at the end of every seven years, when every creditor must release what he has lent to his neighbor;[13] the requirement to build a parapet for one's roof, so that one may not accidentally fall from it;[14] the law relating to gleanings and to leave the corner of the field for the poor and the stranger.[15] These are instances of legal duties that vest or entail legal rights in the beneficiaries. They are instances of what the Hebrew Scriptures speak of as *mishpat*. The moral commands, on the other hand, are general and are not reduced to specific enactments; they entail duties toward God that are fulfilled by love toward the neighbor. They are referred to as *tsedakah*. While mishpat is directed negatively as a prohibition upon the deprivation of the neighbor's rights, tsedakah looks to the positive realization of the good.[16]

The moral and legal strands may intersect. An explicit example of interdependence is to be seen in the formulation of the law calling for the year of release. The rich man, knowing that the year of release is approaching, may refuse to lend to his needy neighbor; thus the benign purpose of the law may stand in the way of the rich extending credit or lending to the poor. At this point the Bible calls upon the moral law written on the tablets of the heart to sustain the enacted or positive law of the year of release:

> Take heed lest there be a base thought in your heart, and you say, "The seventh year, the year of release is near," and your eye be hostile to your poor brother, and you give him nothing, and he cry to the Lord against you, and it be sin in you. You shall give to him freely, and your heart shall not be grudging when you give to him; because for this the Lord your God will bless you in all your work and in all that you undertake. For the poor will never cease out of the land; therefore I command you, you shall open wide your hand to your brother, to the needy and to the poor, in the land.[17]

The law, morals, and religion are wonderfully interwoven. The commandment is one—to have a year of release when all debts are wiped out and when the poor are relieved of their grinding burdens of debts and can look to a fresh start; but the one commandment, when looked at with our modern eyes, clearly has built into it categories that we tend to keep distinct and often even separate.

We should, however, emphasize that we are reading back into the ancient sources concepts and principles that came to be articulated only in modern times. The biblical and ancient rabbinic mind would have found it distasteful, and perhaps even reprehensible, to separate—in thought and institutionally—what God has joined.

What God had joined, according to the biblical theodicy, was fact and value, evil and punishment, good deed and reward. Insofar as possible, the connection is to be effected by the human agency of the ruler and his government. Their essential function is to judge and to execute judgment, as God's surrogates on earth. However, what the human rulers and judges leave undone, God himself would do; for God is the Supreme Ruler, the King of kings and the all-wise and omnicompetent Judge. God would use even nations as his agents to execute his judgments, lifing up one nation and using its power and ambitions to cast down, trample upon, and even wholly destroy other nations. Wicked men and nations are held to strict account. Execution of judgment may be delayed; it may even be postponed for generations—but the day of reckoning finally comes.

This Hebraic theodicy, made explicit by the eighth-century prophets, puts law, morals, and religion into an organic whole. Thus, every deed is subject to God's law, and man lives in a law-centered and law-enveloping world, a law from which there is no escape or hiding place. If the earthly ruler will not execute God's law and judgment, then God himself will do so.

The theodicy encompasses the community as an entity. If the group will live by God's commandments, then God will send the rain in its season, the people will have their corn, wine, and oil and the cattle will have grass, and everyone will eat and be satisfied. If the heart of the people strays, however, then the anger of God will be kindled, and he will shut up the heavens so that there will be no rain and the earth will not yield her fruit.[18] The retribution may also come through "the rod of God's anger":

> Ah, Assyria, the rod of my anger,
>   the staff of my fury!
> Against a godless nation I send him,
>   and against the people of my wrath I command him,
> to take spoil and seize plunder,
>   and to tread them down like the mire of the streets.[19]

The individual, too, is directly subject to God's law, to judgment and its execution. Immediately preceding the above-quoted verses from Isaiah, the prophet foretells the curses that will come down upon the perverters of justice and upon the evil-doers:

> Woe to those who decree iniquitous decrees,
>   and the writers who keep writing oppression,
> to turn aside the needy from justice
>   and to rob the poor of my people of their right,
> that widows may be their spoil,
>   and that they may make the fatherless their prey!
> What will you do on the day of punishment,
>   in the storm which will come from afar?
> To whom will you flee for help,
>   and where will you leave your wealth?[20]

Many of the Psalms emphasize the same theme of reward for the good and punishment for sin and for evil—the providential rule of man's world by the Creator and Ruler of that world. Psalm 37, for example, asserts this faith in providential rule without waver or question:

> Fret not yourself because of the wicked,
>   be not envious of wrongdoers!
> For they will soon fade like the grass,
>   and wither like the green herb. . . .
> Commit your way to the Lord;
>   trust in him and he will act. . . .
> For the wicked shall be cut off;
>   but those who wait for the Lord shall possess the land.[21]

The friends of Job, with the exception of Elihu, express the same theme. Eliphaz says to Job:

> Think now, who that was innocent ever perished?
>   Or where were the upright cut off?
> As I have seen, those who plow iniquity
>   And sow trouble reap the same.[22]

As we have noted, from the standpoint of an all-encompassing theodicy —which is a dominant biblical theme—there is no need for a differentiation among values, for a distinction between law and morals; *all* acts are subject to the law of God, who will find a way to bring to judgment every man and every nation—"for all his ways are justice,"[23] "for the Lord is a God of justice,"[24] "for all his works are truth, and his ways are justice."[25] However, there is also in the Bible a counterpoint to this theme. After all, the evidence of the eye often contradicts this simple faith in a providential rule, a faith that could assert: "I have been young, and now am old / Yet I have not seen the righteous forsaken or his children begging bread."[26] The critical voice cannot be altogether silenced in the face of the evidence that flagrantly contradicts this faith in Providence. "Why," cries out Jeremiah, "does the way of the wicked prosper? Why do all who are treacherous thrive?"[27]

One explanation for the fact that the righteous often suffer is the belief, expressed by Elihu to Job, that undeserved suffering may be a form of moral education or discipline.[28] This would not, however, explain why the wicked prosper. On the group or national level, Isaiah (or Deutero-Isaiah) made a similar approach with his belief in the

Suffering Servant, the idea that a nation may suffer not for its sins but for the purpose of teaching mankind.[29]

A much more daring line is taken by Psalm 73. The author candidly admits that he was envious when he saw the prosperity of the wicked. They enjoy good health; "they are not in trouble as other men are"; they speak with malice and threaten oppression and they act arrogantly. "Behold, these are the wicked / always at ease, they increase in riches." Though his spiritual torment continues—for rationally there can be no abatement of his perplexity—the psalmist does not fall into despair. He makes a staggering leap from the realm disclosed by his senses to a totally different level, from the I/world relationship to the level of I/God. In the face of the evidence of his eyes, the psalmist cries out:

> Thou dost hold my right hand. . . .
> And there is nothing upon earth that I desire besides thee.
> My flesh and my heart may fail,
> but God is the strength of my heart and my portion for ever. . . .
> But for me it is good to be near God;
> I have made the Lord God my refuge.[30]

The psalmist does not see the work of Providence, "nevertheless" he believes; for the I/God relationship suffices as the strength of his heart, as his portion, as his refuge. The order of things is not changed; the righteous go on suffering, the wicked continue to flourish; the connection between deed and reward does not manifest itself; "nevertheless" life is justified, as long as man can say: "I am continually with thee." To be near God is to live, to be far from God is to be spiritually dead—to be dead within the heart. To see things and events from the perspective of the I/God level is to free oneself from the need to find retribution mechanically operating in the world, it is to rise far above the worldly level of the friends of Job. For God's habitation is in the inner man, not in the outer; His holy place is in the heart, not in the marketplace.

The implications of this view are immeasurably great; for our purpose it is sufficient to see that it emancipates morality from the bookkeeping approach that the theodicy seemingly necessitates. Law can depend on utilitarian considerations and on outer sanctions, but morality will depend on God's judgment, which the heart will know. There is the law that men enforce, as God's agents; there is the law, the higher law, the moral commandment, for which the only sanction will be in the conscience or heart.

The same resolution through a "nevertheless" comes to Job when he is finally able to rise above his friends, his dung-heap, his suffering, and his devastating realization that Providence simply does not work in ways manifest to the bodily eye. Job rises to another level of meaning, to the pure I/God level, where pomp, honor, prosperity, health, degredation, dishonor, poverty, sickness—where all the things that men may see, measure, or count—simply do not matter; it is *there* that Job, stripped of his flesh, sees God.[31] On the I/God level, the world and life have meaning—but a meaning that is visible only to the inner eye; and on any other level, though there may be all the sound and trappings of life, there is only death, for God is not there. This is the wisdom that at last comes to Job and that liberates him from ignorance and saves him from cynicism and from atheism.

It is this kind of wisdom and liberation that is required for a distinction between law and morals. For as long as man is bound to a theodicy, then God's law orders every act and event; His law is perfect and will work mechanically to give each man his just deserts and for each act his just reward. Such an order has no need of a differentiation between law and morals. Once the facts of life are faced, however, and it is seen that there is no necessary tie (outside the realm where the policeman and the police court have jurisdiction) between deed and reward, then a separate realm is needed for morality—a realm that only God's eye can penetrate, a realm in which God stands directly before man as His maker, ruler, and judge, a realm in which the outward signs of reward and punishment have no meaning.

A separation probably also was forced upon the Hebraic consciousness as the Jews lived in exile or under foreign rule in their home land. This comes out clearly in the New Testament maxim: "Render therefore to Caesar the things that are Caesar's, and to God the things that are God's."[32] The difference between positive law as the enactment of the state and all other commandments—religious, moral, or legal—that emanate from God is necessarily assumed, as it probably was also assumed by the prophet Jeremiah as he gave counsel to the Jews who were in exile in Babylon.[33] As the Jews mingled with non-Jews, they were compelled to formulate a moral theory of man that, by implication, marked off religion, morals, and law as distinct spheres. Such a view of man's moral nature clearly appears in the Talmudic tradition of the seven commandments to Noah and his descendants, which asserts that *all men* are commanded to observe seven fundamental principles. These prohibit idolatry (which was, in the Jewish tradition, always associated with immoral practices), murder, theft, blasphemy, incest, and eating the flesh of living animals, and require the promotion of justice.[34]

However, as we shall see in part 4 of this essay, always inherent in the Hebraic conception of positive law was the idea that although this law was an expression of the good, of justice, and of righteousness, the law was transcended by the good, the just, and the righteous—a view of law, of morals, and of the relationships between them that Plato and Aristotle would have found understandable and congenial.

2

The ancient Greeks, too, failed to differentiate between law and morals. Just as the Jews found divine sanction for the chosen people and for the Torah, so the Greek dramatists and philosophers found divine sanction for the Greek city-state and its laws. Their city of men was their city of God—a social order that embodied all that was best for man, or at least best for the Greek citizen. The city-state, writes Aristotle, "comes into existence for the sake of mere life, but exists for the sake of the good life."[35] Basic to the good life for the Greeks, as for the Jews, was the rule of law.

For the Jew, the teaching, the Law, Torah, "is a tree of life to those who lay hold of her; those who hold her fast are called happy."[36] It was the Lord Himself who "became king in Jeshurun, when the heads of the people were gathered, all the tribes of Israel together";[37] to obey the law was to be blessed: "If you obey the commandments of the Lord your God . . . then you shall live and multiply, and the Lord your God will bless you."[38]

Socrates, in prison, condemned by the Athenian jury to die by poison, praised the laws and constitution of his city and held fast to them with his last breath. He heard the laws say to him that by their virtue they had given him his very life, by their power his father had married his mother; it was the laws that had directed them how to bring up their son and to educate him. Indeed, Socrates was the child of the laws, their ward and their servant, and he would sooner drink the cup of hemlock and die than destroy his country's laws by breaking them.[39]

The laws had their origin in ancient customs and traditions, in back of which was the will of the gods. "All human laws are fed by the one divine law," said Heraclitus.[40] It was this belief that gave Antigone the strength to defy the decree of Creon, shouting: "It was not Zeus who gave the order." Creon, and not Antigone, was the one who violated the law; he, and not she, was indeed the criminal:

> Nor did I think that your pronouncements were
> So powerful that mere man could override

> The unwritten and unfailing laws of heaven.
> These live, not for today and yesterday
> But for all time.[41]

The rule of law, as conceived by the Greeks, in theory excluded no phase of life or conduct from its province. Its reach was coextensive with tradition and custom, institutions that historically encompassed the totality of man and society. There was no room in this view for any differentiation between morals and law.

As in the case of Hebraic thought and experience, however, a critical element gradually penetrated into the accepted theory, so that in due course philosophical analysis began to point to a differentiation between law and morals. There was nothing explicit in the process. There was a groping, a reaching out, a positing of elements that could later be interpreted as implicitly involving a differentiation (and possibly even a separation) between law and morals.

In Plato's *Republic,* the law is clearly subordinate and accountable to the supreme Form, the Good. The purpose of the law is the production of men who are altogether good. To have such law, philosophers must be kings, and kings must be philosophers. Although this view merges law and morals, the merger is possible only in the ideal state, in which the philosophy of the good life and the art of statecraft coalesce in the same persons. The implication is that in a society that falls short of the ideal, the law, when judged by the ideal moral order, will be found wanting. There is, therefore, an implied differentiation between law and morals.

Given that the ideal social order is beyond human attainment, Plato's *Laws* constructed a society that would be subject strictly to the rule of law. In its formative stage, this society would select the best laws under which the people could live and be ruled; once the code of laws is instituted, there are to be no departures from it. Easy and hard cases alike are to be decided according to the promulgated law. The ideal or moral element is to be kept out.

It was either/or to Plato: either the moral, ideal, intellectual judgment makes the decision, or the decision is made in accordance with the strict law. Philosophy can justify only the former; expedience can justify only the latter. In a crucial passage in the *Laws,* Plato says: "No law or ordinance whatever has the right to sovereignty over true knowledge [of the Good]; 'tis a sin that [moral] understanding should be any creature's subject or servant; its place is to be ruler of all, if only it is indeed, as it ought to be, genuine and free." This is the voice of pure reason, of reason as it listens only to the Form of the Good. It is the voice heard in the *Republic;* this leaves no room for law except for law as the enforcement of the moral judgment. The above passage, however, goes on: "But, as things are, such [moral] insight is nowhere to be met with, except in faint vestiges, and so we have to choose the second-best, ordinance and law."[42]

For the second-best system, then, the moral judgment is important only as the code of laws is being prepared at the founding of society, and the moral judgment pretty well exhausts itself in this constitutional and legislative process. Once enacted, the law has no concern with anything outside its own order. Moral wisdom brings the code of laws into existence, but the laws do not look before or after—they see only themselves.

The reason for Plato's preference for the rule of wisdom, if that were possible, is succinctly stated in the *Politicus:*

> There can be no doubt that legislation is in a manner the business of a king, and yet the best thing of all is not that the law should rule, but that a man should rule, supposing him to have wisdom and power. Do you see why this is? . . .
>
> Because the law does not perfectly comprehend what is noblest and most just for all and therefore cannot enforce what is best. The differences of men and actions, and the endless, irregular movement of human beings, do not admit of any universal and simple rule. And no art whatsoever can lay down a rule which will last for all time. . . .
>
> But the law is always striving to make one.[43]

The law, in other words, should ideally be indistinguishable from the moral wisdom. Moral wisdom will be flexible; it will respond to the infinite variety of human beings, human needs, human situations, human changes. The law cannot achieve this ideal; it will enact what is for the general good but not what is good for each particular case. Laws, some of them written and some of them unwritten, are in a general form, intended for the majority, and they only roughly meet the cases of individuals.[44] Because the laws are based upon long experience and upon the wisdom of counselors who have recommended them and who have persuaded the multitude to enact them, to allow either an individual or the multitude to break the law in any respect would be a far greater crime and a more ruinous error than any adherence to them could be.[45]

Although Plato recognized that harm could come from making trifling acts into crimes, he was not satisfied with seeing any limit on the omnicompetence of the rule of law. He saw in any exclusion from the reach of the law an evil for the public as a whole, for while the frequency and triviality of such faults makes it both improper and undignified to penalize them by law, they are a real danger to such law as we do impose, since the habit of transgression is learned from repetition of these petty misdeeds. Hence, though we are at a loss to legislate on such points, silence about them is also impossible.[46]

Thus, Plato provided regulation of almost every conceivable aspect of life from cradle to grave. It did not occur to him that the effect of placing almost every human action under the law may be the attrition of the moral sense and the loss of human freedom and responsibility. Even a well-trained dog is permitted a large measure of liberty for spontaneous play. Plato recognized the fact that the preparation of the code of laws required extraordinary moral wisdom; once the code is promulgated, however, Plato makes no provision for keeping the moral sense alive in the citizens or in its rulers. All are to be strictly under the rule of law, and any act contrary to law is to be punished by death.[47] "For nobody," says Plato, "should be wiser than the law"—that is, once it is agreed that the rule of the wise must give way to the rule of law, once it is agreed that the best order is impossible and must give way to the second-best.[48] Plato left no room for a combination of wisdom and law, for compromise, for accommodation, for an order of society, institutions, and thought based on both law *and* morals.

However, as we shall see in part 4 of this essay, some serious qualifications to this conclusion must be made. After all, Plato's idealism was too deeply felt by him and was too widely pervasive of his thought to warrant a formulation of jurisprudence that might serve as a model for Hobbes, Austin, or Kelsen. Plato could be an absolute idealist in the *Republic* but he could never be, in any dialogue, an absolute positivist. Indeed, as we will see, his ultimate resolution of the problem of the relation of law to ideal was not in essence different from the biblical position.

3

Probably with an eye on Plato, under whom he had studied for twenty years, Aristotle faced up to the choice between the rule of law and the rule of man and chose the former. In a famous passage in the *Politics*, Aristotle writes:

He who commands that law should rule may thus be regarded as commanding that God and reason alone should rule; he who commands that a man should rule adds the character of the beast. Appe-

tite has that character; and high spirit, too, perverts the holders of
office, even when they are the best of men. Law [as the pure voice
of good and reason] may thus be defined as "Reason free from all
passion."[49]

If faced with a choice between the *Republic* and the *Laws*, Aristotle
would choose the latter; not, however, as the second-best, but as the
best; for even the best of men, philosopher-kings, cannot be free from
appetite and from high spirit.

In fact, however, for Aristotle the rule of law did not need to be as
absolute, as all-encompassing, as Plato in the *Laws* thought it had to
be. Indeed, keeping always in mind the mean or the middle way as
the best disposition and the mixed polity as the best government,
Aristotle could not be expected to choose wholly one extreme or another, either the rule of law or the rule of man. His choice was for an
open-ended, not an enclosed, rule of law. Basically, then, Aristotle
would prefer the approach of Plato as formulated in the *Laws*, provided that the formulation expressly left room for some open doors
and windows, but he would reject without hesitation the line of
thought in the *Republic* that led to the rule of the philosopher-king.

What open doors and windows does Aristotle provide to go with
the rule of law? The answer to this question will show the subtle
interplay of law and morals in Aristotle's thinking.

First, there is the distinction between legal justice and natural justice. Legal justice is justice according to law; it is achievable in a state
among citizens whose relations are regulated by law and who enjoy
free and equal status. In such a polity, the administration of the law
means the discrimination of what is just and unjust. To act unjustly
means to appropriate too large a share of what is good and too small
a share of what is evil: "This is why we do not permit a man to rule,
but the law, because a man rules in his own interest, and becomes a
tyrant; but the function of a ruler is to be the guardian of justice, and
if not of justice, then of equality."[50] Legal justice is conventional and is
therefore variable, but once the law is settled one way or another, its
binding force is not reduced by the fact that its origin was institutional. A rule, says Aristotle, is conventional "that in the first instance
may be settled in one way or the other indifferently, though having
once been settled it is not indifferent; for example, that the ransom for
a prisoner shall be a mina, that a sacrifice shall consist of a goat and
not of two sheep."[51]

Are all rules of justice merely conventional? No, there is also natural justice, according to laws of nature that are immutable and that
have validity everywhere. Rules of justice are variable, yet there is

such a thing as natural justice. What Aristotle means, I believe, can be made clear by an example. It is by natural justice that murder is prohibited and punished. No society can treat homicide indifferently and agree that legal justice shall look the other way when a human being is killed. It is, however, a matter of convention whether the punishment shall be death or life imprisonment or imprisonment for a number of years. The definition of murder and its breakdown into classes or grades—willful or negligent, first degree, second degree, the distinction between murder and manslaughter, and the punishment of each grade or type—these are all variable, though the law against murder is a matter of natural justice. This is, I think what Aristotle means by his statement that the laws of natural justice are immutable and are valid everywhere, yet all rules of justice are variable.

In the *Rhetoric*, Aristotle speaks of "particular" laws as those established by each people in reference to themselves, and of "general" laws as those based upon nature. "In fact," Aristotle continues,

> there is a general idea of just and unjust in accordance with nature, as all men [are] in a manner divine, even if there is neither communication nor agreement between them. This is what Antigone in Sophocles evidently means, when she declares that it is just, though forbidden [by a "particular" law], to bury Polynices, as being naturally just: "For neither today nor yesterday, but from all eternity, these statutes live and no man knoweth whence they came." And as Empedocles says in regard to not killing that which has life, for this is not right for some and wrong for other, "But a universal precept, which extends without a break throughout the wide-ruling sky and the boundless earth."[52]

Although this statement might be somewhat reduced in value on account of its possible forensic context, nothing can be asserted against the import of the statement in the *Nicomachean Ethics* that

> there seem to be some acts which a man cannot be compelled to do, and rather than do them he ought to submit to the most terrible death: for instance, we think it ridiculous that Alcmaeon in Euripides' play is compelled by certain threats to murder his mother! But it is sometimes difficult to decide how far we ought to go in choosing to do a given act rather than suffer a given penalty, or in enduring a given penalty, rather than commit a given action; and it is still more difficult to abide by our decision when made, since in most of such dilemmas the penalty threatened is painful and the deed forced upon us dishonorable, which is why praise and blame are bestowed according as we do or do not yield to such compulsion.[53]

This statement could not have been made in its context unless Aristotle had in mind some such distinction as that between conventional, enacted, or particular laws and laws of natural justice. His statement assumes the existence of some kind of higher law, or a morality that transcends positive law. Aristotle might have cited here once more the example of Antigone, without necessarily approving her invocation of the higher law under the circumstances; or he might have cited the use made of the higher law by Socrates when he related to the jury the instances in which he ran the danger of facing the death penalty rather than obey unconscionable superior orders, or when he said to the jury:

> Where a man has once taken up his stand, either because it seems best to him or in obedience to his order, there I believe he is bound to remain and face the danger, taking no account of death or anything else before dishonor. . . . "Gentlemen, I am your very grateful and obedient servant, but I owe a greater obedience to God than to you.". . . And so, gentlemen, I would say, "you can please yourselves whether you listen to Anytus [the prosecutor] or not, and whether you acquit me or not; you know that I am not going to alter my conduct, not even if I have to die a hundred deaths."[54]

As the second of his open doors in the rule of law, besides classifying law and justice into conventional and natural, Aristotle classifies justice into the unwritten kind and the kind according to law. From the context it would appear that Aristotle meant justice according to morals and justice according to law; the examples he offers make this clear. On the one hand, he says, there is the usual type of business contract, when it is clear that there is a *quid pro quo* involving either an exchange on the spot or future delivery. On the other hand, there is the "moral type" of agreement in which a gift or other service is given "as to a friend." Because the latter transaction is not on stated terms, it often generates misunderstanding, for the giver may in fact expect to receive an equivalent or greater return, as though he had made a loan and not a gift. The reason for this is "that all men, or most men, wish what is noble but choose what is profitable; and while it is noble to render a service not with an eye to receiving one in return, it is profitable to receive one."[55]

Although, admittedly, Aristotle is not precise in his use of the terms "written" and "unwritten" in the *Nicomachean Ethics*, it is hard to see how Ernest Barker could interpret the terms so that "unwritten" becomes merely the "customary."[56] In the *Rhetoric* Aristotle again gives a classification of the just in terms of laws that are written and those that are unwritten. One kind of unwritten justice, he says, "arises from an excess of virtue or vice, which is followed by praise or blame, honor or dishonor, and rewards; for instance, to be grateful to a benefactor, to render good for good, to keep one's friends, and the like."[57] There is, it seems clear, an unwritten law that belongs not to the law enforced by the state with rewards and penalties but to the moral sphere, where the sanctions, if any, are left to public opinion.

There is still, however, another kind of unwritten law, one which is within the positive legal order and which, therefore, does entail sanctions enforced by the state. This is a type of law that bridges the moral sphere and the sphere of enacted law. It is the type called by Aristotle *epikeis* or equity. The *locus classicus* of the notion is in the *Nicomachean Ethics*, where Aristotle defines equity as the correction of the law in cases in which the law is deficient by reason of its generality. In addition to the legally just, there is also then the equitably just, which is a correction of the former.[58] There is a need for equity because a law must always be drafted as a universal proposition but life produces unusual or unanticipated sets of facts, and the judges will feel that these ought not to be subsumed under the generality of the enacted law. The judges will, in these circumstances, seek to correct the omission from the enacted law by writing into it what the legislator himself would have said if he had known what the judges know.

As we have noted, in the *Rhetoric* Aristotle states that there are two kinds of unwritten justice. We have already mentioned one kind, that which arises from an excess of virtue or vice, which is followed by honor or dishonor. The second kind of unwritten justice is the equitable, or that which "goes beyond the written law," that which was omitted in the written law. Aristotle's elaboration in the *Rhetoric* clarifies the notion of equity:

> Actions which should be leniently treated are cases for equity; errors, wrong acts, and misfortunes must not be thought deserving of the same penalty. Misfortunes are all such things as are unexpected and not vicious; errors are not unexpected, but are not vicious. . . . And it is equitable to pardon human weaknesses, and to look, not to the law but to the legislator; not to the letter of the law but to the intention of the legislator; not to the action itself, but to the moral purpose; not to the part, but to the whole; not to what a man is now, but to what he has been, always or generally . . . to prefer arbitration to the law court, for the arbitrator keeps equity in view whereas the dicast looks only to the law.[59]

In a later passage in the same treatise, writing specifically of forensic oratory, Aristotle says that when the written law is against one's case, then we should argue from the general—meaning natural—law and from equity,

> as more in accordance with justice; and we must [then] argue that, when the dicast takes an oath to decide to the best of his judgment, he means that he will not abide rigorously by the written laws; that equity is ever constant and never changes, even as the general law, which is based on nature, whereas the written laws often vary. This is why Antigone in Sophocles justifies herself for having buried Polynices contrary to the law of Creon, but not contrary to the unwritten law: "For this law is not of now or yesterday, but is eternal."[60]

Students of Aristotle do not agree as to where equity was meant to be located—within or outside of the legal order. For the purposes of our discussion, it is not imperative that we take a definite stand on this issue. For us it is enough to note that the concept allows Aristotle to build a bridge from law to morals, so that law could at times be transcended or could transcend itself. On the one hand, equity has a legislative function, permitting the judge to act in place of the legislator, to write into the enacted law a provision that would cover the omitted case. This would seem to put equity within the legal order itself. On the other hand, equity suggests a transcendance of the enacted law to natural justice. This could mean that equity is in the moral sphere but is imported into the legal order to fill a vacant space or to displace a legal enactment.

The answer to the question as to the proper location of equity will come, I think, more easily if we consider the primary question of the relation of law to justice, a question that affords an opportunity to see the essential unity in the legal-moral thought in the Hebrew Bible, in Plato, and in Aristotle—the topic to which we now turn.

4

In the Hebrew Bible, as we have seen, the law embraces the whole life of man and of the community, but there is room left for the good that exceeds the measure commanded by the law. Indeed, the law itself commands its own transcendance by placing before man and society the ideal of holiness: "Be holy. . . ."[61] For the law is Torah; it is law but it is also teaching, instruction, a way of life, because behind the legal code is God the Lawgiver and the Judge; Torah is teaching about God and His ways and His wishes, and it is God's plan or constitution for Israel. Torah is, then, in its most pervasive sense, God's instruction. The study of Torah is itself a basic commandment: "These words which I command you this day shall be upon your heart, and you shall teach them diligently to your children, and shall talk of them when you sit in your house, and when you walk by the way, and when you lie down, and when you rise."[62] Torah is, therefore, both law and religion.[63] As religion, Torah reveals something of the nature of God, the author of Torah, but the revelation of God's nature is made, at least in part, through the law which He gave to Israel. Thus law and religion are inextricably intertwined.

The most fundamental character of the law and of God is justice, or more correctly, righteousness. Whatever righteousness may mean, its most enduring meaning is the quality that makes for what is *right*. The law is perfect because it flows out of God who is always *right*, and because it points to what is *right* for man. God is not one who turns out codes of law as a machine may turn out pins or nails; God's laws bear His imprint; they disclose His justice, His righteousness: "And what great nation is there, that has statutes and ordinances so righteous as all this law [Torah] which I set before you this day?"[64] The theme is repeated with many variations: "The law of the Lord is perfect . . . the precepts of the Lord are right . . .the commandment of the Lord is pure . . . the ordinances of the Lord are true, and righteous altogether."[65] One could quote hundreds of passages that express this theme, but perhaps nothing in the Bible does this so fully or more movingly than Psalm 119 with its one hundred seventy-six verses—a rapturous, sometimes even sensuous, love song to the law:

> At midnight I rise to praise thee,
>   because of thy righteous ordinances.
> I am a companion of all who fear thee,
>   of those who keep thy precepts.
> The earth, O Lord, is full of thy steadfast love;
>   teach me thy statutes![66]

The law, then, points to God, its author; it points to goodness, to justice, to righteousness. The virtue of the law is not simply in its lawness, for other people, too, have their laws, as they have their gods. The Torah, however, is God's law; as His law, it points to His justice, His righteousness. The law is, therefore, inherently transcendant: it is worthy of being law because it has the quality and partakes of justice, of righteousness, and yet it allows itself to be transcended by justice, by righteousness.

> And I will restore your judges as at first,
>   and your counselors as at the beginning.
> Afterward you shall be called the city of righteousness,
>   and faithful city.

> Zion shall be redeemed by justice,
>> and those in her who repent, by righteousness.[67]

It is because justice or righteousness includes observance of the law and at the same time points to that which transcends the commandments that, I think, the prophets when they castigated the people seldom spoke of the commandments but spoke rather of justice and of righteousness, or gave unmistakably clear examples of moral injustice and oppression, which are a denial of righteousness. Thus Amos accuses the nation:

> because they sell the righteous for silver,
>> and the needy for a pair of shoes—
> They that trample the head of the poor into the dust of the earth,
>> and turn aside the way of the afflicted.[68]

To those who heard him, it was sufficient for Amos simply to say, without offering any elaborate bill of particulars:

> Seek good, and not evil,
>> that you may live;
> and so the Lord, the God of hosts, will be with you,
>> as you have said.
> Hate evil, and love good,
>> and establish justice in the gate.[69]

It was precisely because the law pointed to *something within itself and yet also beyond itself*—justice or righteousness—that Job could be portrayed not as a Jew but as "a man in the land of Uz" who was "blameless and upright, one who feared God, and turned away from evil."[70] When he recalled the events of his past life, Job could defend himself by asserting "[I] put on righteousness, and it clothed me / my justice was like a robe and a turban."[71] The Hebrew readers of Job did not find it strange that when this non-Jew thought of examples of justice and righteousness, he could say:

> I was eyes to the blind,
>> and feet to the lame.
> I was father to the poor,
>> and I searched out the cause of him whom I did not know.
> I broke the fangs of the unrighteous,
>> and made him drop his prey from his teeth.[72]

Thus, centuries before Paul told the churches of Galatia that it was possible to transcend the distinctions between Jew and Greek, slave and free, male and female,[73] the Hebrew Scriptures had unmistakably taught the same lesson in transcendence—only what they had in mind was not justification by faith but justification as exemplified by the life of "a man" named Job.

It may be that because (after the exile in the sixth century) the prophets could no longer point to the neglect of the poor and needy through nonobservance of the particular commandments relating to gleanings, dedication of the corners of fields, the sabbatical year, and similar "welfare" provisions—laws binding only in the land of Israel—the prophets were compelled to go beyond these specific commandments to the more general moral principles of justice and of righteousness. The fact, however, is that it seemed to make no difference to the prophets whether they addressed Jews in Babylonia or in their homeland, they hardly ever thought of the specific commandments, not even of the Ten Commandments; their cry was always that righteousness, and only righteousness, redeems a man and exalts a nation; therefore, "Let justice roll down as water, and righteousness as a mighty stream."[74] They did not, of course, mean to downgrade the Ten Commandments or the code of laws, let alone imply that they were abrogated. This would have been a repudiation of the Torah. Just as the specific enactments concerning, e.g., the poor assumed a commitment to the more general moral principles of justice and of righteousness, so the moral principles imply their implementation through specific, detailed provisions. The genius of the Hebrew Scriptures is such that, despite its diverse authors and subjects, it repeatedly interweaves the general and the specific, the legal enactment and the moral principle, the law in the books and the law in the heart, the letter and the spirit, the law as enactment and the law as teaching.

In Plato, the Form of the Good plays the role that righteousness plays in the Bible. The law is, or should be, nothing less than an emanation from the Good, and the closer it approximates this ideal Form, the better it is. The main effort of the *Republic* is to show this.

In the parable of the cave, human beings appear chained, with their faces to the wall. In back of them the cave has an opening; outside the cave and at a distance, there is a blazing fire. The prisoners, watching the wall, see the shadows of the things that pass outside the opening of the cave, and they see too their own shadows. It is these shadows that the prisoners accept as the truth. One of the prisoners is released, and eventually he discovers the sun as the source of light and as somehow the creator of the shadows. Having seen the truth, he no longer wants to go back to his place in the cave; he is taken back, however, and he is now a misfit. As he tries to free others from their illusions and lies, they punish him, and finally they kill him.[75]

The sun is, of course, the Form of the Good, which is the ultimate creator of all things and of all truth. The purpose of the *Republic* is to project a society in which the man who has seen the sun will be accepted as the ruler: the philosopher-king. Such a society is an embodiment, as it were, of the Form of Justice. At the same time as Justice is a virtue of the soul, it is also the virtue of a polis in which the philosopher is king. The good polis is the good man writ large. The laws of the good polis are true to the Form of the Good.

The dominant position of the moral, and the dependence of the law on the moral, are clear in the *Republic*. The *Laws*, because it projects a law-centered society, at first blush presents a problem as to the role of the moral; however, on closer examination it becomes apparent that even here the law is subordinate to and dependent on the moral. For though the city imagined in the *Laws* will not be ruled by a philosopher-king, its constitution and its code of laws are the work of a philosopher-statesman and of his associate commissioners. The rule of law in this imagined city is justified only because the city's code of laws is an expression of the philosophic, moral mind; its author is one who has seen beyond the shadows on the wall to the sun that is the creator of all things and of all truths. The code of laws is as close to the Form of the Good as anything other than the philosopher-king can be. Just as in the *Republic* the law may be said to be assimilated into the moral, so in the *Laws* the moral may be said to be assimilated into the law. In each instance the Good remains preeminent and the generator of all values.

The moral function performed by the philosopher-lawgiver appears clearly in the requirement that the laws be introduced by ethical preambles that will teach the citizens the moral reasons for their enactment. The legal code as a whole has such a preamble or prelude, which is intended to teach that after his gods, the most divine thing a man has—and what is most truly his own—is his soul; that a man must, above all else, advance the interests of his soul; that excess of wealth and property will breed public and private feuds; that we should leave our children rich in reverence but not in gold.[76] It is these and similar moral truths upon which the legal code is said to be based and that it seeks to advance.[77] Then, too, many of the specific laws have their own preambles, which attempt to appeal to the citizen's reason and emotions.[78] For the laws must aim not only to order the polity, and not only to produce virtue in the soul of the citizen, but also to teach. Indeed, the code of laws is a great textbook in religion, morals, and politics, for "any man who treats of law in the style we are adopting, *means* to educate his fellow-citizens rather than [merely] to lay down the law to them."[79] The Curator of Law and the Minister of Education are to instruct the schoolmasters to teach the code of laws to their pupils.[80] This is hardly different from the view that Torah is both law and teaching!

Thus, though in the second-best polity there is to be the strict rule of law, law and morals remain in intimate symbiosis, as though they are body and soul, God and man, the law of the state and the law of nature—things dissimilar yet like one another, different and yet the same.

At the end of the *Nicomachean Ethics* Aristotle writes what is in effect an introduction to the *Politics*.[81] Having discussed happiness and virtue, friendship and pleasure, has he completed his investigation? Perhaps yes, says Aristotle, if all men could be depended upon for nobility of character and for genuine love of what is noble. The fact is, however, that most men are amenable to fear rather than to honor and abstain from evil not because it is base but because of the penalties it entails; generally, passion can be stopped not by reason but by force.

The young must, of course, be educated in virtue, but this means in part that they must be brought up under right laws; moreover, these laws are as necessary for adults as they are for the young. Obviously referring to Plato's *Laws*, Aristotle says that while the lawgiver ought to encourage and to exhort men to virtue on moral grounds, he must also impose sanctions for disobedience. Men's lives are, therefore, to be regulated by the moral intelligence and by a code of laws; the law itself is a rule that emanates from wisdom and from intelligence and that has compulsory force. There must be, then, a public order established by law, "and only good laws will produce good regulations."[82] Legislation is a branch of political science; laws are a product of the art of politics. Ethics is, therefore, a part of politics. However, the reverse proposition is just as true: politics is a part of ethics. A code of ethics needs a code of laws, and a code of laws assumes a code of ethics.

For one thing, law aims at justice, and justice at times can be achieved through equity rather than through the strict law; through the spirit rather than through the letter of the law; through, as it were, reliance on an understanding of the "preamble"—written or unwritten—rather than on only the enactment itself. There must be the rule of law, but the *aim* of the law must not be overlooked, its connection with justice (in the nonjural, in the moral sense) must be kept in view.

The end in view of the laws and of the rule of law is to make the citizens "good by training them in habits of right action—this is the aim of all legislation."[83]

Thus society needs a code of laws as teaching, for the formation of good habits and of virtuous character; it needs the code of laws for its specific provisions for justice in social relations; it also needs the "general" justice that is provided for by the laws of nature, by equity. Law is, therefore, thoroughly intertwined with morals; the rule of law is not altogether separable from the need of men and of society to aim at the good, to seek and to fulfill the demands of justice and of righteousness. For it must always be remembered that the purpose of the state is not mere life but the *good life*—"a good quality of life";[84] the aim of the state must be to "secure a system of *good* laws well obeyed."[85] What conclusion is to be drawn from this?

> The conclusion which clearly follows is that any polis which is truly so called and is not merely one in name, must devote itself to the end of encouraging goodness. Otherwise, a political association sinks into a mere alliance, which only differs in space from other forms of alliance where the members live at a distance from one another. Otherwise, too, law becomes a mere covenant—or (in the phrase of the Sophist Lycophron) "a guarantor of men's rights against one another"—instead of being, as it should be, a rule of life such as will make the members of a *polis* good and just. . . . The end and purpose of a *polis* is *the good life*, and the institutions of social life are means to that end.[86]

In each system of thought that we have considered, there is simplicity and complexity: law and morals are one, and yet are not one. The rule of law is sovereign, yet there is in some sense a higher law, a morality, a general or universal law, which no particular law may contradict. The law is good, yet it aims at goodness, at justice, at righteousness. There is goodness immanent in the law, yet, at least at times, the law must be transcended in order to achieve the goodness at which the law aims. The law is good in itself, yet it is subservient to the ideal of the social order, which is to make the people a holy nation, a just people, a righteous people. The law is the result of a covenant, an agreement, yet it is not (if it is truly law) *merely* conventional, for it was covenanted *because* it was good. The law is coercive, it imposes pains and penalties, yet it is Torah, it is teaching, it is wisdom in living, it is *etz hayyim*, a tree of life—it "will enable all sorts of men to be at their best and live happily,"[87] its object is "supreme virtue" or what "we may call . . . complete righteousness."[88] The law is a compendium of regulations but it is also a textbook in virtue, in righteousness, or in holiness. The code commands "law and order," but the order must be a just order or the law is not "right" law.

Immanence and transcendence are both involved in the relations between law and morals in the Hebrew Scriptures, and in Plato and Aristotle. The ideal must take some tangible form in the here and now; the ideal must somehow become intrinsic in the existing, living order; facts, in some way, must themselves be holy, good, true, and beautiful. Still, the ideal is always promise rather than achievement; it is beyond; it is the object of our quest; it belongs to a higher order; it is yet to emerge; it is the City of God and not the city of man. And yet through love; through knowing, which is a form of action; through teaching, which is a form of possession and of creation; through action, which is a form of loving, knowing, and teaching—the particular and the universal come to possess one another; conventional justice and natural justice, the human and the divine embrace one another. Together they are one, and yet each is separate—but each needs and seeks the other. There remains paradox, contradiction—and reconciliation; for the real is always itself, and yet infinitely more.

6

Natural Law and Judaism

The Case of Maimonides

This essay was written in honor of Dr. Aharon Rabinowicz, of the Faculty of Law of the Hebrew University in Jerusalem, and was included in the festschrift edited by Moses Aberbach and published by Mosad Bialik, Israel, in 1996. A major part of the essay also appeared in the winter 1996 issue of Judaism: Quarterly Journal of Jewish Life and Thought.

1

Sophocles' play *Antigone*, written in about 442 B.C.E., tells how the young girl Antigone, daughter of Oedipus and Jocasta, defied the Theban king Creon by burying the corpse of her brother—an act that the king had forbidden under penalty of death. Confronting the king, she said:

> For me it was not Zeus who made that order.
> Nor did that Justice who lives with the gods below mark out such
>   laws to hold among mankind.
> Nor did I think your orders were so strong that you, a mortal man,
>   could over-run the gods' unwritten and unfailing laws.
> Not now, nor yesterday's, they always live, and no one knows their
>   origin in time.[1]

Of this drama, and of these words spoken to the king by his young prisoner, George Steiner has said: "Whenever, wherever, in the western legacy, we have found ourselves engaged in the confrontation of justice and of law, of the aura of the dead and the claims of the living, whenever, wherever, the hungry dreams of the young have collided with the 'realism' of the ageing, we have found ourselves turning to words, images, sinews of argument, synecdoches, tropes, metaphors, out of the grammar of Antigone and of Creon." The words spoken by Antigone have, for some twenty-five centuries, served as a classic, prime expression of the philosophy of natural law.

The theory that some laws are fundamental to human nature and are discoverable by human reason, independent of supernatural revelation or of governmental enactment, is one of the great contributions of ancient Greek civilization. More than other schools of philosophy, Stoicism formulated and taught the theory of natural law. From Greek philosophy, the theory passed into the theory of *jus naturale* of Roman law. Cicero, writing in the first century B.C.E., gave the most influential definition of the theory:

> True law is right reason in agreement with Nature; it is of universal application, unchanging and everlasting; it summons to duty by its commands, and averts from wrong-doing by its prohibitions. . . . It is a sin to try to alter this law, nor is it allowable to attempt to repeal any part of it, and it is impossible to abolish it entirely. We cannot be freed from its obligations by Senate or People, and we need not look outside ourselves for an expounder or interpreter of it. And there will not be different laws at Rome and at Athens, or different laws now and in the future, but one eternal and unchangeable law will be valid for all nations and for all times, and there will be one master and one ruler, and that is God, over us all, for He is the author of this law, its promulgator, and its enforcing judge.[2]

In another treatise, Cicero made the point that a single human nature pervades all men. For this reason, all men can be subject to the same law that is fundamental to human beings everywhere:

> No single thing is so like another, so exactly its counterpart, as all of us are to one another. . . . And so, however we may define man, a single definition will apply to all. . . . For those creatures who have received the gift of reason from Nature have also received right reason, and therefore they have also received the gift of Law, which is right reason applied to command and prohibition.[3]

The essence of the theory of natural law as expressed by Sophocles and by Cicero may be stated in the following propositions: There is a higher law that is supreme, that is superior to any positive law made by king, by legislature, or by judge. This higher law cannot be abrogated. It is made by God and written into the very nature of man. What makes man different from all other animals is his reason. Law must therefore conform to reason; it must not violate human nature or violate reason. Because men are everywhere essentially the same, that is, participate in a common reason, they are all subject to the same higher law or natural law—all men are under one ruler, "and that is God," who is "over us all," for God is the author of the higher law, the promulgator of the law of nature "and its enforcing judge."

In an essay on the history of natural law, Sir Frederick Pollock has formulated "the central idea" of natural law as being "an ultimate principle of fitness with regard to the nature of man as a rational and social being, which is, or ought to be, the justification of every form of positive law."[4] George Sabine, accepting Pollock's statement of the essence of the theory of natural law, adds: "Throughout the whole of the Middle Ages and well into modern times the existence and validity of such a higher law were taken for granted." Natural law, according to Sabine, "meant interpretation in the light of such conceptions as equality before the law, faithfulness to engagements, fair dealing or equity, the superior importance of intent to mere words or formularies, the protection of dependents, and the recognition of claims based on blood relationship." With respect to a belief in natural law, there was no difference between Christianity and Stoicism, for both believed in "the providential government of the world, the obligation of law and government to do substantial justice, and the equality of all men in the sight of God."[5] The absolute authority of "right reason" or the force of justice is a proposition found implicit in all statements of natural law, but it is made most explicit by Grotius in his *De jure belli ac pacis,* published in 1625: "The law of nature is a dictate of right reason, which points out that an act, according as it is or is not in conformity with rational nature, has in it a quality of moral baseness or moral necessity; and that, in consequence, such an act is either forbidden or enjoined by the author of nature, God. . . . Just as even God, then, cannot cause that two times two should not make four, so He cannot cause that that which is intrinsically evil be not evil."[6]

The implications of the last sentence by Grotius are of transcendent importance, for it means (in addition to what it says explicitly) that two times two make four whether God exists or does not exist and furthermore that evil is evil whether God exists or does not exist. Although not expressly, Grotius in effect, as Sabine points out, liberated natural law theory from theology.[7] The wish or the command—*sic volo, sic iubeo*—of God or of man does not create the obligatory nature of law. Grotius, referring to the Hebrew Bible, distinguished between commands that God gave to the Jewish people as the chosen people and that depended merely upon His will and other laws that can be explained by reference to "reason" and to the "nature of man."[8] The theory of natural law in Grotius can be said to be Janus-faced, for on the one hand, it can be read in its theological context, and on the other, as straining towards a secular context.[9] One need not, however, apply an either/or logic to Grotius; his theory of natural law can be both theological and secular, for he certainly believed that, in Horace Kallen's phrase, secularism is the will of God.[10]

A new twist to the theory of natural law was made largely by John Locke when he translated natural law into natural rights. This meant a shift in emphasis from natural duties to natural rights. Given that most rights and duties are correlatives, the move was bound to take place as an emphasis on the individual came to the fore. The theory of natural rights asserts the claim that each individual has innate, indefeasible rights. They are not given by government or by society; they inhere in the individual from the time of his birth. The principles asserted by Locke came to be embodied in the English Bill of Rights of (1689), the English Toleration Act (1689), the American Declaration of Independence (1776), the French Declaration of the Rights of Man and Citizen (1789), and the Bill of Rights of the United States Constitution (1789–91).

Following World War II and the shocking disclosures of the crimes against humanity and the war crimes that had been committed by the Nazi and Fascist governments and armies, the United States, Great Britain, France, and the USSR established a tribunal at Nürem-berg to try military and civilian Axis leaders. Defendants were found guilty of acts that were considered legal, or even required, by their governments at the time. The trials at Nüremberg in 1945–46 (and the trial in 1946–47 in Tokyo) would not have taken place had not the principles of natural law and of natural rights taken deep root in Western thought and institutions.

Just as there has been a translation of natural law into natural rights, so too has there been a translation of natural rights into human rights. On December 10, 1948, the General Assembly of the United Nations adopted the Universal Declaration of Human Rights. With this act, the higher law claim of the young girl Antigone came to be recognized and proclaimed as though the meeting of the states that comprised the United Nations were a conclave at the foot of Mount Sinai. Although no supernatural voice was heard, a super-national voice was, indeed, heard. The preamble to the declaration states:

> *Whereas* recognition of the inherent dignity and of the equal and inalienable rights of all members of the human family is the foundation of freedom, justice and peace in the world,
> *Whereas* disregard and contempt for human rights have resulted in barbarous acts which have outraged the conscience of mankind, and

the advent of a world in which human beings shall enjoy freedom of speech and belief and freedom from fear and want has been proclaimed [by President Franklin D. Roosevelt's Four Freedoms as asserted in his message to Congress January 6, 1941, and embodied in the Atlantic Charter in August 1941] as the highest aspiration of the common people . . .

ARTICLE 1 proclaims that "All human beings are born free and equal in dignity and rights. They are endowed with reason and conscience." ARTICLE 2 proclaims that "Everyone is entitled to all the rights and freedoms set forth in this Declaration, without distinction of any kind, such as race, colour, sex, language, religion, political or other opinion, national or social origin, property, birth or other status."

The Council of Europe, on November 4, 1950, adopted the (European) Convention for the Protection of Human Rights and Fundamental Freedoms. Similarly, the Ninth International Conference of American States in 1948 adopted the American Declaration of the Rights and Duties of Man. In 1975 the Helsinki Final Act was signed, followed in the next year by the creation of the fifty-three-nation Commission on Security and Cooperation in Europe (CSCS), which monitors and reports on the implementation of the Helsinki accords, with emphasis on basic human rights such as freedom of expression, freedom of religion, and freedom of movement—rights viewed as the "first tier" of fundamental freedoms that had to be addressed especially by the former communist countries before their commitment to further obligations will be taken seriously.

These developments probably will be considered by future historians as the most important aspect of the twentieth century. Although admittedly human rights are by no means universally respected, it is of the utmost significance that they are recognized as *rights* and not merely as ideals or aspirations: "An ideal is something to be aimed at, but which, by definition, cannot be immediately realized. A right, on the contrary, is something that can and, from a moral point of view, *should* be respected here and now. If it is violated, justice itself is abused."[11] So, it is not surprising that the president of the United States should threaten the government of China with loss of its trading privileges unless it demonstrates a reform in its human rights record.[12]

It is important to note, however, that the international declarations of human rights do, in fact, assert not only rights but also ideals. For example, the Universal Declaration of Human Rights provides in Article 23 that "[e]veryone has the right to work, to free choice of employment, to just and favorable conditions of work, and to protection against unemployment." The same article also provides that "[e]veryone, without any discrimination, has the right to equal pay for equal work." Article 24 reads as follows: "Everyone has the right to rest and leisure . . . including periodic holidays with pay." These as well as other articles are honored in the breach much more than in the observance. They are not in any meaningful, legal sense enforcible rights. They are, and are likely to remain, ideals, worthy but in this imperfect world impossible of attainment. For the purposes of our present discussion, it will be best not to focus on human rights—perhaps not even on natural rights—unless we bear in mind the Lockean philosophy that grounds natural rights in natural law.

> The traditional political and civil rights are not difficult to institute. For the most part, they require governments, and other people generally, to leave a man alone: let him live as he decides to live and enjoy what is his; let him speak, meet with others, publish what he wishes, and worship as he chooses. Do not injure, arrest, or imprison him. To respect a man's right to life, liberty, and property is not a very costly exercise. As Locke and others have explained, it requires a system of law that recognizes those rights to protect those rights.[13]

Thus, we must go back to where we started—to Antigone addressing her uncle Creon, to Cicero and the Stoic philosophers, to Grotius—and remember that the "central idea" of natural law, as summarized by Sir Frederick Pollock, is that there is "an ultimate principle of fitness with regard to the nature of man as a rational and social being, which is, or ought to be, the justification of every form of positive law."

2

Is there natural law in Judaism? Leo Strauss has given a partial answer to this question by saying:

> Where there is no philosophy, there is no knowledge of natural right as such. The Old Testament, whose basic premise may be said to be the implicit rejection of philosophy, does not know "nature": the Hebrew term for "nature" is unknown to the Hebrew Bible. It goes without saying that "heaven and earth," for example, is not the same thing as "nature." There is, then, no knowledge of natural right as such in the Old Testament. The discovery of nature necessarily precedes the discovery of natural right. Philosophy is older than political philosophy.[14]

This passage bristles with problems. First, let us admit that the term "natural right" does not appear in the Hebrew Scriptures; that is, not "as such." However, just as one could have been speaking prose for forty years without knowing it, so too the Bible can contain natural law (or natural right) without explicitly avowing the theory or conception. The Hebrew Scriptures do not identify erotic or romantic love "as such," *eo nomine*, but can one argue that it is missing from, e.g., the Song of Songs? Furthermore, as we have noted in the passages from Cicero and Grotius, natural law is not dependent upon philosophy nor upon a philosophy of nature but upon the *nature of man*. It is based upon a belief that the *nature of man* necessarily involves certain *natural laws*. The theory does not involve general nature, a philosophy of nature, but only man, the nature of man. Let me repeat the passage from Cicero: "No single thing is so like another, so exactly its counterpart, as all of us are to one another. . . . And so, however we may define man, a single definition will apply to all." What is the "single definition" that is applicable to all men? Every man has "right reason"—every man has intelligence, rationality; every man has reason and can be reasoned with: "For those creatures who have received the gift of reason from Nature have also received right reason." Moreover, if every man has reason and can be reasoned with (right reason), "therefore they have also received the gift of Law, which is right reason applied to command and prohibition."

The background for Strauss's strange statement is his belief that men cannot live without knowledge of the good to guide them individually or collectively; this knowledge can be had either by "the unaided efforts of their natural powers" or by "Divine Revelation." Strauss puts these alternatives as stark, separate choices; there is no overlap, no middle ground: "No alternative is more fundamental than this: human guidance or divine guidance." Human guidance is characteristic of philosophy, divine guidance is presented by the Bible:

> The dilemma cannot be evaded by any harmonization or synthesis. For both philosophy and the Bible proclaim something as the one thing needful, as the only thing that ultimately counts, and the one thing needful proclaimed by the Bible is the opposite of that proclaimed by philosophy: a life of obedient love versus a life of free insight.[15]

This is a fine example of the either/or logic. Things are either black or white; there are no shades of color. Strauss falsifies both religion and philosophy, and thus he gives a perverted view of natural law. He does not consider the possibility that "free insight" could lead to "obedient love."

Even a cursory examination of the history of Greek philosophy shows the complex and intimate relation of philosophy and religion. Greek philosophy began in religion, and Greek philosophy, as in Plato and Aristotle, ended in religion. From a concern with external nature the ancient philosophers moved to a concern with the nature of man, to psychology, logic, politics, ethics, and epistemology. They discovered the soul, added the dimension of spirituality to the nature of man, and projected immortality for the soul. The philosophical thought of the Platonists, of the Pythagoreans, of the schools of Parmenides and of Heraclitus cannot be discussed without focusing on their religious perspectives. Indeed, as much can be said even of leading twentieth century philosophers: Samuel Alexander, Henri Bergson, Alfred North Whitehead, William James, Josiah Royce, George Santayana, John Ellis McTaggart, F. H. Bradley, Bernard Bosanquet, Thomas Hill Green. All were concerned with the nature of man; all, in one way or another, were concerned with the spiritual nature of man; all were, in one measure or another, concerned with religion.

Let us return to what Cicero says about the definition of man: "No single thing is so like another, so exactly its counterpart, as all of us are to one another. . . . And so, however we may define man, a single definition will apply to all." What does the Bible say about man? How is man defined? "And God said: 'Let us make man in our image, after our likeness. . . .' And God created man in His own image, in the image of God created He him; male and female created He them."[16] Then, after the Flood, God addressed Noah and his sons and said to them: "[A]nd at the hand of man, even at the hand of every man's brother, will I require the life of man. Whoso sheddeth man's blood, by man shall his blood be shed; for in the image of God made He man."[17] As interpreted by classical Jewish commentators, the Hebrew Bible defines man as sharing in the divine character. As Judaism is a religion of *ethical* monotheism, so man has the gift of choosing between good and evil (the blessing and the curse). As God is in some sense a Person, so man, too, is a person, a *thou* and not an *it*. As God acts in accordance with reason, so man is capable of acting according to reason, according to "right reason." Because man is an ethical person and can act in accord with right reason, he was given dominion "over all the earth"; no other creature could be entrusted with such power. Mind and spirit will rule over matter.

From God's address or revelation to Noah and his sons, the Talmud deduced what the rabbis called the seven commandments to Noah and his descendants: a positive commandment, to establish courts of justice, and six negative commandments, prohibitions on blasphemy, adultery (or incest), idolatry, murder, robbery, and eating flesh cut from a living animal.[18] These seven commandments are said to constitute the essentials of natural religion.[19] These commandments are binding on all men, Jews and non-Jews alike. Observance of them by a non-Jew qualifies him to be called a righteous gentile. Do these Noahide laws constitute a recognition of natural law in Judaism? As we have seen, Leo Strauss would deny this claim; so does Marvin Fox, as we shall see later. However, I see no reason for accepting their view. These laws no doubt have as their root the belief that man *qua* man made in the image of God, having a nature that partakes of divinity, must be subject to these commandments or laws. The fact that these laws are said to emanate from God does not deprive them of their rational ground. Antigone did not say to Creon that her right to bury the body of her brother was grounded on reason; she cried out that Creon's order was not made by Zeus, that it violated "the gods' unwritten and unfailing laws." Cicero asserted that true law is valid for all nations and for all times, "and there will be one master and one ruler, and that is God, over us all, for He is the author of this law, its promulgator, and its enforcing judge." Grotius, too, stated that the law of nature, being a dictate of right reason, makes an act either forbidden or enjoined "by the author of nature, God." The line of argument is straight: What reason demands, God demands; or in more biblical phrasing, What God demands, reason demands. (God may demand more of Jews, but our focus here is on what God demands of man, what He commands or prohibits for all mankind.)

In *Mishneh Torah*, Maimonides restates the Talmudic law with respect to the Noahide laws, as follows:

> A heathen who accepts the seven commandments and observes them scrupulously is a "righteous heathen," and will have a portion in the world to come, provided that he accepts them and performs them because the Holy One, blessed be He, commanded them in the Law and made known through Moses our Teacher that the observance thereof had been enjoined upon the descendants of Noah even before the Law was given [at Sinai]. But if his observance thereof is based upon a reasoned conclusion he is not deemed a resident alien, or one of the pious of the Gentiles, but one of their wise men.[20]

3

I find it difficult to accept the proviso that Maimonides has read into the Talmudic statement. For Maimonides gives with one hand and takes back with the other. If the non-Jew is to fulfill the condition—if, e.g., he is to refrain from adultery (or incest) not because of a "rea-soned conclusion" that such an act is evil but only because it was prohibited by the Torah as made known to Moses and enjoined upon Noah and his descendants—it seems to me that he would essentially be a Jew and not a gentile. It would not satisfy the Maimonidean proviso if the gentile merely believed that it was sinful, that it would be a violation of a divine law (like Antigone, or Cicero, or Grotius); no, he must refrain from the act because it was enjoined in the Torah as given to Moses. I find this an insupportable condition and contrary to the spirit of the Bible and of Judaism.

It must never be forgotten that the first man was Adam, the first woman was Eve. They, and not Abraham and Sarah, are said to be the progenitors of humanity. It was they, Adam and Eve, who were made by God in His own image. Nowhere in the Bible is it stated or intimated that by choosing Israel, God abandoned the rest of man-kind. For God is not a tribal deity, He is the Creator of the whole universe. He is *echod*, the one and only God, not only for Israel but for all nations, all peoples.

Noah was a righteous man. He lived hundreds, perhaps thou-sands of years before Moses. Did he avoid doing evil and observe all the commandments (or at least the seven specially marked as the Noahide commandments) only because God "commanded them in the Law and made known through Moses our Teacher that the obser-vance thereof had been enjoined upon the descendants of Noah even before the Law was given [at Sinai]"? Without having this impossible thought in mind, Noah could not be a "righteous heathen"!

The Bible makes many references to righteous heathens. For ex-ample, when pharoah ordered the midwives to kill all male children born to Hebrew women, "the midwives feared God and did not as the king of Egypt commanded them, but saved the men-children alive."[21] The midwives listened to the voice of conscience—"they feared God." Are we to deny them the distinction of being righteous heathens? In Leviticus we read: "Ye shall therefore keep My statutes, and Mine ordinances, which if a man do, he shall live by them: I am the Lord."[22] Commenting on this passage, Rabbi Meier (according to the Talmud) was accustomed to say: "Whence do we know that even a heathen, if he obeys the law of God, will thereby attain to the same spiritual communion as the High Priest? Scripture says, 'which if a *man* do, he shall live by them'—not priest, Levite, or Israelite, but *man*."[23]

Marvin Fox, in an essay on "Maimonides and Aquinas on Natural Law," agrees with Strauss and argues the case against the proposition that there is a theory of natural law in Judaism, asserting especially that there is no natural law in the Bible. He recognizes the fact that in postbiblical rabbinic texts there are some statements that have been interpreted as teaching that there is a conception of natural law; these statements, however, says Fox, should be properly interpreted as maintaining "the classical biblical teaching that divine commandment is the only ultimate source of law. Even positive human legislation is seen as legitimate and binding only insofar as it is an application or extension of rules or principles set forth in the divinely revealed law."[24]

Fox quotes from the Talmud the following passage: "'Mine ordinances shall you do' (Lev. 18:4), i.e., such commandments which, if they were not written [in Scripture], they should by right have been written, and these are they: [the laws concerning] idolatry, sexual immorality, bloodshed, robbery, and blasphemy."[25] Fox says that there is nothing in this passage to suggest that human reason by itself could have known that these acts are evil. He does not note that these are five of the Noahide laws. They are known and respected by pagans. How did they get to know them? They were not at Sinai. If pagans could know them by "right reason," why cannot Israelites? Why should Israelites be unable to arrive at such laws by "right reason"? This, I submit, is the plain meaning of the Talmudic passage. Why should it be subjected to a strained—yes, unreasonable—meaning?

Moreover, given that these are Noahide laws, their context is non-Jewish people. Jews have the Torah, which contains these commandments. The Talmud in effect says that if Jews did not have the Torah, they could have arrived at these commandments in the way that gentiles arrive at them, that is, by "right reason."

One might agree with Fox that Jews should consider themselves bound by these commandments not because "right reason" dictates them but because they have been ordained by God; however, this concession does not compel one to deny that human reason could have known by itself that these acts are evil.

In the Amidah, which is recited three times each weekday, there is the following prayer: "You graciously endow man with wisdom, and teach insight to a frail mortal. Endow us graciously from Yourself with wisdom, insight, discernment. Blessed are You, Hashem, gracious Giver of wisdom."[26] The Hebrew words used are *daat, binah,* and *haskel,* which may be better translated as knowledge, understanding, and discernment.[27] When a Jew arrives at the commandments by "right reason," by the use of his God-given gift of reason, he knows that he ought to thank the Giver of Reason for arriving at right understanding and wisdom. As we have seen, this is exactly what was said by Antigone, by Cicero, and by Grotius. Even for the pagan, natural law need not be atheistic; its ultimate ground can be a firm belief in God as the source of wisdom—and of law.

The Bible says, "I am the Lord that healeth thee."[28] This has not kept Jews from cultivating medicine and surgery as a profession, nor has the belief that God is the healer kept Jews from consulting physicians, nor pious, saintly rabbis from becoming physicians—e.g., Maimonides and Judah Halevi, and before them in the Talmudic period, Rabbi Ishmael, Rabbi Hanina ben Dosa, Samuel ben Abba ha-Kohen. All believed—both doctors and patients—that healing is in the hands of God but also that physicians are His instruments. By the same reasoning, one can say that wisdom is in the hands of God, but wise men and women are His instruments. Just as one may use "right medicine," so too one may use "right reason." God is not displaced by such service; instead, God's purposes are fulfilled by such instruments.

Christianity asserts that "God gave us eternal life, and [that] this life is in his Son. He who has the Son has life; he who has not the Son has not life."[29] Does Judaism make the same claim for Moses? Does Judaism proclaim that eternal life is possible only through Moses, that he who has the Mosaic faith has life, and that he who has not this faith has not life? Christianity asserts that the gate is narrow and that only few can enter.[30] This, however, is the teaching of Judaism:

> Rabbi Jeremiah said: Whence can you know that a Gentile who practices the Law is equal to the High Priest? Because it says, "Which if a *man* do, he shall live through them." And it says, "This is the Law [Torah] of man." It does not say, "The Law of Priests, Levites, Israelites," but, "This is the Law of man, O Lord God." And it does not say, "Open the gates, and let the Priests and Levites and Israel enter," but it says, "Open the gates that a righteous Gentile may enter"; and it says, "This is the gate of the Lord, the righteous shall enter it." It does not say, "The Priests and the Levites and Israel shall enter it," but it says, "The righteous shall enter it." . . . So even a Gentile, if he practices the Law, is equal to the High Priest.[31]

Isadore Twersky, in his magisterial *Introduction to the Code of Maimonides (Mishneh Torah)*, states that Maimonides does not operate with a concept of natural law. (As we have seen, this is, indeed, the case.) According to Maimonides, intellect is a tool for uncovering "the congruence between reason and revelation and the ultimate meaning of divine laws . . . the religious philosopher operates on the assumption that the Torah—i.e., moral-ritual law created by God—is rational and intelligible."[32] This, however, does not address the problem of the righteous gentile. Can *he* use his intellect to arrive at the "right reason" for the Noahide laws? Would that suffice or must he justify his observance of these laws by avowing his belief that they were enjoined by God's revelation to Moses? These questions are not addressed, but, it seems to me, they loom large as one reads Maimonides and is perplexed by what he says.

Haim Cohn, former justice of the Israel Supreme Court, a leading jurist and authority on Jewish law, in an essay on "Authority and Reason in Ancient Jewish Law" considers the question of the source of the oral law when no scriptural text and no tradition, custom, or judicial precedent is available. In such a case, recourse is to "independent reasoning (Sevara)." The sages, Cohn writes, classified such laws within the oral law, "but as a matter of fact and tradition, they were actually classified as Written Law, as if they emanated not from delegated but from direct divine authority." Cohn does not approve the variety of rabbinic rationalizations. He writes:

> The true explanation seems to me to be . . . : it is God who has imbued human beings with reason and has written it "on our hearts in broad and indelible characters"; and as the human capacity of reasoning is divine and godsent, so is the use of this capacity an exercise of divinely bestowed power, and its normative result a divine law. Or, in more typically Jewish jurisprudential terms, as the revealed word of God established divine law, so must the divine will be inferred from and reflected by God's deed and creation, including the human mind and its reasoning capacity. It is the very same idea which underlies Spinoza's concept of lex divina naturalis.[33]

As I interpret this passage, Cohn asserts that, despite appearances and legal or jurisprudential fictions, the ancient rabbis did in fact operate within a theory of natural law, as the theory has come down to us from the Stoic philosophers through Grotius, Scholastic thinkers, Richard Hooker, and Spinoza.

In another essay, "Legal Change in an Unchangeable Law: The Talmudic Pattern," Cohn discusses briefly the passage from Maimonides that we have been considering. "It has been said," writes Cohn, citing Leo Strauss,

> that the Old Testament had no knowledge of any "natural law" or "natural right." No divine revelation can possibly be invalidated by any "superior" law; nor can any law, however "superior," serve as model for the divine will. The Oral Law, like the Written, is a form of positive law; and since it, likewise, is held to be divine, no unwritten "natural law" can ever transcend the Oral Law, either. The rejection of all natural law concepts is vividly demonstrated by a dictum of Maimonides to the effect that a Gentile who observes the Noahide laws has a portion in the world to come, and is reckoned as one of

the righteous of the nations, provided that he accepted these laws as binding upon him *because* they were divinely ordained; but that if he observes them because of his own conclusions based on reason or compassion, he is not deemed either righteous or wise. At the same time the talmudical jurists, too, distinguished between laws which, if they had not been expressly laid down, would have had to be observed in any event according to the common standards of mankind (such as the prohibitions of homicide, idolatry, larceny and incest), and laws which had to be laid down for the suppression of natural human urges . . . and which nobody would observe were it not for their enactment as positive law (such as dietary and purity laws). But the easily understandable reasons underlying the former laws are as irrelevant for their validity as is the ostensible lack of reason distinguishing the latter: all of them are expressions of God's unfathomable will.[34]

Our concern is not with the question whether the ancient authorities recognized the possibility of a claim that there is a law higher than the Torah—of course such a claim is inconceivable within the realm of traditional Halakha. Our concern is with the question, When does a gentile become a righteous gentile, entitled to a place in the world to come? Cohn does not focus on this question, but it should be noted that in stating what the rabbis required of the gentile he leaves out the proviso that the gentile must not only believe that the Noahide laws were commanded by God but that, in addition, he performs these commandments *because* God commanded them in the Torah and made them known to Moses, "that the observance thereof had been enjoined upon the descendants of Noah even before the Law was given [at Sinai]." The proviso that has been omitted is the troublesome condition. For if one takes the proviso seriously, one can then question whether Judaism takes seriously the statement that there is a common humanity, that every man and every woman is made in the image of God, *betzelem Elokhim*. The proviso must raise the question, Does Judaism allow for salvation, for immortality only for those of the Mosaic faith? For, as we have noted, natural law is based on the belief that there is a common human nature, that there is a common humanity, that all men participate in "right reason," under God (not under Moses!). Perhaps Cohn, a staunch advocate of human rights, purposely left out the proviso as a necessary cleansing of the Maimonidean statement?—as if to say that the great codifier of Jewish law could not possibly have meant seriously what he said, or that perhaps a scribe overzealously injected the proviso as a "fence" against a liberal application of the Noahide laws and the honorific title of "righteous gentile"?

Apart from other serious questions that we have noted concerning the proviso, it should be obvious to persons familiar with Christian dogma that the proviso injected by Maimonides into the doctrine of the Noahide laws disturbingly looks very much like justification by faith. To the Christian, it is through faith—especially faith in the death and resurrection of Jesus—that he separates himself from Judaism. In his letter to the Galatians (Jewish converts), Paul wrote:

> Now, before faith came, we were confined under the law [of Judaism], kept under restraint until faith [in Christ] should be revealed. So that the law was our custodian until Christ came, that we might be justified by faith. But now that faith has come, we are no longer under a custodian; for in Christ Jesus we are all sons of God, through faith. . . . There is neither Jew nor Greek, there is neither slave nor free, there is neither male nor female; for you are all one in Christ Jesus. And if you are Christ's, then you are Abraham's offspring, heirs according to promise.[35]

The dogma of justification by faith is in sharp contrast to Jewish belief. "With what shall I come before the Lord," the prophet Micah asks, "and bow myself before God on high?" He answers the question with a resounding affirmation of the ethical nature of Jewish monotheism:

> He has showed you, O man, what is good;
>   and what does the Lord require of you
> but to do justice, and to love kindness
>   and to walk humbly with your God.[36]

Unlike Christianity, the emphasis in Judaism is not on faith but on "works," on righteousness, on justice—*tsedakah, mishpat*. How did Amos say it?

> Take thou away from Me the noise
>   of thy songs;
> And let Me not hear the melody of
>   thy psalteries.
> But let justice well up as waters,
>   And righteousness as a mighty stream.[37]

The Noahide laws are consistent with the ethical essence of Judaism. There is the one positive commandment, to establish courts of justice. There is no positive commandment to believe in any dogma. There are two negative commandments that today we would say fall into the realm of religion; viz., a prohibition on idolatry and a prohibition

on blasphemy. Again, however, they are prohibitions, they are nega-
tives; the heathen, to be a righteous heathen, is not commanded to
make any confession of faith. The other four commandments are
strictly ethical; viz., prohibitions on immorality, murder, robbery, and
cruelty to animals. Taken on their face value as stated in the Talmud,
they eminently qualify as a statement of natural law in its pure, classical sense.

Philo, a contemporary of Jesus, was probably the first Jew to have
formulated articles of faith.[38] With regard to Philo's five principles of
Judaism, Rabbi Louis Jacobs has noted that Philo acted to formulate
them because he felt that these principles were denied in his day and
it was necessary to combat their denial.

> This was to happen again and again in the history of Jewish Creed
> formulation. It was never a question of examining the classical
> sources of Judaism in an objective manner in order to discover the
> basic principles of Judaism. This would have been an almost im-
> possible task since the Biblical sources are neither speculative nor
> systematic but organic and dynamic. It was rather a question of em-
> phasizing the ideas and beliefs which required to be stressed as prin-
> ciples of faith in a given age because it was in these areas that the
> challenge to the Jewish spirit was felt to be acute. In reality this is
> only another way of saying that dogmas in the Catholic sense, for
> instance, are impossible in Judaism because Judaism has no Church,
> no central authority with the power to formulate beliefs.[39]

Maimonides in the twelfth century formulated his "Thirteen Articles of Faith," which has become the most famous creedal formulation
within Judaism. His statement accompanying the formulation was a
caveat that a person who held to these beliefs should be loved with
affection and with brotherly sympathy—even if he be guilty of every
possible transgression through his desires and lack of self-control. He
will be punished according to the measure of his perversity but he
will nonetheless enjoy a portion in the world to come. However, if a
man breaks away from any of the fundamental principles of belief,
then he loses his membership in the body of Israel; he is a heretic
who should be hated and extirpated.

Maimonides thus made correct faith supreme over all other aspects of Judaism and of Jewish life: "The believing sinner is included
in 'the general body of Israel.' The unbeliever [though a righteous
and just person] is excluded."[40] This, I submit, is a nonbiblical position. I hazard the thought that Maimonides was driven to take this
position by his rationalist approach, by his great power of conceptual-
ization, and perhaps also by his fear that the danger of apostasy to

Islam or to Christianity was so great and so imminent that a strong and unusual measure had to be taken. Because Islam and Christianity emphasized creedal faith, there had to be, to meet the emergency, a formulation of Jewish creedal beliefs.

When considered against this background, the proviso injected by Maimonides into the formulation of the Noahide laws is consistent with Maimonides' philosophy of Judaism: It is not enough for a gentile to be righteous in order to merit a place in the world to come; he also must have the right belief as the foundation for his righteousness. If the righteous Jew with heretical beliefs has no place in the world to come, why should the righteous gentile who lacks the right beliefs have such a place?[41] Perhaps one may venture to say that Maimonides was rational to an extent that was irrational?

4

The proposition that Judaism does not recognize natural law or natural right has not gone unchallenged. In recent years two esteemed scholars have questioned and opposed the conclusion dogmatically asserted by Leo Strauss.

In an essay with the significant title "Does Jewish Tradition Recognize an Ethic Independent of Halakha?" Rabbi Aharon Lichtenstein, Rosh Yeshiva of Yeshivat Har-Etzion in Israel, states that the ancient rabbis recognized the existence of "natural morality": "The fact remains that the existence of natural morality is clearly assumed in much that is quite central to our tradition."[42] Although Rabbi Lichtenstein uses the phrase "natural morality" instead of "natural law" or "natural right," I do not think that this is a material difference, for the theory of natural law in fact was a theory of natural morality; it concerned itself with the rules of right or virtuous conduct and with the moral quality of character.

To the issue stated by the title of the essay—whether natural morality is recognized by the Jewish tradition as an ethic independent of Halakha—the answer, says Lichtenstein, "need hardly be in doubt." As proof texts he quotes the famous saying of Rabbi Johanan as given in the Talmud: "If the Torah had not been given, we would have learnt modesty from the cat, [aversion to] robbery from the ant, chastity from the dove, and [conjugal] manners from the cock."[43] According to Lichtenstein, the passage implies (at least) three things: that ante-Halakhic virtues exist; that they can be inferred from natural phenomena; and that they are not only observable in nature but inherent within nature.

The author then refers to the concept of *derekh eretz*, which may be broadly defined as civility, proper ethical conduct, conduct "which is right and fitting toward people." Derekh eretz is important not merely as conduct that is conventionally approved but "as prescriptive *lex naturalis.*" He quotes the statement of Rabbi Eliezer ben Azaria as it appears in the Mishna, that "without Torah, there is no *derekh eretz,* and without *derekh eretz,* there is no Torah."[44] The Midrash, Lichtenstein comments, goes beyond this dialectical reciprocity, stating that *"derekh eretz* preceded Torah"—not merely chronologically but axiologically:

> As the Maharal put it, "From this [i.e., the Mishna] we learn that *derekh eretz* is the basis of Torah which is," as explained by the Midrash, "'the way of the tree of life.'" Their link [of Torah and derekh eretz] reinforces our awareness of the Rabbis' recognition of natural morality.[45]

A rejection of natural morality, says Rabbi Lichtenstein, cannot mean that apart from Halakha—in the absence of divine commandment—"man and the world are amoral. . . . At most, the Rabbis rejected natural law, not natural morality. They may conceivably have felt one could not ground specific binding and universal rules in nature but they hardly regarded uncommanded man as ethically neutral. . . . One might contend, maximally, that natural morality is contextual rather than formal. It does, however, exist."[46]

5

Along other lines of argument, Robert Gordis likewise finds a legitimate place for natural law (or natural morality) in Judaism. According to Gordis, the Noahide laws antedate in Judaism the Talmud. The apocryphal Book of Jubilees (written sometime before the Christian era) attributed to Noah moral instruction binding on all men: "In the twenty-eighth jubilee [year] Noah began to enjoin upon his sons' sons the ordinances and commandments and all the judgments that he knew and he exhorted his sons to observe righteousness."[47] This instruction became in the Talmud the seven Noahide laws. Gordis also cites a passage in the New Testament (perhaps written by a Jew) that seems to refer to the Noahide laws.[48] The doctrine of the Noahide laws, Gordis writes,

> represents in essence a theory of universal religion which is binding upon all men. Characteristically Jewish is its emphasis upon good actions rather than upon right belief as the mark of the good life. Ethical living rather than creedal adherence is the decisive criterion

for salavation. Its spirit is epitomized in the great rabbinic utterance, "I call Heaven and earth to witness, that whether one be Gentile or Jew, man or woman, slave or free man, the divine spirit rests on each in accordance with his deeds."[49]

In a chapter of his book *The Root and the Branch* entitled "Natural Law in the Modern World," Gordis makes a strong argument for a rightful place of the theory of natural law in our time.[50] The theory of natural law, Gordis states, is based on three elements: human nature, justice, and reason. Laws must be in harmony with human nature, which is believed to be constant through time, universal, and knowable. Laws are not always identical with justice but they must be just if they are to meet the demands of natural law. Finally, law must satisfy reason. It has been assumed over the centuries that the sources of natural law are to be found only in ancient Greek and Roman thought, and thus possible Hebraic roots have been entirely neglected and forgotten. The Hebraic sources exist, however, and are to be found in the Hebrew Bible, in the apocryphal books, and in the Jewish deposit in the New Testament. This was known to seventeenth- and eighteenth-century scholars (e.g., John Selden, who in 1665 identified the Noahide laws with natural law),[51] but generally it has been bypassed as if nonexistent.

In our own time the theory of natural law has been in disrepute because it has generally been used to sustain the status quo: because human nature was assumed to be unchanged and unchangeable, what was reasonable and just two thousand years ago must be reasonable and just at all times and everywhere. According to Gordis, however, the Jewish contribution can correct this misapprehension, because "the dynamism of the Judeo-Christian world view, the sense of history moving toward a great consummation, was not present in Greek and Roman thought, which saw life as unchanging and human history as going through repetitious cycles."[52] To the extent that it was Greco-Roman civilization that produced natural law, its static character seemed to be indispensable; to be viable today, the theory needs to be reinterpreted to incorporate the Jewish contribution. The demands of human reason and of justice remain as essential elements; human nature, however—though it contains aspects that are constant, universal, and knowable—must be seen as potentially changeable: "Human nature is dynamic and rich in potentialities which must be reckoned with in any viable theory of natural law."[53]

Some elements of human nature are, indeed, constant, such as friendship, love, reason, and culture. These are not artificial grafts upon human nature but are inherent elements of it. Without such intellectual, aesthetic, and spiritual aspects human nature is not human.[54] However, there are also darker sides to human nature: "Human nature exhibits the qualities of friendship, love, co-operation, the appreciation of beauty, the hunger for righteousness. But it also reveals aggressiveness, greed, lust, irrationality."[55] Which set of traits are the basic elements of human nature to be recognized as such by natural law?

To answer this question, Gordis considers man in a cosmic setting, in which

> as we ascend the evolutionary ladder from ameba to man, we encounter an ever greater complexity of physical structure . . . and an ever more developed nervous system with a heightened degree of consciousness, which reaches the maximum of self-awareness in man. Nor is this all. This self-awareness in man is more than a consciousness of self; it expresses itself in the love of beauty, in moral aspiration, and in the capacity to reason.[56]

As we observe the phenomena of human behavior, we are compelled to make value judgments, and we make the value judgment that the basic traits of human nature are reason and justice rather than irrationality, greed, and cruelty. In doing so, we make value judgments that "have their source in a world view fashioned by a theistic metaphysics."[57]

The jurist may not wish to push his inquiry into such a seemingly remote area as "theistic metaphysics," but he should recognize the fact that, as Gordis says,

> [g]ranted the existence of rationality and creativity within man, far-reaching consequences do emerge with regard to the nature of the universe of which man is the offspring. The nature of man *in esse* sheds light upon the character of the universe *in posse*, which, therefore, emerges as rationally created, dynamic, and possessing within itself the seeds out of which have developed the specific human traits in human nature. These are pre-eminently the attributes of rationality, moral aspiration, and creativity.[58]

6

That our view of human nature cannot be static has become clear in the twentieth century. After Freud, our knowledge of human nature is much more complex than it was before psychiatry, psychoanalysis, and psychology took into serious consideration the existence and the effect of the subconscious. We know much more about human sexuality. The status of women has undergone a radical change. Since the

Holocaust, we can no longer be as trusting in man as were the philosophers of the Enlightenment; we are constantly reminded that, as Jeremiah said, "the heart is deceitful above all things, and desperately wicked."[59] Still, as the charter of the United Nations and the various domestic and international bills of rights affirm—and as the Book of Genesis portrays—there is a common humanity, a human nature in which all men and women participate despite their differences with regard to race, color, creed, nationality, ethnicity, sex, political opinion, language, culture, or class. This belief is the bedrock on which any theory of natural law must be based.

It is this view of a common human nature on which is based the concept of the Noahide laws. Moreover, the seven laws given by God to Noah and his descendants are as clear and pure an example of what was meant by the theory of natural law as is the cry of Antigone in her confrontation with Creon or the formulations of the theory by Cicero or Grotius.

As Jacob Katz has noted, Moses Mendelssohn felt forced to reject the view of Maimonides that there is no salvation for righteous gentiles who do not acknowledge that their moral beliefs and actions are founded on divine revelation (or, even more perplexing, on the revelation by God to Moses). In a letter to Jacob Emden, Mendelssohn wrote: "For shall not the inhabitants of the earth, from the rising of the sun unto the going down thereof, except ourselves [the Jewish people], descend into the pit and become an object of abhorrence to all flesh, if they do not believe in the Torah which has been given as an inheritance to the congregation of Jacob only?"[60] Mendelssohn's "deep belief in the common humanity of all men" was rooted in the Hebrew Scriptures.[61] It was not rooted in Enlightenment philosophy but only confirmed and invigorated by it.

However, as eminent a scholar as Jacques Maritain could still write that the idea of natural law

> is a heritage of Christian and classical thought. It does not go back to the philosophy of the eighteenth century . . . but rather to Grotius, and before him to Suarez and Francisco de Vitoria; and further back to St. Thomas Aquinas; and still further back to St. Augustine and the Church Fathers and St. Paul; and even further back to Cicero, to the Stoics, to the great moralists of antiquity and its great poets, particularly Sophocles. Antigone is the eternal heroine of natural law, which the Ancients called the *unwritten law.*[62]

There is no mention of the substantial contribution that Judaism has made, for, with rare exceptions, Jewish thinkers have either ignored the subject, have abandoned any claim to the theory, or have muddied the waters. The theory of natural law is a legitimate and significant part of the Jewish legacy, and it ought to be reclaimed, with conviction of its demonstrability and with a sense of justified self-esteem.

In a profoundly scholarly essay published in 1979, Rabbi Norman Lamm, president of Yeshiva University, concludes that with respect to a belief in natural law, the position of Maimonides is ambiguous: in some passages he seemed to deny natural law, while in others he seemed to affirm it, "but even then, natural law does not at all assume for him the significance it does in other traditions."[63] Aside from Maimonides, however, Lamm places Saadye Gaon, Joseph Albo, and Bachye ibn Paquada, as well as some unspecified Geonim, as proponents of natural law. These, one may think, constitute a respectable, substantial, even formidable phalanx of authority in support of the proposition that there is room in Judaism for a belief in natural law.[64]

In an essay published in 1994, Eugene Korn, of the Shalom Hartman Institute in Jerusalem, struggles over the Maimonidean texts and summarizes his findings as follows:

> In the 16th century, Yosef Karo accepted Maimonides' opinion [that a righteous gentile will have a place in the world-to-come only if he observes the Noahide laws because he believes that they were revealed to Moses] but could not find a source for it within Jewish tradition.

> In the 17th century Spinoza accepted Maimonides' opinion as authoritative, but found it so obviously incorrect that it provided the basis for his argument undermining the validity of Judaism.

> In the 18th century Mendelssohn could not accept the opinion as correct, considered it to be idiosyncratic and rejected it as an element of true Judaism.

> In the early 20th century [Hermann] Cohen realized that he could not reject Maimonides in the name of Judaism and exploited the fact that some texts were corrupt. He proceeded to change the text, so that he could interpret Maimonides to say that belief in the Mosaic revelation was required only of gentiles wishing to live under Jewish sovereignty (resident aliens) [the ger toshav], but not required for righteous or wise gentiles.

Korn goes on to say that in the twentieth century "there was one Jewish figure [Chief Rabbi Abraham Isaac Kook] who made a bold interpretive move, attempting to be faithful to Maimonides, the text and to considerations of justice." The reference is to a passage in one of Rabbi Kook's letters, the point of which is that a gentile who observes the seven Noahide laws through the rational process—rather than through a belief that these commandments were "given by God"—merits not only a share in the world-to-come but also recognition as being one "of their wise men."[65]

Whether or not Rabbi Kook's interpretation of the Maimonidean texts effectively puts to rest the true meaning of Maimonides, it is comforting to have Rabbi Kook on the side of natural law.

PART TWO

Judaism and Pluralism

7

Many Are Called and Many Are Chosen

The belief in the "election" of Israel—that God "chose" Israel as His am
segulah, *His "treasured people"—seems to conflict with the spirits of modernity and of democracy, although the Christian dogma that God has transferred the election from Israel to Christianity has caused less feeling that the concept of election by God is a "scandal." Within Judaism, the Reconstructionist movement has discarded the belief, and the Reform movement has softened the concept by emphasis on the universal ethical mission of Israel. This essay develops the pluralistic approach, the idea that the election of Israel does not foreclose the availability of the claim by others. A smallish movement in this direction was, I think, made by Vatican II in its "Declaration on the Relationship of the Church to Non-Christian Religions," when it stated that "although the Church is the new people of God [i.e., the new "chosen" people], the Jews should not be presented as repudiated or cursed by God, as if such views followed from the holy Scriptures." This essay was first published in the quarterly journal* Judaism *in 1955.*

Years ago, as I studied ancient Greek civilization—especially Greek philosophy and drama—I began to wonder about the meaning and validity of the claim that Jews are the "chosen people": that God elected the Jews to be his "peculiar treasure," that Israel was chosen from among the families of the earth.[1] No greater claim of spiritual distinction could possibly be made by any people. Yet here I was discovering that Jeremiah and Solon were near contemporaries; that Ezekiel lived only about a century before Socrates; that at the time Ezra was attempting the restoration in Judea, Aristotle was teaching in the Lyceum. The question came to me with startling and shattering force: Could it possibly be that the Lord of the universe, the Creator

119

of light and darkness, the God who brings and takes life, He who has created and sustains all things, the heavens and the earth and all the host of them—that the Creator of the universe and the Lord of history could possibly say: "And I will establish My covenant between Me and thee"?[2] Suppose the ancient Greeks had made the claim of election, would not then the Jews have cause to wonder how God could love with a special love the people of Homer, Hesiod, Solon, Pericles, Socrates, Plato, Aristotle, Aeschylus, Sophocles, Euripides, Aristophanes, Phidias, Heraclitus, Euclid, Democritus, Pythagoras, Herodotus, and Thucydides, and not love *with an equal love* the people of Abraham, Moses, Joshua, David, Solomon, Isaiah, Jeremiah, Ezekiel, Hosea, Micah, Amos, and Jonah? Did the Jews give their great spiritual treasure to the world under a special providence, while the Greeks worked and created without God seeing or hearing? True it is that the life of Western man would seem empty if the Jewish heritage were suddenly withdrawn, if there were a brainwashing and the Bible were cast out from mind and heart; but would not life become equally impoverished, if not barren, if the Greek heritage were eradicated from consciousness?

These questions disturbed me greatly, and, I must confess, they still do. Some years later, when I began to study the literature of Christianity, the election problem began to disturb me from another standpoint. I saw that from the point of view of the man who attempted to think and live as a Christian, who tried to live a holy life in "the imitation of Christ"—say a Saint Francis of Assisi, an Albert Schweitzer, a Tolstoy, or a humble carpenter or cobbler, a Christian Bontscha Schweig[3]—the rejection of Jesus by his own people must seem to have been, as John C. Bennett expresses it, "strangely providential," for this meant that Jesus "belonged to no national group"; no race, nation, or class could lay special claim to him; he belonged "to all who received him, who believed on his name," for to all such persons "he gave power to become children of God." Could it be, I asked myself, that God had no hand in all this; that God, as it were, looked the other way as Saul of Tarsus became Paul, the bearer of the name of the Living God to Cyprus and Salamis and Galatia and Lystra and countless other places, remote and near, where men had not heard the name before? Is it possible that the Righteous Ruler of the universe—not a local deity, a mere tribal god—could have dropped an iron curtain before His mind's eye so that He would know what Jonah did, but not what Paul did? Could the Lord of whom we say "Blessed art thou, O Lord, our God, King of the Universe, Who openest the eyes of the blind," have been indifferent when the eyes of blind barbarians were opened to a vision of His kingdom and power and glory?[4]

My perplexity was compounded even more when I learned how radically pluralistic one who adheres to the philosophy of democracy must be. For this philosophy starts from the premise that according to "the Laws of Nature and of Nature's God,"[5] all men are created equal; that every man anywhere and any time is made in the image of God; that God is equally solicitous for the welfare of every race, nation, and tribe—that all people and all men have their place in the sun; that God wants variety and differences, for otherwise He would have made a different kind of world. When it was asked, "From which part of the earth's surface did God gather the dust from which He made the first man?" Rabbi Meir answered, "From every part of the habitable earth was the dust taken for the formation of Adam," so that men everywhere are brothers—yet different one from the other. Had God wanted uniformity He could have made Adam of an unmixed dust, and then each man would resemble every other man, even as one coin resembles all other coins struck from the same die.[6]

Finally, there was the problem of squaring the doctrine of the election of Israel with a global view of history. As long as one's interest in history is limited to the biblical period, it may be possible to look upon all recorded events as revolving about Israel. God could then use Ethiopia or Assyria as actors in an Israel-centered drama. In such a world, America, Africa, China, and India do not exist. Can one be so parochial, however, as to believe that the Jewish people are today at the center of events as these happen before God? Does God see the sun rise and set primarily for the sake of His people, Israel? Is Communist China, for example, significant only as it serves God's purpose for the role and destiny of Israel? To believe this today is to make of God, the Creator and Ruler of the universe, a mere means to Israel's ends; and even though these ends may be posited by God and not by Israel, this view reduces the moral power of God to that of a tribal deity with imperialistic pretensions. To believe in such a God is to blaspheme; for it means making Israel greater than God Himself, even as the folk imagination has at times made God subject to His Torah—a captive of His own creation.

How does one solve these problems?

The early Christians, who were also Jews, thought that they solved the problem through interpreting the covenant with Israel in such a way as to make possible a "new covenant." In his epistle to the Romans, Paul gives what has become the classical Christian position. God chose Abraham, but not for the personal aggrandizement of

Abraham; rather, he was chosen so that in him and in his seed all families of the earth may be blessed. The covenant was not handed down to Ishmael, the firstborn son of Abraham, but to Isaac; not to Esau, who was equally with Jacob seed of Isaac, but only to Jacob. At Sinai, Israel was again chosen—not because it deserved any special favor and not for itself but as a means of blessing to the other nations. Israel as a nation, as a collectivity, failed to be the blessing, but here and there were individuals who lived up to the promise of "all that the Lord hath spoken we will do." Such persons were the "remnant" of whom the great prophets spoke, and it was the remnant who bore the covenant; they were the kernel, and the rest were the husk—"for they are not all Israel that are of Israel."[7] Election, then, is not a virtue that is attached to a nation or group; it is personal. God chose Israel, true enough; but the individual Jew must choose God, or the covenant is not effective. Election becomes a matter of inner conviction, of personal faith or commitment. This inward faith, after Paul, is built on Christ; and the Church, as a voluntary congregation of believers, is the "new Israel," bound to God by the "new covenant." Everyone, without regard to race, nation, class, or language—Greek or Jew, bound or free—may elect himself into the new Israel and become bound by the new covenant. Thus, in the Christian view, self-election by the grace of God displaces election by God; and each believer becomes a "vessel of election" to bear Christ's name to the Gentiles.

This view leaves the Jew standing outside the covenant, old or new, for the old covenant no longer obtains after the coming of Christ, and the Jew's stiff-neckedness excludes him from the new covenant. However, each Jew can by his own will choose to become a member of the new Israel, and it is the mission of Christians to bring this about.

However, the Christian claim of election does not, for the Christian, solve the problems that we have stated: (1) Before the Christian era, were the Jews alone the chosen people? Were the Greeks, for example, not, in some significant sense, also chosen by God? (2) Does God love only the Christian saint? Does God not have a special love for good, decent people wherever He may find them, within or without a designated church? Is there no salvation for the righteous Jew, Hindu, Moslem, or "humanist"? (3) In a world of "united nations," in which a man is a man "for a' that" and the equal of every other man, can it be maintained that God has "elected" only those who are members of the Christian church? And, by the way, which church is the true Christian church? For even among those who profess to be Christians there are rival claimants for the covenant and for the election. The democratic challenge thus faces the Christian in a twofold way, in relation to other Christian denominations and in relation to the whole Christian world. (4) Does God manipulate history, in some sense or other, so that His election will ever remain at its center? Is there a special providence that looks after His chosen church?[8]

Paul thought that he was solving the problem of the covenant by his Janus-faced interpretation of the election doctrine, which makes it look two ways—the old way and the new. It is no solution, however; it only aggravates the quarrel between Jew and Christian over who enjoys the election and the covenant. Each now claims to be *the* Israel, *the* people of *the* covenant. The substitution of a church for a nation-church does not eradicate or even lessen the "scandal" of the doctrine of election.

The rabbis themselves were to a degree aware of this problem. They satisfied themselves by emphasizing that Israel was elected not for honor but for service. Israel was called upon to be a holy nation, a kingdom of priests. It was no life of ease and luxury to which they were called. To live by the word of God may mean living on a morsel of bread; and to have honor in the eyes of God may mean to have shame in the eyes of men. The Jews were elected to be servants to God and not to be rulers of men; the election offers no privileges, it only imposes duties. The only crown that Israel can wear is "the crown of a good name" as Israel lives in a way that sanctifies the Name, and Israel can do this only if all of its deeds are done for the sake of heaven.[9] The life lived in accordance with the Torah is a hard life—no other people "allowed" itself to be chosen for this covenanted way of life.

This interpretation removes the possibility of Israel claiming to be a *Herrenvolk:* it removes from the election any taint of conscious race superiority or national arrogance. It leaves, however, the *mission* of Israel at the center of the universe. Not the messenger but the message is to be honored; the world exists not for the sake of Israel but for the sake of the holy life to which Israel is dedicated. Insofar as the message must be borne by a messenger, however, insofar as the holy life must be lived by people of flesh and blood and bone, Israel significantly stands at the center of creation. A man is elected president of a country not so that he may live in an executive mansion and exercise the prerogatives of rulership; no, he is elected for service—he must work harder, worry more, and often suffer more (e.g., Abraham Lincoln and Woodrow Wilson) than most men. He is elected for *service*—that is what Israel says of its own election. But how can one possibly escape from concluding that preeminent dignity and honor must enwrap him whom God has chosen for a mission? He who is chosen may be "despised and rejected of men,"[10] but before God he has the riches of royal glory and the splendor and pomp of majesty; and "if God be for us, who can be against us?"[11]—or rather if God be for us, what does it matter if all others are against us?

The rabbinic interpretation of election is, however, a necessary one, for it puts the emphasis where it belongs—on service and not on prerogatives. If the president were elected for anything other than service, he would be unbearable; the election concept would then be totally discredited. It is the same with the election of Israel. The doctrine can be saved only by the interpretation made by the rabbis—an interpretation entirely in the spirit of the Bible: Israel was elected to live up to its promise to "walk after the Lord . . . and fear Him, and keep His commandments, and obey His voice" and to "serve Him and cleave to Him."[12]

However, the rabbinical interpretation, though necessary, is insufficient, for it leaves our questions unanswered: the unity of God, Creator and Ruler of the universe, and the election of any one people—even if the election is for service—seem inconsistent one with the other.

Saadye Gaon, it seems to me, was also troubled by this problem. A passage in Deuteronomy, "For the portion of the Lord is His people, Jacob the lot of His inheritance," provided him with a text around which to weave an extremely significant homily.

> As regards [the matter of] *possession,* inasmuch as all creatures are God's creation and handiwork, it is not seemly for us to say that He possesses one thing [Israel] to the exclusion of another, nor that He possesses the one [Israel] to the exclusion of another, nor that He possesses the one [Israel] to a greater and the other to a lesser degree. If we, nevertheless, see the Scriptures assert that a certain people [Israel] is His peculiar property and His possession and His portion and inheritance . . . —that is done merely as a means of conferring honor and distinction. For, as appears to us, every man's portion and lot are precious to Him. Nay, the Scriptures even go so far as to declare God, too, figuratively to be the lot of the pious and their portion, as they do in their statement: "O Lord, the portion of mine inheritance and of my cup." This is, therefore, also an expression of special devotion and esteem.

Furthermore, says Saadye, Scripture speaks of "the God of Abraham, of Isaac, and of Jacob." Is He not the God of all men, of all creation? At the same time, the Scripture designation of God as the God of Israel "is entirely in order," says Saadye, "since God is the Master of all." When Scripture says "God of Abraham" or "God of Israel," it merely intends to use "an expression of His esteem and high regard."[13]

In other words, what these passages mean, I think, is that the election of Israel by no means implies the rejection of the rest of mankind, no more than saying "God of Abraham" means that God is not the God of Terah, Abraham's idol-worshipping father. Israel was chosen by God for a special purpose, and Scripture is the record, in part, of Israel's mission. It is, therefore, proper, in *this context*, to speak of Israel as God's "peculiar treasure" or "possession." In other contexts, other people may be equally God's "peculiar treasure." God is the God of all mankind, and "the worth of each man and his lot are equally precious before Him." All men are equally His creatures; God does not possess one people or one person to a greater and the other people or the other person to a lesser degree. Israel is conscious of the fact that God delivered them from Egypt, but God also delivered the Philistines from Caphtor and the Syrians from Kir.[14] There is nothing that can keep the Philistines from saying: "I will sing to the Lord, for He has triumphed gloriously; the horse and his rider He has thrown into the sea."[15] Had the Philistines seen "the great work which the Lord did" against Caphtor, they too would have sung of their deliverance in the manner of Moses. So too the Syrians, the Persians, the Egyptians, and the Greeks: God possesses them all and equally, and each, in one context or another, is God's "peculiar treasure." Damascus is punished "because they threshed Gilead with threshing instruments of iron";[16] Gaza is punished because "they carried away captive the whole people to deliver them up to Edom";[17] and Nineveh might have been punished had its people not listened to Jonah. God is the Lord of all history; had the history of Egypt or Greece been written *from the standpoint of God*, each of them would have its own Bible. They lacked, however, the consciousness of their dependence upon God, and so their Bibles remain unwritten—the deliverance of the Philistines from Caphtor and of the Syrians from Kir remains unsung. Just as *every man* can say to God "My father," so *every people* can say: "Our God, and God of our fathers." The only requisite is the consciousness of one's relation to God—a relation that makes every man and every people God's "peculiar treasure," His "chosen people."

God's covenants may be oral as well as written, implied as well as expressed. God had a mission for the Greeks, just as He had for Israel; and perhaps God has a mission for America, "the new nation," as Emerson said: "One thing is plain for all men of common sense and common conscience, that here, here in America, is the home of man."[18] To Emerson, America was the home with open doors for the immigrant, the place on earth where there would be the abolition of kingcraft, priestcraft, caste, and monopoly.

Gladstone, studying simultaneously the ancient civilizations of the Jews and the Greeks, thought that God had made a double revelation of Himself to *both* peoples and that through the Homeric poems God had meant to supplement the revelation of true religion imparted by the Bible.[19]

This concept of multiple elections was partially seen by the great Saadye Gaon. It was also, in a limited way, projected by Maimonides, who—while he firmly believed in the truth of Judaism, and that when the Messiah comes, the followers of other religions will recognize and acclaim this supreme truth—nonetheless believed that somehow Christianity and the Muslim religion play important roles in God's scheme. In his *Mishneh Torah*, Maimonides wrote:

> But it is beyond the human mind to fathom the designs of the Creator; for our ways are not His ways, neither are our thoughts His thoughts. All these matters relating to Jesus of Nazareth and the Ishmaelite [Mohammed] who came after him, only served to clear the way for King Messiah, to prepare the whole world to worship God with one accord. . . . Thus the Messianic hope, the Torah, and the commandments have become familiar topics—topics of conversation [among the inhabitants] of the far isles and many peoples. . . . They are discussing these matters and the commandments of the Torah.[20]

Is not Maimonides here claiming for Christianity and for Islam some form of election, a mission to bring the knowledge of the true God and of His revelation to the far corners of the earth? In the twentieth century Franz Rosenzweig used this idea when he considered Christianity as Israel's apostle to the nations, to bring them to God.[21]

The noted Semitics scholar H. Wheeler Robinson gropingly tended toward this idea of the multiple election:

> That one man, or one nation, should enjoy a closer and more intimate knowledge of God than others, presents no more difficulty than the fact that one man or nation may possess a finer artistic consciousness, or a deeper passion for freedom. They will all have their place in the embracing purpose of God, and "all service ranks the same with God." The problems of divine election, which re-state the problems of human experience, are very real, but they must not be exaggerated by ideas of partiality and favouritism. Where God finds men able and willing to receive Him, there He finds an instrument for His purpose.[22]

The French Renaissance theologian, mystic, and orientalist Guillaume Postel argued that the Muslims had come into a special covenant with God, for everywhere they were waging a war on all idolatries and on temples of idols and were bringing men to a knowledge and love of God.

All these interpretations, both by Jewish and by non-Jewish theologians, are in the spirit of the ancient Jewish tradition that every word uttered by God at Sinai was at once translated into seventy languages, to make it clear that God did not speak only to Israel but to all mankind.[23] However, it remained for Justice Louis D. Brandeis to state clearly this concept. I give here in full his statement on this topic:

> I should think it presumptuous for any people in this century to assert that it alone had a mission for all peoples, but that none of the other peoples had any mission for it. Every people, it is becoming more and more evident, has its own character. And insofar as it has a character of its own it has a mission. For it has that elusive something, its essence, which the other peoples do not have and of which they may stand in need. But all other peoples should have those elusive somethings, of some of which the Jewish people certainly stand in need. In the realm of things material one people may be a solitary benefactor and not a beneficiary. In the realm of the spirit there is no such solitary philanthropist. Here all people give and take, some more and some less, each giving what it has, and if it is wise it takes what it needs.
>
> The experience of the Jewish people is unique. It is Jewish. Consequently the Jews have much to contribute toward the solution of the problems that perplex and confound all men. As a comparatively small people the Jewish people may be in a position to do better than bigger peoples. Palestine, when the Jews constitute the majority there, may, because of its very smallness, serve as a laboratory for some far-reaching experiments in democracy and social justice. But let us not forget that there are other small peoples who have in recent decades performed miracles in soil reclamation, in the rebuilding of their lands and peoples, and in advancing popular education and democratic ideals. Nor can we as Americans forget what our country has already done for the world and what it may yet do. The Pilgrim Fathers, in their day, and many of our most representative men since then, all conceived of America as God's gift to humanity. President Wilson spoke with deep conviction of America's mission. Perhaps Mr. Wilson had learned to speak this way because he was a constant reader of the Bible. Well then, let us teach all peoples that they are all chosen, and that each has a mission for all.[24]

At another time, Justice Brandeis said: "If the Greeks and Romans had been favorably disposed toward the Jews and there had been understanding and sympathy on both sides, the rabbis would have recognized the immense contributions those two peoples made to the advancement of civilization, and might not perhaps have rejected the possibility of their having been 'chosen' in some way."[25]

Israel requires—*as does every people*—the doctrine of election, but there is nothing in the genius of Judaism that makes impossible or undesirable a belief that other peoples too have been chosen. We are not God and we do not know all His ways, His plans, His thoughts, yet we know enough to believe that God is in some significant sense the Lord of all history, and so no one people can rightly claim that only it is the center of all history, especially if the mission of this people is to serve all others. A means to an end cannot be the center of all history.

Perhaps there is no one center; perhaps God sees many centers. Or maybe the center is yet to be made, when it will no longer be necessary—when God's righteous rule will prevail throughout the world in the Kingdom which is yet to come; for then only will it be seen by all that "There are varieties of gifts but the same Spirit."[26] As in the legend of Saladin and the three rings, each people will be able to say that it has the true inheritance, God's true law and commandments—and God will sustain the claims of each. My election is not negated or diminished when I know that others, too, have been elected by God; nor are our differences wiped out. On the contrary, as we recognize each other's quality of chosenness, we see that our right to be different—our right to be differently gifted—is rooted in the very nature of things as God created them. There need not be, as Walt Whitman wrote, "only one Supreme." We affirm with Whitman that "there can be unnumbered Supremes, and that one does not countervail another."[27]

Just as I may say "For me was the world created"[28] without implying that my neighbor may not make the same claim, so Israel may say "For our Torah was the world created" without denying the equal right to other peoples and religions to make the identical claim.

Leo Baeck has rightly reminded us that the covenant of God with the universe and with mankind came before the covenant with Abraham and with the people of Israel. "Man lives within the universe and within history," wrote Baeck. The people of Israel

> understood that history and universe testify to a oneness, and reveal a totality and order. One word has dared to be the one expression for that which keeps everything together: "covenant"—"the enduring," the covenant of the One God. It is the covenant of God with the universe, and therefore with the earth; the covenant of God with humanity, and therefore with this people [Israel] contained in it; the covenant with history and therefore with everyone within it; the covenant with the fathers and therefore with the children; the covenant with days which were and therefore with days which are to come.[29]

8

Tradition and Change in American Judaism

A Letter to David Daiches

David Daiches is a highly regarded English literary scholar, critic, and author. His grandfather was rabbi in Leeds; his father was rabbi in Edinburgh and was recognized as the spiritual leader of Scottish Jewry. David Daiches himself was a professor at Chicago, Cornell, Cambridge, and Sussex universities. In 1951 he published in Commentary *an autobiographical essay in which he explained why he was unable to accept the Orthodox Judaism of his forefathers and why he avowed agnosticism. At the time we were colleagues at Cornell and friends (our friendship has continued over the years); soon after his essay was published we engaged in a public discussion in the presence of several hundred professors and students, in which he elaborated on the contents of his essay and in which I responded with a lecture that became this essay, which was also published in* Commentary. *Notwithstanding agnosticism, Daiches maintained a strong commitment to Judaic and Hebraic studies; his book* Moses: The Man and His Vision *was published in 1975, and his Gifford lectures,* God and the Poets, *were published in 1985.*

Dear David,

Had your article in the February 1951 *Commentary* been only an exposition and defense of agnosticism, it would have awakened in me echoes of Thomas Huxley and Bertrand Russell, but I would not have felt myself personally involved. Your article, however, because it is your "personal view" of American Judaism, has started up in me reverberations from some of the deepest layers of my mind; I find myself profoundly and inextricably involved. For you and I have had pretty much the same upbringing, experiences, and education. My

129

father too, as you know, was a distinguished Orthodox rabbi who enjoyed the respect and confidence of both Jew and Christian; my education too was in several cultures, sacred and profane; my career too has brought me, in my vocation as a teacher, to an American university campus. However, though I accept some of the incidental things you say in your article, if your fundamental assertions are right, then I have been misliving my life; I have gained from my background, experiences, and education only a bushel of tares, while you possess the wheat. I feel myself, therefore, personally challenged.

Cutting away some of the underbrush, I find that our differences arise from our different attitudes toward tradition, particularly as to the function of tradition in Judaism. Our differences here are over fundamentals.

One extreme view of tradition may be characterized as the Platonic view. Plato held that the good is what preserves, that evil is what changes. Change leads away from what is perfect, the Form or the Idea; change tends toward the imperfect, evil. Any change whatever, Plato says in the *Laws*, "is the gravest of all the treacherous dangers that can befall a thing—whether it is now a change of season, or of wind, or of the diet of the body, or of the character of the soul." This statement, he says, applies to everything except to what is evil. Again in the *Laws*, he says: "The lawgiver must continue by hook or by crook a method which ensures for his state that the whole soul of every citizen will resist, from reverence and fear, changing any of the things that are established of old."[1] In the *Philebus*, Plato says "that all men who have a grain of intelligence will admit that the knowledge which has to do with being and reality, and sameness and unchangeableness, is by far the truest of all."[2]

An opposite extreme view of tradition may be characterized as the Emersonian view. If "a man claims to know and speak of God," says Emerson in his essay "Self-Reliance," and yet

> carries you backward to the phraseology of some old mouldered nation in another country, in another world, believe him not. . . . Is the parent better than the child into whom he has cast his ripened being? Whence then this worship of the past? . . . When we have new perception, we shall gladly disburden the memory of its hoarded treasures as old rubbish. . . . This one fact the world hates, that the soul *becomes*; for that forever degrades the past . . . . Say to them: "O father, O mother, O brother, O friend, I have lived with you after appearances hitherto. Henceforward I am the truth's. Be it known unto you that henceforth I obey no laws less than the eternal law. . . . I appeal from your customs. I must be myself. I cannot break myself any longer for you, or you."[3]

Emerson, who knew his Plato, was here, I believe, answering him by substituting one extreme view for another. Plato was on a quest for certainty, Emerson was on a quest for change. Plato identified the good with being; Emerson identified the good with becoming.

If one is offered a choice between these two extremes, a person with a warm attachment to life and to experience must do what Emerson counseled: break with the past completely, tell the dead to bury the dead, kiss one's parents good-bye, and turn one's face in the direction of the future and the unknown.

In a way, David, it seems that this is what you have done. The Orthodox Judaism of your father was, you say, "the real thing." Judaism is that religion that you associate with your father—"the full historical Judaism with its richness, its ceremonial, its discipline, and its strange beauty." When you think of Judaism, you are a Platonist and would put a curse on anyone who removes his father's landmark. Judaism is a perfect Form or Idea; it is unchanging; any change is a step toward imperfection: "The men of old . . . were better than we are now, and . . . lived nearer to the gods."[4] If Jews wish to continue as Jews, they should go back to your father's *shul*, his way of life, and his ways of looking at life and at the world.

But you yourself, David, because of your intelligence and spirit, find your father's ways and views no longer congenial or acceptable. You, therefore, feel that you must break with the past completely, and so you go over to Emerson's side. For you, there can be no worship of the past. You say to your father: "O father, henceforward I am the truth's." You have made the leap from Judaism to humanism, from the dead past to the live present and future, from being to becoming.

If Judaism is something that is finished, completed, a Form that will not reflect anything that is alive and throbbing today and this minute, how could one blame you? If Judaism is only a mummified corpse, what could you personally do with it except hack it to pieces, free yourself from it, and run outdoors for a bit of fresh air and sunshine?

In a way, however, your position is extremely equivocal. You still want the cake, but only for *others to eat*. Identifying Judaism with your father's shul and home, you want others to sustain it for "its richness, its ceremonial, its discipline, and its strange beauty." For others, Judaism is a Platonic Form, perfect in its being. But not for you. For yourself, you are on an Emersonian quest of becoming; you shatter the past, you have disburdened yourself of its hoarded treasure as so much old rubbish.

Now I say, David, if the choice were only between Plato and Emerson, I would be on your and Emerson's side. However, you have narrowed the possible choice to two impossible extremes.

There is a third way. It is the way of all that is best in Judaism. For a description of this third way I shall go to T. S. Eliot's essay "Tradition and the Individual Talent"—and I go to him rather than to, say, Solomon Schechter, because his discussion will bring home to you the fact that you have treated tradition in Judaism differently from the way you would treat tradition in English literature or culture, for I believe you share the views Eliot expresses in this essay.

Tradition, says Eliot, cannot be inherited as a dead weight—the way a son inherits his father's house or his books. The inheritance of tradition involves a number of things. First of all, it involves the historical sense. This sense involves a perception "not only of the pastness of the past, but of its presence." The historical sense "compels a man to write not merely with his own generation in his bones, but with a feeling that the whole of the literature of Europe from Homer and within it the whole of the literature of his own country has a simultaneous existence and composes a simultaneous order." This historical sense is "a sense of the timeless and of the temporal together." No writer or artist can be seen as standing alone: "His significance, his appreciation is the appreciation of his relation to the dead poets and artists. You cannot value him alone; you must set him, for contrast and comparison, among the dead."[5]

This is only one side of a two-sided transaction. "The existing monuments form an ideal order among themselves, which is modified," says Eliot, "by the introduction of the new (really new) work of art among them. The existing order is complete before the new work arrives; for order to persist after the supervention of novelty, the whole existing order must be, if ever so slightly, altered; and so the relations, proportions, values of each work of art toward the whole are readjusted; and this is conformity between the old and the new." The past, then, "is altered by the present as much as the present is directed by the past."

In Judaism we find—at least I offer it as my personal view—both sides of the creative transaction described by Eliot. We have the historical sense, which gives to Jewish history a simultaneous existence and which composes of Jewish history a simultaneous order. Let me illustrate this point from the Passover Haggadah: "We were the slaves of Pharaoh in Egypt; and the Lord our God brought us forth from there with a mighty hand and an outstretched arm. And if the Holy One, blessed be He, had not brought us forth from Egypt, then surely we, and our children, and our children's children, would be enslaved to Pharaoh in Egypt." We are taught that every Jew in every generation must think of himself as having gone forth from Egypt: "It was not only our forefathers that the Holy One, blessed be He, redeemed. Us, too, the living, He redeemed together with them."[6] The past, then, changes the present: I, an American, have been redeemed from slavery and from Egypt. The past is significant to me not in its character of pastness but in its existential presentness.

On the other side, the past in Judaism is changed by the present. When Moses was shown the Torah as it was to be interpreted and applied by Rabbi Akiba many centuries later, he looked at it in amazement and consternation, for he could not—the rabbis tell us—recognize in it the Torah that he had transmitted to the Jews at Sinai.[7] The Torah as it has passed through the alembic of the minds of the prophets, of Maimonides, of Saadye Gaon, and of the thousands of rabbis of the Talmud and of the centuries since then, has undergone profound sea changes. "Turn it over, turn it over," we are told, "for everything is in it."[8] Judaism can no more be reduced to a number of dogmas and practices—or even, as you seem to intimate, to monotheism, humanism, and a sense of righteousness—than English poetry can be reduced to a textbook of abstract generalizations.

In Judaism, then, the past is altered by the present, and the present is altered by the past. Had you considered Judaism in this light, you could not then have permitted yourself to identify Judaism exclusively with your father's beliefs and practices. To freeze Judaism into any form is to give substance to Toynbee's charge that Judaism is a fossil; for it means identifying Judaism with the past as utter and dead pastness; it means inheriting Judaism from one's father as one inherits one's father's house or books. There is only one thing to do with one's father, and that is to stand upon his shoulders—and to see farther. For a child to carry his father upon *his* shoulders is to identify his father with obsolescence and to invite nihilism. "He who does not himself remember that God led him out of Egypt," said Martin Buber, "he who does not himself await the Messiah, is no longer a true Jew."[9]

Let me for a moment look at this matter from another point of view. It seems to me that an identification of Judaism with the shul and the forms of observance of one's father lays one open to the charge of idolatry. "And thou shalt love the Lord thy God with all thy heart, and all thy soul, and all thy might." We have not been taught to love our synagogues, or our *kiddush* cups, or our Sabbaths and holy days, or our rabbis, or even the Bible or the Torah, with all our hearts, with all our souls, and with all our might—only God. (We are taught to *honor* our fathers and mothers; we are not taught to *love* them with all our hearts, with all our souls, and with all our might.) Holy places, holy days, holy books, and holy men are important, but their importance is of a secondary, relative, contingent nature. To identify Judaism with them is to confuse form with substance, shadow with reality. To worship the Bible is to practice bibliolatry—witness the Jewish judgment on the Karaites. To worship an infallible church or pope, a Sanhedrin, a land, or a book—or an infallible father—is to love something other than God with all one's heart, all one's soul, and all one's might.

It was Cardinal Faulhaber—though it could have been a great rabbi—who said, "We cannot separate the Law of the Lord from the Lord of the Law." To give centrality in Judaism even to the Law of the Lord is to set up an idol. Only the Lord of the Law is entitled to centrality as an absolute.

This, incidentally, is one reason why I object to making the Law of the Lord the law of the state of Israel, for it means separation of the Law of the Lord from the Lord of the Law; it means the intervention of a policeman between Jew and God and the displacement of God by the state. The intention of the rabbis is, of course, to enthrone God, but the effect would be precisely the opposite. When you, David, say that the separation of church and state in Israel may be good Jeffersonian Americanism but is not good Judaism, you are again fossilizing Judaism, refusing to admit that the Judaism of thousands of years ago has been changed by the centuries and by the many millions of Jews—and non-Jews, including Jefferson—who have lived and died since the destruction of the Temple.

It is in a nonidolatrous, Jewish spirit that we observe rites and ceremonies. "The commandments," said Rab, "were given to Israel only in order that men should be purified through them. For what can it matter to God whether a beast is slain at the throat or at the neck?"[10] Even the Temple was used by our forefathers as an idol. "Trust ye not in lying words, saying: 'The temple of the Lord, the temple of the Lord, the temple of the Lord are these,'" said Jeremiah to them. "I will do unto the house, whereupon My name is called, wherein ye trust . . . as I have done to Shiloh."[11] To call a place the temple of the Lord and to trust in it in such a way as to displace God is to engage in idol-worship. (We see here an essential reason why Jews find it impossible to reconcile themselves to a religion that says that the way to the Father is only through the Son—or through the Church; for this means the positing of an absolute alongside God. The Jew, *per contra*, says: the way to the Father is through your heart and your deeds. Nor does he add: and through your father's synagogue and his observances.)

I want to quote to you a Psalm that you know very well—Psalm 15:

Lord, who shall sojourn in Thy tabernacle?
Who shall dwell upon Thy mountain?
He that walketh uprightly, and worketh righteousness,
And speaketh truth in his heart;
That hath no slander upon his tongue,

Nor doeth evil to his fellow,
Nor taketh up a reproach against his neighbor;
In whose eyes a vile person is despised,
But he honoureth them that fear the Lord;
He that sweareth to his own hurt, and changeth not;
He that putteth not out his money on interest,
Nor taketh a bribe against the innocent.
He that doeth these things shall never be moved.

I quote this psalm not so much for what is in it as for what is *not* in it. You will note that there is not a word in it about the Temple, about forms of worship, not even a word about Jews or Judaism. And it was this Psalm that, according to the rabbis of the Talmud, summarized the 613 commandments.[12] It was in the spirit of this psalm (and such passages in the Bible are legion) that Saadye Gaon said that he who observes the commandment regarding honest weights and measures may, for all we know, be as righteous as he who observes the ritual commandments;[13] and that Rabbi Kook held that the religious duty to labor for the Zionist ideal of rebuilding Israel deserved the highest priority as a supreme command of God.[14] I cite these examples not to prove that deeds are more important than rituals but only for the purpose of demonstrating that it is a falsification to give to rituals, to any institution, or to any person or book a position of exclusive centrality in Judaism.

You, David, are no worshipper of ancestors and no worshipper of idols. Your intelligence is free and brave, so you have shattered the image of Judaism that you had projected upon the image of your father; and by shattering one, you have shattered both. You were wrong, however, in the beginning when you identified Judaism with your father's thoughts and practices. Had you climbed up to your father's shoulders, you would have seen farther—you would have seen yourself as changed by him and as changing him. From the standpoint of a tradition that is not inherited as a dead weight but that is alive and creative, it may be said that even as he is the child of the man, the child is also the father of the man. A sanctity, Santayana said, hangs about the sources of our being; piety is loyalty to those sources, and "it must never be dislodged; spirituality without it is madness. We must . . . suffer reflected light from other ages . . . to lighten a little our inevitable darkness."[15] This is the piety that characterizes the direction of sentiment from son to father. This is only half the story, however. The other half is the piety that characterizes the direction of sentiment from father to son. Either half alone is impiety; the two taken together give us a tradition in which the present is enriched by the past and the past is enriched by the present, thus saving us from nihilism as well as from idolatry.

Seen this way, Judaism is no hindrance to humanism. On the contrary, it affords one a stance from which one can say with Terence: *Homo sum; humani nihil a me alienum puto.* Jews and Christians have been great humanists without feeling that either their religion or their humanism was compromised. A proper perspective makes possible a perception of the timeless and the temporal together, and of man and God together. When a man knows with Saadye Gaon that God is "the God of all mankind" and that "the worth of each man and his lot are equally precious before Him," and with Ben Azzai that the verse in Genesis "This is the book of the generations of Adam" is the greatest principle in the Torah,[16] then nothing human—not even agnosticism—can be alien to him. Judaism, as thus conceived, stands committed to all that is open and free and is the enemy of all that is closed and restricted. If you will say that this is not the Judaism of your father and mine but a Jeffersonian Judaism, I will answer that I am not at all sure that they were not Jeffersonian Jews. Though at times they felt themselves possessed by God, they never acted as if God were possessed by them.

There is, of course, much that is wrong—and even rotten—in American Jewish life. However, this is equally true of American life in general (as it is true also of British, French, Asian life, and of every man's life, wherever his local habitation and whatever his name). Yet we do not, by any means, despair of American life. Why, then, should we despair of Jewish life in America? If we are not better than others, are we worse? Amos, Hosea, Jeremiah, and Ezekiel saw no less evil in their own days, yet they were prophets of hope as well as prophets of doom. Their mission was to call for and to promise a renewal. American Jews today, as Jews everywhere and at all times, prefer the lesser to the greater good, see the better but follow the worse. There is so much good that must be done and so much evil that is being done that one wishes to cry out, "But yet the pity of it . . . !"

One is torn between pity and anger—at oneself as well as at others—but Judaism is committed to both anger and pity. For just as pity alone may weaken the will so that it becomes tolerant of evil, so anger alone may destroy the world—with all the good that is in it and all its promise of good for the future. It is not only Judaism but sanity that compels us to stake all we have on the good, and on the future—eschatological or natural. Judaism will yet flourish, even in America—perhaps especially in America. There is much vexation of spirit, and that which is wanting cannot be numbered. Yet the crooked *can* and *will* be made straight.

9

What Is Jewish Living?

Until modern times, Jews everywhere had a distinctive, recognizable style of life; when it became possible for Jews to live and work and move freely among non-Jews, however, Jews believed that it was possible or even desirable to live as Jews at home but to live outside of their homes as nondescript Germans or Frenchmen, Englishmen or Americans. Thus a Jew can preserve his Jewish religion and Jewish identity while at the same time seek and achieve integration into the general society and its culture. It was thought possible and desirable for a Jew to live in a happy harmony of the sacred and the secular. Even modern Orthodoxy, as exemplified by the teaching of Rabbi Samson Raphael Hirsch, projected the ideal of Torah im derekh eretz, *or as the motto of Yeshiva University in New York proclaims,* Torah U-Madda— Torah and Culture. *Now, however, there is strong evidence that secularism has become so pervasive that Torah is more of an ideal than a reality. This is the condition in Israel no less than in the United States. It is against this background that this essay faces the question "What is Jewish living?" The essay was first published in* Judaism *in 1952.*

Perhaps from the beginning of their history Jews have felt a great compulsion to find a way of Jewish living, a way of life that they could call their own. It is this compulsion that is, I believe, the propulsive force of prophecy in Judaism. The search for a Jewish way of life is based upon the premise that it is not enough merely to be a Jew; rather, Jewish existence must be validated and justified by a norm that transcends mere being, even as poetry transcends mere emotion. The term "Jewish" points to two intentions: (1) to serve as a merely descriptive term, and (2) to point to a norm or an ideal. There is an implication throughout Jewish literature that though one may be a Jew, he may yet fail in his duty to live as a Jew ought to live.

This distinction, which has always created a spiritual tension in the lives of individual Jews and in Jewish history, is felt with a special poignancy by American Jews. In ghetto life, when one was born into a Jewish community as well as into a family of Jews, one took his Jewishness for granted. Jewishness had for our forefathers the character of inevitability. It was only the exceptional Jew (e.g., Spinoza) who felt that there was a distinction between fact and norm. Today, however, the situation is the reverse: American Jews are aware of the distinction between the fact of Jewishness and the norm of Judaism, and they ask: "Since I *am* a Jew, how *ought* I to live in order to give significance to my Jewishness?"

The situation is one that compels the American Jew to seek existential meaning in his Jewishness. He cannot take for granted his status, role, or destiny. Like Jacob, he must wrestle with the angel until his name is changed to Israel and he receives the key to the meaning of his name. This is the blessing for which he will wrestle with the angel of the Lord. Living in freedom in a non-Jewish community, the American Jew asks why he must continue to bear the name Jacob, why he must continue to strive with God and with men. This means that each Jew seeks to win for himself the name Israel. It is no longer a sufficient answer to his problem to be told that his grandfather Jacob had wrestled with the angel and had won the blessing. To change the metaphor: The American Jew feels himself compelled to stand at the foot of Sinai; he himself must see and hear, the covenant must be made with him, he himself wants to hear what it is that the Lord requires of him.

The average American Christian is a Christian without knowing why or to what end. The average American Jew cannot accept the fact of his Jewishness in the same matter-of-fact way, for he has the freedom to become a nominal Christian. This *freedom* to choose imposes upon him the *necessity* to choose Judaism as something more than a fact—to choose it as a norm or an ideal. The American Jew, being in fact a Jew, chooses to *become* a Jew by a commitment of his whole person. The process of becoming a Jew is, in fact, the search for a Jewish way of living.

Jewish or Human Ethics?

As we consider the question of Jewish living, we ought to bear in mind that there is an instinct, so to speak, that keeps us from asking how an American ought to live. If one were to ask how an American ought to live, the answer would be given quickly that he ought to live as befits a *man*. The same answer would be given if the question related to an Englishman, a Frenchman, or an Italian. It is generally assumed, and correctly so, that norms or ideals of conduct are significant in so far as they are universal (if the essential circumstances are duplicated). Kant may not have been altogether convincing in his precise formulation of the categorical imperative, but the drive of his thought is beyond reproach insofar as it is based on the assumption that, as Emerson said, in essence all men are One Man. It is no longer possible to say that there is one standard for the Athenian and another for the "barbarian," one for Marcus Aurelius the Emperor and another for Epictetus the slave.

Is it possible to say, however, that there is one standard for the Greek and another for the Jew? It is doubtful whether the ethical genius of the Jew would ever have permitted an affirmative answer to this question. This is not the place for a historical examination of the evidence, but I would mention several points merely to indicate the lines that an answer on a historical basis might take.

The rabbis, when they construed the covenant with Noah, concluded that all mankind—all being descendants of Noah—are bound by the seven commandments: (1) to establish courts of justice; (2) to refrain from blasphemy; (3) to refrain from idolatry; (4) to refrain from incest; (5) to refrain from bloodshed; (6) to refrain from robbery; and (7) to refrain from eating flesh cut from a living animal. The commandments are part of the covenant with "all flesh that is upon the earth." This interpretation of Genesis 9 makes possible or even necessary, from the standpoint of Jewish tradition, natural law, natural rights, and a universal ethics in which a distinction between Jew and Greek would be intolerable.

In Ezekiel we find that Tyre, Egypt, and other nations are judged by God in the same way in which He judges the Jewish people. They too feel the rod of His justice and the balm of His mercy. When the heart of the prince of Tyre was "lifted up" because of his riches, God promised to bring upon him strangers and "the terrible of the nations." Says the prophet: "Behold, I am against thee, O Zidon, / And I will be glorified in the midst of thee; And they shall know that I am the Lord, when I shall have executed judgments in her, and shall be sanctified in her."[1] Because Egypt had grown arrogant and had said, "The river is mine, and I have made it," God said, "I am against thee, and against thy rivers." The biblical position is that although Israel has a special role to play in God's plan, and the "nations" stand in a relation to Israel that is different from that in which they stand to one another, God's justice and mercy are universal in their sweep, and their essence does not admit of partiality or discrimination.

A final instance I shall cite is the incident of the *heathen* who came to Hillel and said, "Teach me the whole Law while I stand on one foot." "What is hateful to you do not to your fellow," replied Hillel. When a *Jew* came to Rabbi Akiba with the same question, he received essentially the same answer: "What is hateful to yourself, do not to your fellow man. If you wish that nobody should take from you what is yours, take not from another what is his." The ethical norms formulated by Akiba and by Hillel allow of no distinction between Jew and non-Jew, and in spirit they anticipate Kant's categorical imperative, which, as we have said, assumes the ethical equality of all men.

Jewish living, then, insofar as it means living in accordance with ethical norms, is not to be differentiated from American or British or African—or human—living. Ethical norms know only man as the universal subject and object of rights and duties. The Declaration of Independence speaks of the laws of Nature and of Nature's God under which all men are created equal and are equally endowed with certain inalienable rights. The Declaration of the Rights of Man and of the Citizen states that "men are born, and always continue, free and equal in respect of their rights." The general assembly of the United Nations, in the Universal Declaration of Human Rights, gave recognition to "the inherent dignity" and "the equal and inalienable rights of all members of the human family," which are "the foundation of freedom, justice, and peace in the world."

These great pronouncements of the universal character of ethics, of human nature, and of human rights and freedoms reflect and implement the great teachings of Judaism. These pronouncements should give us special joy not merely because they contribute to our personal survival and security but because they are fruit of our seed. Our jealous interest in them should not be diminished because other people too (e.g., the ancient Greeks) contributed to their formulation and acceptance. Greeks too are of the sons of Noah, and Jews in particular ought not to permit themselves and others to forget that every man can and ought to trace his ancestry back to Noah and back to Adam and Eve. What are the Declaration of Independence, the Declaration of the Rights of Man and of the Citizen, and the Universal Declaration of Human Rights but modern versions of the great book of Genesis, with the books of the prophets as commentaries on the text?

The first plank in a program of Jewish living should be the affirmation of the universal character of man and of his rights, freedoms, and duties. There must be no thought of a code of Jewish ethics, of a code of Jewish ethical conduct. Such a thought would do violence to the genius of Biblical and rabbinic philosophy. From the ethical standpoint Jewish living means human living—living with full awareness of the dignity and glory that should accompany human existence. We should recall and remember what Rabbi Joshua ben Levi said: "When a man goes on his road, a troop of angels proceed in front of him and proclaim: 'Make way for the image of the Holy One, blessed be He!' "[2]

Recently, a student asked me to recommend some works on Jewish ethics. I thought of one or two books and named them reluctantly. My impulse was, however, to send the student to the works of Spinoza, Kant, John Stuart Mill, William James and several others, and to say to him: "Study these works. In them you will find the human spirit searching for ways to find its peace with God through peace between man and man, each made in the image of God. This search is found in many hearts and minds. The Bible is the record of such a search; in a sense, the quest is a Jewish quest, the hunger for justice and righteousness is a Jewish hunger. In a sense, Amos and Isaiah sought for a Jewish ethics. No sooner does a man start on this quest, however, than he discovers that what he is looking for is that which will make impossible a distinction between Jew and Greek, even as it will make impossible a distinction between emperor and slave. There is, then, no such thing as Jewish ethics, and there ought to be no book with such a title; for insofar as a book is about ethics, it cannot be about Jews but only about human beings."

Jewish living, then, implies a denial of any special Jewish ethics and implies a commitment to a system of universal ethics that embraces all mankind, without distinction of race, color, creed, national origin, sex, or economic status, and that is pledged to an observance of the rights and freedoms of all men everywhere.

This commitment justifies and is the reason for the singularity of Israel. The Jews are, Reinhold Niebuhr has rightly said, a group "with a universalistic religious faith which transcends the values of a single people but which they are forced to use as an instrument of survival in an alien world." It is the Jew's destiny to bear witness to this universalistic ethic and to the belief in the equality and freedom of all men. This destiny does not make the Jews any more "chosen," in an invidious sense, than does the mission of the Quakers to give their peace testimony before men in arms make them "chosen" in an offensive sense.

This ideal of Jewish living, the essence of which is a prophetic universalism that would dissolve Jewish singularity, has not always been clearly revealed to us. It appears to us more clearly than it did to our forefathers. This does not, however, by itself make it a new ideal. "It belongs to the nature of historic ideals," Ralph Barton Perry has written, that they should point toward the future, and that their meaning should be progressively revealed. There is an insight which is reserved for those who look back over the path already traversed, and which will escape the most prophetic imagination of earlier times as well as the experience of contemporaries. . . . There is such a thing as the "light of perspective."[3]

Kiddush-Ha-Shem

There is, then, the Jewish ideal that demands of the Jew that he bear witness to the truth of a universal system of ethics and universal freedoms, based on a commitment to equality and to the equal freedom of all men. This ideal Jews share with many men all over the world, and insofar as this ideal wins wider acceptance and implementation, the historical fact of Jewish singularity gains greater justification. However, this ideal must be maintained and fought for every day in the life of the Jew, otherwise his singularity will be without reason and without virtue.

There is also a special Jewish *sanction* that supports and gives religious truth to the expression of this ideal; namely, the concept of *sanctification*, kiddush. The idea behind this concept is that the divinity of God is, so to speak, incomplete; it may, in a sense, be increased or decreased by the acts of men. According to the rabbis, God says: "When you do My will, My divinity is increased; when you violate it, it is decreased." (In our own century, William James gave the clearest expression of this thought. God, he said, depends on our conduct: "God himself, in short, may draw vital strength and increase of very being from our fidelity."[4]) When a Jew does a wrong, he sins not only because the act in its nature is evil and sinful but also because he reduces the presence of God in the world. Thus, Ezekiel says that when God expelled the Jews from their homeland because of their evil ways, God Himself suffered an injury:

And when they came unto the nations, whither they came, they profaned My holy name; in that men said of them: These are the people of the Lord, and are gone forth out of His land. But I had pity for My holy name, which the house of Israel had profaned among the nations, whither they came. Therefore say unto the house of Israel: Thus saith the Lord God: I do not this for your sake, O house of Israel, but for My holy name, which you have profaned among the nations, whither ye came. And I will sanctify My great name, which hath been profaned among the nations, which ye have profaned in the midst of them; and the nations shall know that I am the Lord,

saith the Lord God, when I shall be sanctified in you before their
eyes.[5]

In this spirit the rabbis taught: "It is worse to steal from a non-Jew
than to steal from an Israelite because of the profanation of the Name
(*Hillul Ha-Shem*)."

Sanctification of the Name (*Kiddush Ha-Shem*) is the supreme Jewish duty, and *Hillul Ha-Shem* is the supreme sin.

Certainly, one of the meanings of this tradition is that the Jew
always bears the character of witness to the lordship of God, to His
sovereign rule in the realm of conduct. When he sins, he is like a
servant who has brought his master's name into disrepute. God is
dependent upon the Jew for the glory of His name. When the Ca-
naanites threatened the existence of the Jews, Joshua demanded of
God, "What wilt Thou do for Thy great Name?"

Here we detect a facet to Jewish living. The Jew is required to
view himself as living in a God-centered world, in which he is under
constant divine judgment. Each of his acts must be sacred or must be
viewed as a sacrament, as testimony to the rule of God. (The distinction between sacred and secular is not one that the Jewish tradition
permits except as a manner of speaking. The distinction is *ben-kodesh
le-kodesh*, between one sanctification and another sanctification. One
can see this clearly when one recalls the blessings required to be expressed even in connection with the performance of bodily functions.)
Thus any act can be a religious act if one sees it as the fulfillment of a
divine commandment, if one sees it as oriented towards God.

"One should, and one must," Martin Buber has said,

> truly live with all, but one should live with all in holiness, one
> should hallow all that one does in one's natural life. No renunciation
> is commanded. One eats in holiness, tastes the taste of food in holi-
> ness, and the table becomes an altar. One works in holiness, and he
> raises up the sparks which hide themselves in all tools. One walks in
> holiness across the fields and the soft songs of all herbs, which they
> voice to God, enter into the song of our soul. One drinks in holiness
> to each other with one's companions, and it is as if they read to-
> gether in the Torah. One dances the roundelay in holiness, and a
> brightness shines over the gathering. A husband is united with his
> wife, and the Shekinah rests over them.[6]

To the holy man, it is said, every river is the Ganges. To the Jew
who is aware of the holiness dimension of life, every day is a High
Holy Day, every place is a Holy of Holies, every language is a *loshen
kodesh*, a holy tongue, and every book is a Bible. To his way of seeing

and judging things, there is no conflict between science and religion, for he sees in science, in the intelligence, no less a manifestation of God than in beauty and in goodness; for science is dedicated to truth, and truth too serves the interests and ends of God. Science itself is thus holy. How, then, can there be a conflict between science and Judaism? The scientist who works in his laboratory does God's work even as does the cobbler, the baker, and the carpenter. If God can ordain strength out of the mouth of babes and sucklings, why not out of the mind of the scientist?

It does not do to say that man is but a worm and to let it go at that. Certainly, if man is but a worm, and if the scientist is but a man, the scientist is but a worm, his work is a worm's work, and it does not compare with God's work. This way of looking at things is to glorify God by belittling His handiwork. It is to forget that man is a little lower than the divine, that God has crowned him with glory and with honor, that God made him to have dominion over the works of His hands, and that He has put all things under his feet. *This* is man, and this is why God is mindful of him. The scientist who splits the atom does so with the intelligence that God has given him, and his work is no less sacred—or godly—than was the work of God in the first six days of creation. It is not that God's power is an extension of man's: rather the reverse, man's power and work are an extension and continuation of God's power and work. When the work of the scientist becomes destructive, it is the work of man rather than the work of the scientist that has become destructive. When a book spreads poison to the minds of men, the fault is not that of the printing press nor of its inventor. Every creator must work in fear and trembling, lest he create for death rather than for life, for destruction rather than for enrichment and enlargement of life and of the spirit.

The sense of *sanctification*, of *mitzvot* as the performance of acts that will increase God's divinity in the world of men, is the religious foundation of Jewish living and is the *sanction* of Jewish singularity for the sake of universalism.

This Jewish immersion in God's will and purposes, to expand His domain by bringing glory to His name, by universalizing justice and righteousness, equality and freedom, truth, beauty, and happiness, is what provides strength and resolution to the consciousness and to the will of the Jew. ("There is a continuum of cosmic consciousness, against which our individuality builds but accidental fences," says William James, "and into which our several minds plunge as into a mother-sea or reservoir."[7]) The consciousness of this orientation of our will, purposes, and acts toward God makes possible the interpolation of the ideal into the real world and makes the ideal and real dynamically and causally continuous; it brings together the realm of conduct and the realm of thought; it makes possible the union of Jewish living and Jewish thinking; it brings together ethics and religion. The universal ethic to which the Jew is committed says that all men are brothers; the universal religion to which the Jew is committed says that the brothers are all sons of one Father—and adds that the Father is not only Father, He is also Ruler and Judge (all our prayers are directed towards *Abenu Malkenu*, "our Father, our King").

The Christian, of course, also knows this sense of sanctification. "Whether ye eat or drink," said Saint Paul, "do all to the glory of God." Commenting upon this passage, Jeremy Taylor has said that when this rule is observed,

> every action of nature becomes religious, and every meal is an act of worship, and shall have its reward in its proportion, as well as an act of prayer. Blessed be that goodness and grace of God, which, out of infinite desire to glorify and save mankind, would make the very works of nature capable of becoming acts of virtue, that all our lifetime we may do Him service.

Even when performing the most common action of life, says Taylor, the Christian should act with a "holy intention" and say to himself: "Now I am working the work of God; I am His servant, I am in a happy employment, I am doing my Master's business, I am not at my own dispose, I am using His talents, and all the gain must be His."[8]

The ideal of holy living is probably in its origin—at least for Western man—Jewish, but its universal appeal makes it an ideal that transcends the confines of any one religion or people. Still, just as life, liberty, and the pursuit of happiness may be rightly claimed as American ideals even though they might be similarly claimed by the French and British and other peoples, so holy living may be claimed as an ideal of Jewish living even though it might be similarly claimed by the Christian. I think it was Saadye Gaon who said that the people of Israel may claim to be the chosen people, though the Egyptians may make the same claim *if they but see themselves as chosen by God.*

The Question of Rites and Rituals

Often, when Jewish living is mentioned, one thinks of special rites and rituals, sabbaths and festivals. What place is there in Jewish living for rites and rituals, for sabbaths and festivals? There is room for them if they are used to increase and to sharpen the sense of sancti-

146 I Judaism and Pluralism

fication, to accent the belief that the small, everyday acts of a man's life can offer up a sense of the holy, of the numinous, to the man who is awake to the divine dimension of human existence and life.

Even if such matters are viewed as mere human devices, historically conditioned, their value is not thereby necessarily diminished. The emotions need props, and one may resort to them without feeling shamefaced. Towards the end of his life, Charles Darwin expressed the regret that he had neglected the reading of poetry to the point where he had lost his sense of aesthetic appreciation. The emotions need supports and exercises, and the sense of the holy is not exempt from this need.

To the holy man, we have said, every day is a High Holy Day. This should imply no antinomianism, for the Jew still needs particular sabbaths and holy days to remind him of the holiness of days. He needs particular places of worship to remind him that the glory of God fills the whole world—lift the rock, and there you'll find Him. He needs Hebrew to remind him that God speaks in the language of man.

Furthermore, Jewish rites and rituals, sabbaths and festivals help in the maintenance of Jewish singularity. They thus have a survival value, which ought not to be disregarded. This, however, would be a purely sociological value, which would be hard to justify if the singularity were not itself a means to an ethical end and a religious objective. There is no value, said Saadye Gaon, to a Jew's observing the rituals of the sabbath and of the festivals unless he has preceded them with the observances of the moral law, the deeds of righteousness and truth and equity and the command "Thou shalt love thy neighbor as thyself," which is further clarified by the maxim "That which is hateful to thee do not inflict upon thy neighbor."

Often Jewish tradition has been identified with these rites and rituals, sabbaths, feast and fast days. I suspect that one reason for this identification is that tradition becomes easier to transmit if its meaning is exhausted by these aspects of Judaism. All that the father needs to do is to practice the rites and rituals in the presence of his children; then they will know what it means to have a Jewish home; and then, when their turn comes, they will follow in their father's ways by sheer repetition or imitation. The closer the imitation, the more traditional is the son or daughter, and hence the more Jewish.

This represents a perversion of the meaning of tradition. It identifies tradition with sacerdotalism and mimicry. "A heritage is not transmitted," André Malraux has said; "it must be conquered." The conquest, he adds significantly, is made slowly and unpredictably:

We do not demand a civilization made to order any more than we demand masterpieces made to order. But let us demand of ourselves a full consciousness that the choice made by each of us out of the past—out of the boundless hopes of the men who came before us—is measured by our thirst for greatness and by our wills.

A tradition must be won and must be won over. The process by which one takes it is not possession but repossession. As Goethe put it: *"Was du ererbt von deinen Vätern hast, erwirb es, um es zu besitzen."*[9] A living people—and Jews are a living people: *Am Yisrael hai*—must have no exaggerated fear of change and must not show a desperate clutching of the past.

There are those among us—extreme Jewish nationalists—who preach a gospel of mere future. Such people are as harmful as are those who preach the gospel of mere past. Both these gospels are false. As Ralph Barton Perry has said:

[W]e cannot live in either the past or the future, but only in the present, which is both. We live out of the past and into the future. Our ideals, therefore, must be both old and new—both *memories* and *plans*. They must enable us to preserve our . . . identity, and draw inspiration from heroic days; but they must also find new content in the facts of life about us, reveal our faults, and help us with courage and invention to find new solutions of new problems.[10]

When I lived at home with my parents, whenever it was reported that a Jew had not conducted himself properly or had committed a crime, they would say, *Es passt nisht für a Yid; es is a Hillul Ha-shem"* ("Such conduct is unbecoming a Jew; it is a desecration of the Name").

Today we hardly ever hear these phrases. There is a feeling generally prevailing that Jews, like all other peoples, are "entitled" to their quota of miscreants and criminals. "Why," I have often heard the question asked, "should not the Jews have their portion of criminality and immorality?" The question is, of course, intended to be rhetorical, as if there could not possibly be a negative answer.

More than anything else, it seems to me, it is imperative for us to recapture the sense of sanctification, by which a person identifies himself with God's dependence upon *him* for His work among men and for the maintenance and enlargement of His divinity, as well as with man's dependence upon God for the maintenance and enlargement of the divinity in *him*. The recapture of this sense defines our greatest challenge. Without this sense of kiddush, Jewish being, but not Jewish living, is possible. With this sense of kiddush, the breach between fact and ideal will be healed, though the tension of fact toward ideal can never be completely overcome.

To be an American, Santayana has said, "is of itself almost a moral condition, an education, and a career." This is no less true of the Jew, and it is especially true of the American Jew.

10

Chaim Grade's Quarrel

Chaim Grade (1910–1982) was considered by some critics the leading Jewish poet of his time. He wrote in Yiddish, but much of his work has been translated into Hebrew. Before settling in New York in 1948, he lived in Poland, Russia, and Paris. In the latter part of his life Grade wrote novels that have been translated into English, among them The Yeshiva, The Agunah, The Well, *and* Rabbis and Wives, *along with* My Mother's Sabbath Days *(a memoir). To many readers of Jewish literature, Grade is best known for "My Quarrel with Hersh Rasseyner," which was first published in Yiddish in* Der Yiddisher Kemfer, *the Zionist weekly edited by Hayim Greenberg. It is this so-called story that is the subject of the present essay, which was published in* Midstream *in November 1995.*

1

Chaim Grade's famous "My Quarrel with Hersh Rasseyner" was presented as a short story in *A Treasury of Yiddish Stories*, edited by Irving Howe and Eliezer Greenberg.[1] But is it a story? It is a work that cannot be classified—like Thomas Carlyle's *Sartor Resartus*, like Walter Pater's *Marius the Epicurean*. What is Ecclesiastes? What is the Book of Job? In the Hebrew Scriptures they were wisely placed in the part known simply as "Writings." For the sake of convenience, I shall refer to "My Quarrel" as a story.

The story is a unique mixture of intellect and passion, of rationality and emotion, of religion and philosophy. It is a secular work, originally written and first published in Yiddish, yet it belongs, I would say without hesitation, among our writings that are considered sacred. I would associate it not with the other short stories in the Howe-Greenberg anthology but with the Book of Job. A reading of the story must leave one disquieted, disturbed, jolted out of compla-

149

cence. Chaim Grade challenges not only Hersh Rasseyner but also the reader, because, above all, like Job, he challenges God. His "Krig," his "Quarrel," is with life itself.

Chaim Grade, like Shmuel Yosef Agnon, wrote out of a depth of knowledge of classical Jewish scholarship. To fully understand and appreciate Grade, to be sensitive to the nuances and unexpressed references to Jewish literature, history, and life, one needs to come to him with all one's memories and knowledge. Of course, like all great, important literature, Grade can be read on a variety of levels of meaning. His poems, novels, short stories, and even "My Quarrel" can be read in a straightforward way, as one reads, e.g., a novel by Charles Dickens or by Anthony Trollope, one-dimensional works (this is not said to belittle them; they are great storytellers). Grade, however, wrote not only with his mind and imagination but also with a memory that was both personal and communal, individual and historical, private and social, secret and manifest. He wrote as one who has lived his own life but also as one who has lived the life of his ancestors, all the way back to his forefather Abraham and his foremother Sarah; as one who has lived through the history of the twentieth century but also the history of some three thousand years; as one who has read Tolstoy and Pushkin but also has read and studied the Bible and Talmud, Spinoza and Kant, Rashi and Maimonides.

Erich Auerbach, in his famous book *Mimesis,* said about Homer that he knows no background; what Homer narrates is "the only present, and fills both the stage and the reader's mind completely"; his style leaves nothing that he mentions "half in darkness and unexternalized," nothing remains hidden or unexpressed; there is never a glimpse of "unplumbed depths." In Homer there is only foreground, no background. Homer can be analyzed but cannot be interpreted.[2] The exact opposite is true of Grade. His writings have perhaps even more background than foreground, more darkness than light, more depth than surface. Adapting what T. S. Eliot wrote in his influential essay on "Tradition and the Individual Talent," one can say that Chaim Grade has a strong historical sense; he was able to perceive not only the pastness of the past but also its presentness. He wrote "not merely with his own generation in his bones, but with a feeling" that the whole of Jewish life and literature had a simultaneous existence and composed a simultaneous order. He had a sense of the temporal and the timeless together.[3]

2

Let me illustrate several of the qualities of Chaim Grade as they appear in "My Quarrel."

Two persons, Chaim (obviously the author) and Hersh Rasseyner, engage in a heated discussion (a *krig* in the original Yiddish, a "quarrel" in the English mistranslation), broken up by years when they are separated. Both Chaim Vilner (as Grade referred to himself) and Hersh were survivors of the Holocaust; both had been students in a Musar yeshiva in Novogrudok (in Yiddish, Novaredok), a city in the Grodno oblast that passed from Lithuania to Poland to Bellorussia. It was an important city, of which Isaac Elchanan (for whom the rabbinical seminary affiliated with Yeshiva University is named) was rabbi. Now, the fact that both discussants were musarniks has a strong bearing on the substance and on the spirit of the quarrel, yet the reader is given no explanation that would inform him or her about the nature of Musar and what it meant to be a musarnik. This omission is no reflection on Grade as author, for the story is not an exposition; its motion and rhythm could not be interrupted by an objective statement about the Musar movement. The author was forced to assume that the reader would have the background to appreciate what it meant for the discussants to be sharers of a common education in Musar.

The Musar movement was closely identified with the life of its founder, Rabbi Israel (Lipkin) Salanter (1810–1883). From his early youth Salanter was recognized for his scholarship, piety, and moral sensitivity. He had all the qualities of personality to make a founder and leader of a movement in the lively world of Lithuanian yeshivot. Salanter became distressed that the yeshivot concentrated almost exclusively on Talmudic studies and neglected the study of ethics and morals and the formation of the character of the students. He founded his own yeshiva in Vilna where he would feel free to teach the principles of Jewish ethics, and he established also a Bet Musar that became a model. In the yeshiva and in the Bet Musar students studied ethical classics, especially *Mesilat Yesharim* (The path of the righteous) by Moses Hayyim Luzzatto (1707–1747) and *Hovot Ha-Levavot* by Bachye ibn Paquada (mid-eleventh c.). After some years in Vilna, Salanter moved to Kovno, where he founded a Musar yeshiva. He made some significant changes in the day-to-day lives of the students by abolishing the practice of their going every day to different private homes for their meals and establishing a common refectory, and by insisting that they dress in clean and neat clothes and that they acquire proper manners. Needless to say, Salanter had opponents, but he was intrepid and steadfast.

There are many anecdotes about Salanter, but perhaps the following (the most famous) will give one a measure of his qualities of character and of person: In 1948 there was an outbreak of the terrifying cholera epidemic in Vilna. Rabbi Salanter ordered that notices be posted in all synagogues that Jews were not to fast on Yom Kippur, that they were to shorten the service and to walk about outdoors during the cool hours of the day; and during the morning service, Salanter took in his hand some baked goods, ascended the pulpit, recited the blessing, and ate in the presence of the congregation, so that the worshipers might be induced to do likewise.

Salanter particularly attacked the tendency of people to be strict in their observance of ritual *mitzvot* (commandments) while neglecting the mitzvot relating to ethical conduct. Every morning, seven days in each week, observant Jews repeated from their prayer books a passage from the Talmud that says that a person is required to do acts of kindness, show hospitality to strangers, visit the sick, provide for brides, escort the deceased to their resting places, and bring peace between person and person; yet these and similar commandments are belittled in practice, while men are strict in their observance of rites and rituals. "I am astounded by those people," Salanter once said, "who wish to benefit their fellow by standing outside the synagogue calling out, *'Kedusha! Kedusha!'* [calling them to come in for prayers]. Why do they not also stand at the gates of their homes when a rich and bountiful meal is spread on the table and cry out, 'A feast! A feast! Please come in!'"[4]

In 1857 Salanter left Lithuania and went to Germany. He studied and learned the German language, dressed in the style of German men, acquired German citizenship, and delivered sermons in German. He lectured on the Talmud at Koenigsberg University, studied secular subjects, and urged that the Talmud be made a subject of study in universities. Anticipating by a century the work of Adin Steinsaltz, Salanter advocated the translation of the Talmud from Aramaic into Hebrew and also its translation into all European languages. He corresponded with Rabbi Samson Raphael Hirsch, founder of neo-Orthodoxy, and became a friend of Rabbi Azriel Hildesheimer and an admirer of Hildesheimer's rabbinical seminary in Berlin, where the students studied secular subjects as well as the traditional Jewish religious subjects. Although he approved the Hildesheimer curriculum, he did not recommend its introduction in Lithuanian yeshivot, except for secular subjects that would help students to prepare them for making a living.

Although in his lifetime Salanter faced opposition from heads of yeshivot who were satisfied with the traditional system, gradually all Lithuanian yeshivot became Musar institutions. Some were minimalist and some were maximalist; the Novogrudok yeshiva, where Chaim and Hersh studied, was one of the maximalist Musar yeshivot. This fact influenced each of them differently, for each understood

Musar in his own way, each had his own conception of what it means to be a Jew and a mensch. Moreover, each of them was differently affected by the Holocaust. These differences are at the center of the quarrel between Chaim Grade and Hersh Rasseyner (a real person).

3

A concept that plays a basic role in Musar is the *yezer ha-ra*, generally translated as the evil inclination, the evil impulse, the temptation to sin or to do evil. Many of us are familiar with the effort to find a theory that would deal with this problem from Plato's *Phaedrus*, where Plato uses the myth of the chariot and the two steeds. The chariot is the body, one horse is desire, the other horse is the will. Mind does the driving, holding the reins; it must bridle the two steeds in balance, else the charioteer—the soul—will be driven into the abyss. A similar myth is used in the *Katha Upanishad*. In each case the assumption is that the true soul is essentially rational.

In rabbinic literature, *yezer* can be evil or good. The two kinds are sometimes personified as contenders who fight for rulership over man, over his soul. The yezer ha-ra is the tempter, which, if not controlled or "bridled," will destroy the person. More often than not, the evil yezer is identified with the sexual drive, which is conceived to be the most imperious desire. However, the favored Musar classics do not ignore or underestimate the impulse to be selfish, to aggrandize oneself by greed for wealth and for material possessions, by the will for power and for domination, by pride, and by many other desires.

Grade sets the stage in the very first paragraph of the story. When Chaim visited Bialystock, seven years after he had left the Novogrudok yeshiva, he found many of his old schoolmates weary of their spiritual struggles; they realized that "they had lost the war with themselves. They had not overcome the evil urge [the yezer ha-ra]."[5] Hersh is a maximalist, an extremist, in his concentration on the need to overcome the yezer ha-ra. At their first reunion, in Bialystock, Hersh says to Chaim: "You know the saying among us: Whoever has learned Musar can have no enjoyment in his life." Eleven years later Chaim and Hersh meet in Paris, and now Hersh boasts that he has achieved victory. He had suffered many lusts; the very veins in his head had almost burst from the boiling of his blood. "But I knew," he says, "that whoever denies himself affirms the Master of the World. I knew that the worst sentence that can be passed on a man is that he shall not be able to renounce his old nature [the yezer ha-ra]. And because I truly wanted to conquer myself, the Almighty helped me."[6]

Was it his mind, his reason, that managed successfully to bridle the steeds—to use the Platonic terms? No, says Hersh, the mind is not trustworthy. The mind can rationalize a desire to make it feel that it is a *good* yezer. Hersh uses a rather crude form of expression: "Reason is like a dog on a leash who follows sedately in his master's footsteps—until he sees a bitch. . . . Any man can rationalize whatever he wants to do."

If mind or reason cannot hold in check the evil inclination, what can? Hersh says nothing can be trusted but the Torah. He fasts two days a week, but this does not suffice: "The one way out is this. A man should choose between good and evil *only as the Law [Torah] chooses for him.* . . . Even when a man understands rationally what he should do, he must never forget that before all else he should do it because the Law tells him to do it." But is it not possible to have enjoyment of the world *and* of Torah? No, says Hersh. If you try to have both, you will have neither. It is one or the other. And he has chosen Torah—totally, to the complete exclusion of the world.

Again I am reminded of Plato. When he wrote the *Republic,* he had the fifth century's trust in reason. Towards the end of his life, however, after he had witnessed the degradation of Athens—which had put Socrates to death as if he were a common dangerous criminal—and after his failure to reform the government of Syracuse, he wrote the *Laws,* his last work, in which he depicted a completely closed society, ruled not by reason, not by philosophers, but, under God, by tradition and by religious law. "The principal thing," he wrote, "is that none, man or woman, should ever be without an officer set over him, and that none should get the mental habit of taking any step . . . on his individual responsibility. . . . In a word, we must train the mind not even to consider acting as an individual or know how to do it."[7]

What Hersh says to Chaim is not very different from what Plato in his last years proposed for his ideal commonwealth: "We want," says Hersh, "a more onerous code, more commandments [mitzvot], more laws, more prohibitions. We know that all the pleasures of life are like salt water: the more a man drinks of it, the thirstier he becomes. That's why we want a Torah that will leave no room for anything else."

Even Torah, however, is not enough to keep a person from sinning: "Even a man who has a Law won't be able to withstand his temptation if he doesn't watch over himself day and night. . . . [U]ntil a man has accomplished what he should, the Law does not trust him." While Abraham and Isaac walked towards Moriah, the outcome was still uncertain. It was only after the binding of Isaac by Abraham that the angel could say, "Now I know." "Without deeds all inquiry is vain."

The contention of Hersh assumes that both he and Chaim have in mind the position of Maimonides with regard to the question who is a truly virtuous man. Maimonides distinguished between ceremonial laws and the ostensibly moral laws. With respect to the former, a man should not say, e.g., that he is not at all tempted to eat foods forbidden by the Torah; *per contra*, he should say, "I very much would like to eat this food, but God forbids me, so I shall not eat it." When, however, he is faced with an opportunity to commit adultery, to steal, or to commit fraud, he ought not at all to be inclined to do the act. It should be to him a repulsive notion, which he would not at all entertain. A noble soul, says Maimonides, "has absolutely no desire for any such crimes, and experiences no struggle in refraining from them."[8] With regard to ceremonies, rites, and rituals—the ceremonial law—were it not for the Torah, "they would not at all be considered transgression." The other commandments, however, are such about which the rabbis said—and here Maimonides quotes the Talmud—"If they had not been written in the Law, it would be proper to add them."[9]

It seems, however—although this is not made explicit in the story—that Hersh's position is that *all* commandments, without distinction between ceremonial and moral laws, must be observed only because they are commandments of God: "A man should choose between good and evil only as the Law chooses for him." No trust can be placed in reason, for a person can easily rationalize to do what his heart desires. "Even when a man understands rationally what he should do," says Hersh, "he must never forget that before all else he should do it because the Law tells him to do it." Why? Because, says Hersh, a time comes when reason loses its power of control, when it can no longer have power to command.

This is a crucial point of difference between Hersh and Chaim, and it is clearly articulated in the argument over gentiles—whether gentiles, "who have not the Law," can be trusted to be righteous. Hersh addresses this question immediately after he reminds Chaim of what the Holocaust has done to individual Jews and to the community of Israel. By implication Hersh contradicts Paul, who, in his epistle to the Romans, said: "For it is not the hearers of the Law who are righteous before God, but the doers of the Law who will be justified. When gentiles who have not the Law do by nature [natural law] what the Law requires, they are a Law to themselves, even though they do not have the Law."[10] Maimonides in effect contradicted Paul, and this is part of the intellectual provenience that we must read into the quarrel between Hersh and Chaim.

4

According to the Talmud, all human beings—including Jews—are descendants of Noah, the second Adam; however, after Sinai, Jews were no longer called Noahides, but only gentiles were known by that designation. Noahides were given by God seven commandments, which are according to reason and which may be derived from the Torah; namely, prohibition of idolatry, blasphemy, bloodshed, incest, robbery, eating a limb cut from a live creature, and the command to establish courts of law (*Sanhedrin* 56a). According to the rabbis, whoever observes these seven Noahide laws will be considered a righteous gentile and will have a portion in the world to come. Now, Maimonides added a highly-controverted proviso; namely, that a gentile who performs the seven Noahide laws will have a portion in the world to come *provided* he accepts them and performs them because God commanded them in His Torah and informed us through Moses our teacher that these laws had previously been enjoined upon Noah's descendants. If the gentile's observance is based only on reason, however, he is not regarded as a righteous gentile but only as one of their wise men. Maimonides does not state why he adds the proviso, and no basis for it has been found in the Talmud or other ancient Jewish sources. (See chapter 6 for further discussion of the Noahide laws and of Maimonides' proviso.)

Hersh challenges Chaim to answer the question: "Since, [you say,] the wise men among the gentiles wanted to be good why couldn't they?" He argues that as students at the yeshiva they were taught that man has freedom of the will and that he can attain a state of perfection; then why were not the Germans under Hitler and the Russians under Stalin good persons? The reason is, says Hersh, because the Germans and others who were like them trusted their minds: "They trusted their reasoned assumptions as men trust the ice of a frozen river in winter. Then came Hitler and put his weight on the wisdom of the wise men of the nations. The ice of their slippery reasoning burst, and all their goodness was drowned." The Nazis used their reason to subvert all morality: "So there came in the West a booted ruler with a little mustache, and in the East a booted ruler with a big mustache, and both of them together struck the wise man to the ground, and he sank into the mud." No, it is not man's mind, not his reason, that can be trusted. Only the Law, only Torah can be trusted. "Any man can rationalize whatever he wants to do." Is there no way out from this perplexity? "The one way out," says Hersh, "is this. A man should choose between good and evil *only as the Law chooses for him*."

Thus Hersh explains, by implication, the reason why Maimonides annexed a proviso to his statement about the possibility of a gentile becoming a "righteous gentile"—it is not enough that by his reasoning he has come to the Noahide laws, he must accept them and believe them to be the Law revealed by God to Moses. Only then can the Noahide be trusted. It is not enough to be one of their wise men. To be a righteous gentile, deserving a place in the world to come he must believe in and obey the Law, Torah.

We shall see what Chaim has to say about this, but let me interject my own observation. Hersh himself had admitted: "Even a man who has a Law won't be able to withstand his temptation [his yezer ha-ra] if he doesn't watch over himself day and night." Even a rosh yeshiva, as Grade shows in his novel *The Yeshiva*, is not free from the siege of temptation, and even he can rationalize to do what his temptation propels him to do. Hersh himself has said, "Any man can rationalize whatever he wants to do." Trust in the Law can be as feeble a guard against the yezer ha-ra as is the mind or reason.

"Though God created the yezer ha-ra," says the Talmud, "He created the Law as an antidote against it."[11] But one may ask: since the gentile too has the yezer ha-ra, did God leave him without an "antidote"? Is that possible? Did Socrates, did Plato, did Sophocles—who had no knowledge of the Law as given by God to Moses—have no antidote?

Let us now turn to Chaim and see what he as to say.

5

Chaim is a modernist Jew, a man with a secular education, a writer, an author of books, yet a person who was deeply influenced by his years of study in the yeshiva of Novogrudok. Perhaps his questioning has gone so far as to make him a freethinker, as was Job, or Abraham when he questioned the justice of God; or perhaps he is even a skeptic, but one who has a profoundly religious mind and spirit. He tells Hersh that while he does not place a special merit on having doubts, "I must tell you that just as the greatness of the faithful consists in their innocence and wholeness, so the heroism of thinkers consists in their being able to tolerate doubt and make their peace with it." Chaim, however, does not have peace, he does not enjoy tranquillity of spirit. In a way, he says, his life is more burdensome than Hersh's, for he, Chaim, has a double, not a single, responsibility: toward Judaism and toward secular culture. Hersh was committed to the community of Israel, but Chaim is an individualist; secularists want to free the individual, to have a commonwealth of free and happy individuals. Secularists can point to an endless list of young people who spent their years in dungeons because they would not give up the struggle to make this a better world *(tikkun ha-olam)*. Hersh denied the world, withdrew from it, spurned it, while the secularists loved the world and sacrificed themselves to improve it. With passion, he tells Hersh that he, Chaim, has nothing for which to apologize; on the contrary, it is Hersh who must beg pardon, for by his fanaticism he has pushed out anyone who differed from the tradition in the slightest degree. Chaim reminds Hersh that even the Gaon of Vilna persecuted followers of the Enlightenment, the Haskalah movement of the eighteenth century; that the rabbis hounded and persecuted even Moses Hayyim Luzzatto, author of *Mesilat Yesharim*, which the musarniks venerated. Even now, he asks Hersh, "doesn't your voice have in it something of the trumpet of excommunication?" Chaim reminds Hersh that yeshiva students read *Gates of Repentance* "with such outcries that their lungs were almost torn to shreds; but they never thought to learn its moral, which is not to be fanatical."

Chaim says to Hersh that while he, Hersh, would exclude the *maskilim* (the Jews who were influenced by the Enlightenment) from the community of Israel—and even from the world to come—they were not excluded from persecution by the enemies of Jews, nor does the Master of the World exclude them. "In the other world your soul," he says to Hersh, "won't be wearing a cap or a beard or earlocks. Your soul will come there as naked as mine." He says to Hersh that he, Hersh, thinks of the Jews who perished in the Holocaust as saintly and pure; however, had they survived wouldn't he think of them as wicked and evil?—the same Jews are evil when alive but saintly Jews when murdered!

If Hersh hates Jews who do not agree with him, it is natural that he should also hate all non-Jews. But is it right to hate the non-Jewish world? Were there not gentiles who saved the lives of Jews? There were gentiles who risked their own lives so that they might shelter Jews and save them. They did this "not from pity alone, but for their own sakes as well. They wanted to prove to themselves—no one else could possibly have known—that the whole world does not consist only of criminals and those who are indifferent to the misfortunes of others." Yet Hersh has no room in his mind or heart for righteous gentiles.

What, Chaim asks, has the Holocaust changed in their worlds? For Hersh, his faith has been strengthened. But, Chaim says, that is a whining, paltry reply, which he will not accept, for all the old questions put to God remain, only they are now reinforced. For the righteous man fares ill and the evil man fares well—"only multiplied for a million murdered children." Hersh should cry out with Job: "Though He slay me, yet will I trust in Him; but I will argue my ways before Him!" "As for us, even if we were devils, we couldn't have sinned enough for our just punishment to be a million murdered children." Hersh's answer that his faith has been strengthened is no answer at all as long as he does not demand an accounting of heaven.

Chaim says that for him, his love of Jews has been made deeper and more sensitive. He will not renounce the world, and he will incorportate into himself "the hidden inheritance of our people's strength, so that we can continue to live."

Chaim tells Hersh that there is an even deeper meaning to his cry of impotent anger against heaven, that "because we absolutely refuse our assent to the infamous and enormous evil that has been visited on us, because we categorically deny its justice, no slavish or perverse acquiescence can take root in our hearts, no despairing belief that the world has no sense or meaning."

Chaim ends his part in the dialogue with a statement that is an affirmation of his way of life. The same misfortune befell both, but Hersh has a ready answer, "while we," says Chaim (meaning himself), "have not silenced our doubts, and perhaps we never will be able to silence them. The only joy that's left to us is the joy of creation, and in all the travail of creation we try to draw near to our people."

The exchange between the two former yeshiva students is a dialogue of reason, something rare in literature. It reminded me nostalgically of my pleasure, years ago, in reading the dialogues between Jallez and Jerphanion in the fourteen-volume novel *Men of Good Will* (1933–46) by Jules Romains. Hersh Rasseyner is a truncated man, really a half-man, a person who would live without science, without literature, without philosophy, without art. His God is not the God who cared for the people of Nineveh and even for its cattle, the God who cared for the Ethiopians even as He cared for Israel, the God who brought the Philistines from Caphtor and the Syrians from Kir.[12] Hersh's morals concentrate only on the suppression of sexual desire; as if God had no concern that men should not commit fraud, should not steal, should not hate their neighbors. His God is a legalist, a God who is concerned only with the minutiae of ritual observances; He is not God the Father, not a God of mercy, but the God of Jonathan Edward's sermon on "Sinners in the Hands of an Angry God." He is not the God of the Jews but only of a small congregation of fanatical musarniks.

Indeed, musarniks like Hersh corrupted the teaching of Rabbi

Salanter, who stressed the sin of financial fraud even more than the sin of sexual permissiveness—for the former can also be the cause of a Hillul Ha-Shem, a desecration of the Name, bringing shame and humiliation to the Jewish people. Salanter and his disciples taught their students to suppress feelings of vanity, love of material goods, greed. Salanter was well aware of the teaching of Rabbi Nahman ben Samuel that the yezer ha-ra is indispensable for life, "for if it were not for the [so-called] evil inclination, man would not build a house, or take a wife, or beget a child, or engage in business."[13]

The impassioned, eloquent, deeply moving response by Chaim attests to the poetic genius of Chaim Grade. If it were standing alone, however, not against the backdrop of Hersh's misreadings of Chaim's character and his foolish attack on the philosophy of *Torah im derekh eretz* or *Torah U-Madda*, it would lack the dramatic force that it richly has. Against the provenience of Hersh's accusations and self-pleading, it is a masterpiece of Jewish letters and of Holocaust literature. It is not surprising that its author has been acclaimed by Elie Wiesel, by Saul Lieberman, and by Shneur Zalman Shazar, and that he is considered by some critics as the national Jewish poet of his day, as Chaim Nachman Bialik was in his day.

PART THREE

Zionism and Homelessness

11

Zionism

Homecoming or Homelessness?

This essay, first published in Judaism *in 1956, was originally a lecture delivered at the dedication of the Theodor Herzl Institute in New York. The program of the Institute is to present the Jewish heritage in light of Zionist ideals and experience, to study modern Israel, and to promote research into all aspects of Zionism. The essay is, in part, autobiographical, an* apologia pro vita sua, *for at the time I prepared the address (for an audience of Zionist officials and members of Zionist organizations), I was struggling with the problem whether to accept or to reject an attractive offer of a very distinguished professorship at the Hebrew University in Jerusalem. I felt that I had to explain—to myself, and to my son—how it could be that I, a strongly committed Zionist, could decide (as I did) to remain an* American *Jew, could decide not to make* aliya, *not to "go up" to Zion, but to remain "homeless." The essay that follows, "Of Exile and Double Consciousness"— published in 1980, almost a quarter-century later—shows that I wished to confirm what I had said and decided in 1956.*

1

Passover, at the seder, when I come to the passage in the *Haggadah* that says, "In every generation let each man look upon himself as if he himself came forth out of Egypt," I pause and, following the injunction to "tell" my son in "that day," I explain to him that he and I both participated in the exodus from Egypt, that both of us were there in that night that was a night of watching for all the children of Israel. This personal identification with an event that took place thousands of years ago involves me in an existential commitment that wipes out distances of space and time and puts me on the very brink of the Red Sea, as one who was actually there in the exodus from Egypt.

This personal identification with the exodus from Egypt, consequential as it is, is not the only exodus in which I have participated. It is only one of several.

For in 1948, when the state of Israel was founded, the call went out to every Jew to pack his wordly possessions and to make his way to the reestablished Jewish homeland. Once more the Jew heard the challenge: "House of Jacob, come, let us go up!" The door was open, there was no McCarran-Walter Act to bar the way. We all heard the call; it did not come to our fathers but to us, even us, "who are all of us alive this day." Yet we did not go. I did not heed the call. I have not gone.

In spirit, I am one of millions of Jews who have been in an exodus from Israel, even as once I was in an exodus from Egypt. This exodus from Israel is an act of my free will. I have freely chosen not to go to the Jewish homeland but to make my home freely in another land. I have chosen to be an American Jew and not an Israeli Jew. Thus it is necessary, and ever will be, for me to tell my son that I have myself participated in an exodus from Jerusalem, for I must look upon myself as having come forth out of Jerusalem.

There is, however, one important difference between my participation in the exodus from Egypt and my participation in the exodus from Jerusalem: I cannot go back to Egypt, I left that land thousands of years ago, but each day that I continue to live in the United States as an American Jew I live through, as a fresh experience, my exodus from Jerusalem. I must say, "*Each day* let each man look upon himself as if he himself came forth out of Jerusalem."

Nor is this our first exodus from Jerusalem. Nearly two thousand years ago, as Jerusalem fell, Rabbi Johanan ben Zakkai, together with some disciples, left the city and found their way to Yavneh, where they founded an academy for the study of the Torah. If the Passover seder were not devoted exclusively to the reliving of the exodus from Egypt, this exodus of Rabbi Johanan ben Zakkai would, I think, play a prominent role in our ceremonies; for if it had not been for this exodus from Jerusalem, and if every Jew in every generation had not looked upon himself as if he himself had come forth out of Jerusalem with the great Rabbi Johanan ben Zakkai, Judaism and the Jewish people would have perished with the destruction of the Jewish state and of the Temple. Perhaps a tiny remnant would have remained, but they would be like the pathetic remnant of the Samaritans, who would truly be the "fossil" of whom Toynbee falsely speaks.

We remember the exodus from Egypt, and the exodus from Jerusalem as disciples of Rabbi Johanan ben Zakkai, by reliving them in our own lives, believing, as we do, that *we were there* when these events took place; but our exodus from the state of Israel is an everyday living event in our lives.

It is this exodus from the state of Israel, enacted each day of his life by every American Jew, that agitates our hearts, that gives us no rest. For we have been taught by our rabbis that "He who dwells outside the Holy Land is as though he had no God." Yet, we *freely choose* to dwell outside the Holy Land. Are we as though we had no God?

We have been taught to believe that as long as we live outside the Holy Land, the *Schechina*—the Divine Presence—also is in exile, and weeps. Is it true that the Schechina is in exile and weeps?

There was a rabbi who as he went to sleep always kept his walking stick by his bed in case the Messiah would come in the middle of the night, for he wanted to be sure that his stick would be near at hand, so that he would not need to fumble for it and lose time in getting started on his way back to the Holy Land; and he instructed his servant to sleep near him and to awaken him the instant that he heard that the Messiah had come. This rabbi typified the Jews—everyone lived in a state of restlessness, eager expectancy; one had to be ready to go home, and home, of course, was the place where our father Jacob had his dream and where he said upon waking: "How full of awe is this place! This is none other than the house of God, and this is the gate of heaven." Is it no longer necessary for us to keep our walking sticks within easy reach and to want to be awakened from our sleep in the very instant that the Messiah arrives?

We have heard it said that we American Jews do not live in *Galuth*, in exile, but that we live in *"chutz-le-aretz,"* merely outside the land of Israel. Are we, then, living here—in Chicago, New York, Pittsburgh, Ithaca—at heaven's gate? Are we as near to it as was our father Jacob at Bethel? Are we as near to it as our brethren in Safad, Tiberias, or Tel Aviv?

"We are a people, *one* people," Theodor Herzl said. Jews, he said, must reject the theory that they are only a religious sect, for this view will lead to assimilation; and we must also reject the view that Jews in different countries constitute different communities, for this view will lead to disintegration. Jews, Herzl believed, must emigrate *en masse* and create a Jewish state. In this way, and only in this way, can Jewish life be normalized; and only in this way can we free other nations from their intense preoccupation with what they call the Jewish question. Now, in our own day, the *Judenstaat* that Herzl foresaw has come into existence, and the *Altneuland* that he projected has become a reality. Can we simply proceed, with a clear conscience, as if nothing has happened in the half-century since the death of Herzl?

If we are men who seek to live by principle, what is the principle by which we seek to live? Or are we living a lie? These questions are not lightly put. We must try to answer them. This historic moment in the life of the Jewish people is too sacred for anything but the truth. But what is the truth?

2

I wish to suggest, contrary to the fashion of the day, that we American Jews are living in exile, in Galuth; and that the Schechina too is in exile. Let me not linger on this point, however, for I have stated only a half-truth. The other half is that the Jews in Israel are in no different condition. For the condition of the Jew, every Jew, in or out of Israel, is to live in Galuth, in exile. And the Schechina is in exile—even in Israel; and there too it weeps.

For every Jew, in his character as Jew, is both at home and homeless. The American Jew is at home in the United States, as is every American; he is, at the same time, in exile, as is every Jew. Similarly, the Israeli Jew is at home in the state of Israel, as is every Israeli; he is, at the same time, in exile, as is every Jew. Homelessness for the Jew does not end with the attainment of freedom and equality in a free, democratic country; nor does it end with the attainment of national independence and statehood in Israel. Like Jacob, he is eternally the sojourner.

This is a logic that no non-Jew can easily comprehend. For the biblical, Jewish logic is not built on the Aristotelian law of contradiction, which prohibits the simultaneous affirmation of contradictory propositions. According to the Aristotelian logic a man must be either homeless or at home. It is a logic of either/or. Ours, however, is a logic of both/and:

Man is free; yet everything has been foreseen by God.[1]

If I am not for myself, then who will be for me? But if I am for my myself only, then what am I?[2]

God is a God of justice; yet if He governed the world only by the test of justice, how could the world endure? God is a God of mercy; yet if He governed the world only by the rule of mercy, how could the world endure?[3]

Faithful is thy Employer, to pay thee the reward of thy labor. . . . Be not like servants that minister to their master for the sake of receiving a reward.[4]

For I the Lord thy God am a jealous God, visiting the iniquities of the father upon the children unto the third and fourth generation. . . . Behold, all souls are mine; as the soul of the father, so also the soul of the son is mine: the soul that sinneth, it shall die.[5]

The propositions are contradictory, but we know that the contradiction is only on a verbal level; in our souls we know that the oppositions complete rather than cancel each other. For the truth, we know, has many faces. In the very marrow of our bones we are pluralists. More than others, we know that in our Father's house there are many mansions. Thus we know that a Jew can be at home and homeless at one and the same time; and this paradoxical at-homeness in exile, exile at home, citizenship that is alienage, alienage that is citizenship, is inescapable for the Jew.

Theodor Herzl thought that the establishment of a Jewish state would normalize the Jew, make him like all other peoples. This is true, but only in one respect: The Israeli Jew, in his condition as an *Israeli*, is as normal as is the Greek in his condition as Greek and as is the American in his condition as American. In his aspect as *Jew*, however, the Israeli Jew remains, and will remain, abnormal. For the Jew, there is no normalcy. For the Jew, there is no final resting place. He remains homeless, in exile, a sojourner. Even when the Jew lives in the state of Israel, he yet remains a disciple of Rabbi Johanan ben Zakkai, for the Israeli Jew too once left Jerusalem in the company of that great rabbi, and he must stand ready to leave Jerusalem once again, and as often and as many times as God may try him, even as God tried Abraham at the *Akedah*. Like the American Jew, the Israel Jew who does not permit the Jew to be assimilated by the Israeli can cry out with Jehudah Halevi: "My heart is in the East, while I am in the far West." And the Jew, inside or outside the state of Israel, keeps, as he sleeps, his walking stick by his bed and half listens for the footsteps of the Messiah. Only when Redemption will unite God in His ultimate being and God in His wandering will the Jew find his way to a final homecoming.

There have been those who were wont to teach and to preach that the Jew should be a Jew in his own home but on the street he should be a man—or a German, or an Englishman, or an American. Zionists were quick to react to this point of view and to argue that it opened the door to assimilation, for the Jew would soon tire of his divided existence, being half this and half that. Like his non-Jewish neighbor, he would want to be a whole man—or a whole German. The answer, said the Zionists, was a Jewish state in which the divided nature of the Jew would be ended and the Jew would win back his wholeness.

However, to be a Jew is not to be divided; it is to have a double being. This doubleness has not ceased for the Jew upon his acquisition of Israeli citizenship: he remains a double entity: he is both Jew and Israeli. He can lose his duality by becoming completely assimilated in the Israeli—even as I can become assimilated in the American or the English Jew in the Englishman. A Zionism that denies the inherent duality of the Jew, and that promises an escape from it as a means to prevent assimilation, itself opens a door to assimilation.

For there can be assimilation in Israel as there can be in England, France, or the United States and even more easily. Was this not the issue between the Hellenists and the Hassidim, and between the prophet Elijah and Ahab?

But, it may be asked, is not the reverse process of assimilation possible in Israel; namely, that the Israeli may become assimilated in the Jew? As long as it is possible to be a Christian or a Moslem Israeli—or a "Canaanite" Israeli—and as long as Israel is a free, democratic state, this is unthinkable; thus the dual nature of the Jew remains, even in Israel.

———

An insight into this duality of Jewishness is found in the incident related of Jacob when his father-in-law left him and his household, and Jacob went on his way. Then, says Genesis, angels of God met him. Jacob said when he saw them: "This is God's camp," but he called the name of that place *Mahanaim*, meaning two camps. Rashi says that Jacob saw two bands of angels, the band that was with him in exile and the band that met him as he came into the promised land. For wherever the Jew is, there he is in Mahanaim, in two camps, for he is both at home and homeless; and yet the two camps are *one* camp: "This is God's camp."

It is a great burden to carry homelessness, exile, as part of one's destiny. It makes the Jew the eternal nonconformist, the dissenter, the nay-sayer, the one who is always different, the person who—as Thoreau said of himself—hears a different drumbeat and, therefore, marches in step only to his own music, music that the others do not hear. Because homelessness is so great a burden, the Jew tries to transcend it. He projects a land of his heart's desire, where he too will be able to feel that

> Home is the sailor, home from the sea,
> And the hunter home from the hill.[6]

He, more than Ulysses, seeks to find or to make a land of lotus-eaters:

> Surely, surely, slumber is more sweet than toil, the shore
> Than labour in the deep mid-ocean, wind and wave and oar;
> Oh rest ye, brother mariners, we will not wander more.[7]

The Jew prays, yearns, pleads for the coming of the Redemption that will put an end to his wandering—a wandering that engages him even when he is secure in his home in New York or London or Paris or Tel Aviv. Sometimes, when his heart can contain no more, with Rabbi Israel of Koznitz he cries out to God, with a rapture in which despair and hope are inextricably mingled: "If you will not send the Messiah ben David to redeem us, then send him to redeem the Gentiles! But send him!"

The state of Israel is the most concrete projection of this dream in which we want to transcend our homelessness. Like our homelessness, the dream is an inescapable part of our souls and our destiny; no reality can displace this dream, because no reality can cure us of our homelessness. The *Israeli* can live in and with the reality; but as *Jew*, the Israeli remains possessed by the dream, because as *Jew* he remains in exile.

3

This, it seems to me, is the true basis of Zionism, which makes Zionism as eternal as is the Jew. The Zionist is the Jew—American or Israeli—who sees himself in the fullness of his Jewishness. After he abstracts from himself his Americanism or his character as an Israeli, he sees himself as a Jew, and he begins to feel the pain and the glory of his exile, the pain and the glory of the dream that would bring an end to his homelessness; and this full awareness of his Jewishness— or the awareness of the fullness of his Jewishness—is Zionism.

Moreover, the closer the Jew approximates to the condition of Zionism, the closer does he approximate to the condition of humanity. For every man is in exile, if he only would know his condition; but while the non-Jew must gropingly seek this truth, this truth seeks the Jew and possesses him. For who but a Jew, when he hears a great tumult in the street, begins to think that maybe the Messiah has come?

The Zionism that we, of the post-Herzl era, experience is a deeper, more Jewish, and more human Zionism than he could have experienced in his day. For our Zionism exists at the point of tension between normalcy and abnormalcy, security and insecurity, at-home-ness and exile, reality and dream. Our Zionism recognized the precariousness of our Jewish-human existence; the inescapable restlessness, uncertainties, and conflicts of life; the essential homelessness and alienage of human beings, and especially Jews, wherever we may build our homes—in the United States, in England, in Israel. There is a legend that once Xerxes, the king of kings, as he looked down upon a sea of his subjects, wept to think that in a hundred years not one of them would be left. We too often weep for the same reason, but in our eye's vision are not only myriads of human beings but also states and principalities and powers. For who knows what, a hundred years from now, will be left of all that we see today?

At the same time, however, our Zionism recognizes that the Jew must walk with consciousness of the fact that man's condition is but a little lower than an angel's; that the Jew must walk with head erect and with a dream in his heart; that he must cheerfully and firmly face and affirm life, including the ineluctable tragedies that are on their way to meet him; and that though he lives in two camps, of which one is his home and the other his exile, yet both camps are one camp, and "this is God's camp."

4

David Ben-Gurion says that only the Jew who emigrates to Israel is a Zionist; thus Zionism, instead of uniting Jews, divides them. Nahum Goldmann in principle accepts Ben-Gurion's statement, but he knows that since the establishment of the state of Israel only one percent of those who have gone there to settle came from the United States, Canada, and the other countries of the Western Hemisphere, and that a mass movement of American Jews to Israel is very unlikely. Under these conditions, according to Goldmann, the function of Zionists is to prepare the consciousness of American Jews so that they will want to emigrate to Israel in the future. Zionists are to accomplish this by stimulating Jews to make investments in Israel or to send their children to Israel, for such acts will lead the investors or the parents themselves to emigrate. ("Where your treasure is, there will your heart be also.") Zionists, accordingly, must do everything possible to sustain Judaism (or Jewishness) in their communities, and they must do their work aggressively as the most restless, spirited, agitated, and dissatisfied elements in their communities. In this way will they awaken a desire *in other Jews* voluntarily to emigrate to Israel. Ben-Gurion is the impatient and Goldman is the patient Zionist, but to each of them, Zionism means only emigration to Israel by oneself or vicariously.

American Jews—at any rate, those that I know—will not buy this Zionism. For we want America to be a place where our children will *want* to live, to work, and to build their families and their homes. In this, we but follow the advice of the prophet Jeremiah:

> Build houses and live in them; plant gardens and eat their produce. Take wives and have sons and daughters, and give your daughters in marriage, that they may bear sons and daughters . . . seek the welfare of the city where I have sent you into exile, and pray to the Lord on its behalf, for in its welfare you will find your welfare.[8]

For my son is an American; as an American, he must feel at home here; and I as an American and as his father must do all I can to make his home here secure, peaceful, wholesome, prosperous, and a happy one—*so that he would not want to leave it.*

This involves not merely loyalty with respect to big things but wholeness of heart in little things as well. I must be devoted to America in such a way and with such fidelity of spirit and of love that my son will understand from my gestures, from my smiles and laughter, my sighs and tears, from my silence as well as from my speech, from my rest as well as from my work, that America is my home and his home and his children's home.

Should my son, however, one day wish to emigrate to Israel, I shall then say: "The spirit bloweth where it listeth." I shall be happy that his young and earnest heart will drive him to help build a city of God on the shores of another land on another continent. But if he should choose to remain here, I shall then say: "The spirit bloweth where it listeth." For cities of God need to be built on the shores of this continent, too. On every Day of Atonement, the prophet Jonah teaches us the lesson that Nineveh no less than Jerusalem is part of God's plan. And we must strive, hope, and pray for a free world where every man will enjoy, in full measure, freedom to come and to go, freedom to build his home wherever his heart desires, and freedom there to live and to prolong his days in peace and in security.

In that free world, Israel must have a place of dignity and honor. For it has as much right to exist and prosper as has Holland or Turkey or South Korea. It is as an American, and not necessarily as a Jew, that I want to see Israel grow strong and prosperous and to enjoy no less security than is given in this insecure world to other nations. Toward this end it is right and necessary to seek to win for Israel diplomatic, military, and economic assistance from this country, from other countries, and from the United Nations.

As a Jew, Zionism unites me with other Jews everywhere in the world in a common fellowship of religion, history, and destiny. Zionism unites us in a common Galuth, which transcends differences of language, nationality, or race. In this common Galuth, Zionism has as its task to feed and to feast the heart and mind and soul of the Jewish people with the spiritual riches that are our great inheritance and with the spiritual riches that we must yet create—values that are Jewish, yet universal in their reach and validity. To this end Zionists must dedicate themselves to be the most zealous and constructive builders— builders of Zion in New York, builders of Zion in Tel Aviv—builders of the city that has its local habitation and its name in the memories and aspirations, in the hearts and hopes of Jews everywhere, whether they live by the waters of Babylon or the waters of Manhattan or the waters of the Jordan. Thus, and only thus, can the Jew live in two camps, at home and in exile, and have bands of angels follow him in each of his camps, and yet the two camps shall remain one camp, and this shall be God's camp. Thus, and only thus, can the Jew in Israel and the Jew in the United States join their souls in crying out with one voice: "If I forget you, O Jerusalem, let my right hand wither! Let my tongue cleave to the roof of my mouth, if I do not remember you . . ."

Without this Zionism, Israel may become a state of Israelis but not a Jewish community. Without this Zionism, the Jew in Israel may become assimilated to the Israeli. There is always the danger that such assimilation of the Jew to the Israeli may take place; for Israel may in time develop a civilization that will be Israeli, in which differences between Jew and non-Jew will hardly be apparent. The history of Palestine during the past two thousand years demonstrates that merely living on the soil of that land is not enough to make one a Jew. When Hebrew ceases to be a loshen kodesh and becomes the official language of the state and the convenient language of the street, its use will not any longer distinguish the Jew from the non-Jew. Yes, an Israeli civilization is possible, and it may become sufficiently notable to constitute a contribution to the world. However, an Israeli civilization in which the Jew will have become assimilated to the Israeli will have no more relevance to the lives of American Jews than has, for example, the civilization of Eire to the lives of Americans of Irish descent. The Jew in Israel must ever keep in the forefront of his consciousness the fact that just as it is possible for him to be an Israeli, so too it is possible for the Moslem or the Christian to be an Israeli. The Jewishness of the Israeli Jew must, therefore, if it is to be perpetuated, rise above and reach beyond the borders of the state of Israel. The Jewish soul of the Israeli Jew must remain in exile, it must remain a wandering soul, if the Israeli Jew is to remain a Jew.

Without this Zionism, American Jews may be merely members of one of 256 denominations; members of a small religious denomination most of whom will live without religion, without Judaism, without reason for remaining Jews, and only assimilation will await most of them. The Jew in the United States, like the Jew in Israel, must keep his Jewishness a transcendent quality, which places him in Galuth and preserves his membership in universal Jewry.

The twin evils that Theodor Herzl sought to prevent—assimilation and disintegration—can be prevented by a Zionism that Herzl did not foresee, a Zionism that is not fulfilled—and extinguished—by the founding of a state. He could see then a Zionism based on homecoming; we can see now a Zionism based on homelessness. It is only because we stand upon his shoulders, however, that we can see further than was given to him to see.

12

Of Exile and Double Consciousness

The monthly British magazine Encounter *published in August 1979 a review of my book* Judaism and the American Idea. *The review led the editor of* Encounter *to invite me to submit a brief article that would comment on some observations of the reviewer, Max Beloff, professor at the University of Oxford and noted English historian and political scientist. My response was the following brief essay, published in the October 1980 issue of* Encounter.

If my book *Judaism and the American Idea* is read and reviewed—as was done by Max Beloff—from the perspective of the problem of anti-Semitism, then I can see how it may impress the reader as the expression of "the innocent optimism of an American Jew." However, I would gently protest that to read the book in such a confined context is to subject it to a procrustean treatment. I had thought that I had made it clear at the very outset that my book was concerned "not with being but with ideals and values"; that it proposed to describe "an ideal America" and "an ideal Judaism"; that it was concerned with "human ideals and rights." It is a book that should be classified as a history of ideas rather than as a sociological treatise. Only in one chapter, "From Jewish Rights to Human Rights," do I touch the question of anti-Semitism, without, however, departing substantially from the chief thrust and spirit.

However, Beloff has raised some significant and sharply-focused questions. They touch the problem of "roots" and "Jewish identity" (to use the terms of Beloff's subtitle). He concludes with the challenging statement: "The ambiguity of Jewish existence and the claim to be a people and not just a sect means that anti-Semitism is inherent in its environment—Christian, or Muslim, or Marxist. *Pace* Professor Konvitz, no Bill of Rights can resolve the problem of Jewish identity."

174

I readily assent to the spirit, though not to the letter, of this statement. Jewish existence is intrinsically ambiguous, but this ambiguity is not necessarily a cause of anti-Semitism. Nor is anti-Semitism the cause of Jewish ambiguity; for even if the Bill of Rights of the United States Constitution were fully observed, so that every American—regardless of his race, color, religion, or national origin—lived peacefully under his own vine and his own fig tree, the problem of Jewish identity would still remain. A Gallup poll (conducted in May 1979) showed that 12 percent of American Protestants and 13 percent of Catholics thought that Jews were trying to gain too much power. This was a significant drop from the figures in polls taken in 1952 and in 1965. In May 1979 only 2 percent of Protestants and Catholics said that they ever had an experience that made them dislike Jews. Even if polls and other investigations were to show that there was absolutely no prejudice against Jews and no instances of discrimination against them, there would still remain, I would say, the problem of "Jewish identity" and the "ambiguity" of Jewish existence. Just as the Emancipation and the Enlightenment did not end the Jewish exile, the *Galuth* of the Jew and of Judaism, even so the establishment of full peace and security for the state of Israel will not end either the exile (Galuth) or the dispersion (*Golah*).

For the Jew's destiny is existence in tension: to be, at one and the same time, attached and detached; to be rooted and yet transcendent; to seek harmonization with his surroundings and yet to be the critic and the prophet and to have no resting place. The haunting verse of Henry Vaughan applies peculiarly to Jews: *"God ordered motion, but ordained no rest."* No one so much as the Jew knows an inner solitude. Emerson in his essay on "Fate" wrote of "double consciousness." But who knows this double consciousness better than the Jew? I can speak of myself as being an American Jew, or as a Jewish American, but in fact I am both an American and a Jew. The two coexist, often in harmony, often in tension. I think of the poignant outcry of John Woolman, the saintly American Quaker: "In my traveling on the road, I often felt a cry rise from the centre of my mind, thus, 'O, Lord, I am a stranger on the earth, hide not Thy face from me.'"[1] The Jew is at home and a stranger. He may be busy in the marketplace or in the office, on the bench or in the legislature, yet at his center there is a tiny heart of loneliness and of solitude. Like Hawthorne's minister who always wears a black veil, the Jew has a private face that he will not show the world. Jews live in a world of action but often are not of it. They are attached to it, and yet a part of them belongs elsewhere. In that elsewhere they know each other, they embarrass and hurt each other, they comfort and keep each other, they strive and hope for each other; in that elsewhere they are a people apart.

In that elsewhere they have, with Sir Thomas Browne, "a glimpse of incomprehensibles, and Thoughts of things which Thoughts but tenderly touch"[2]; their heads lodged with immaterials, and they ascend (or descend) into invisibles. For the Jew, there is no ease in Zion; life is perpetual struggle; existence is actually or potentially precarious; he sees life as constant motion and change, as contention and reconciliation, as damnation and salvation.

What I have said about the American Jew is, perhaps with equal force, true of the Israeli Jew. He is at home in the state of Israel. He is, at the same time, in exile, as is the American Jew, as is every Jew. Homelessness for the Jew does not end with the attainment of freedom, equality, and freedom from prejudice and discrimination—freedom from anti-Semitism—in a free, democratic country; nor does exile end with the attainment of national independence and statehood in Israel. Like Jacob, the Jew is eternally the sojourner. For the Jew, there is no normalcy, not even in the state of Israel. He remains in exile, a sojourner. The Israeli Jew too, like Jehudah Halevi, can cry out: "My heart is in the East, while I am in the far West."

The Jews have always been wandering Israelites. They wandered before they were banished. They were in the Diaspora before they were in the Exile; the golah came before the galut. "Our people wandered before they were driven," says Joseph Kalonymos in *Daniel Deronda*; and hundreds of thousands of Israeli Jews, even *sabras* (native-born citizens), choose to be wanderers, to be in exile in America or in Europe rather than to be in exile in Israel. "The spirit bloweth where it listeth. . . ." It is no different with the Jews who are fortunate enough to be allowed to leave the USSR: some choose home/exile in Israel, some choose to make their home/exile elsewhere. Why would they not remain in their Russian home/exile? Because Russian totalitarianism demands that the Jews, though identified and marked as Jews, destroy one side of their double consciousness; that they do what is for them an impossibility, namely, think of themselves as being altogether at home and not at all in exile; in other words, though identified and marked—and treated—as Jews, that they cease to know themselves as Jews.

The Jew, however, as easily as Kant, and almost by instinct, knows the difference between phenomenon and noumenon, between the world of appearance and the world as it really is—*das Ding an Sich*. This puts him in constant tension between the actual and the possible, between what he sees and what he hopes for. In *The Autocrat of the Breakfast Table*, Oliver Wendell Holmes says that in every dialogue between John and Thomas, there are at least three Johns and three Thomases: (1) the real John, known only to his Maker; (2) John as he ideally sees himself, often very unlike him; and (3) John as Thomas sees him, often very unlike the real or the ideal John. (The same analysis can be applied to Thomas.) One could say that every Jew is many men. There is more than double consciousness in his case. (1) There is the Jew as only God sees him. Maybe that is the real man, the Platonic Idea of myself. (2) Then there is the Jew as I see myself ideally, the man I wish to be, hope to become. (3) The Jew I know myself to be phenomenally, with all my foibles, my habits, my failings. (4) The self that I try to show to my wife and to my family and friends, the self that is sharply controlled and moulded to get close to the ideal self that I would like to be. (5) The Jew that I show myself to be when I am with other Jews. (6) The Jew that I try to be when I am with non-Jews. I contain, I am sure, many other selves, a whole universe of selves. And they overlap, coexist, and are in constant tension among themselves and among the multiple selves of others.

—————

Now I know that much of this is fully applicable to all men, Jews and non-Jews alike, as the reference to Holmes alone would indicate. In the story by Hawthorne, "The Minister's Black Veil," the speaker is a Christian cleric, who speaks, in the following poignant passage, for the human condition:

> "Why do you tremble at me alone? Tremble also at each other! Have men avoided me, and women shown no pity, and children screamed and fled, only for my black veil? What, but the mystery which it obscurely typifies, has made this piece of crepe so awful? When the friend shows his inmost heart to his friend, the lover to his best beloved; when man does not vainly shrink from the eye of his Creator, loathsomely treasuring up the secret of his sin; then deem me a monster, for the symbol beneath which I have lived, and die! I look around me, and lo, every visage a Black Veil!"

The Jew, however, the man of multiple consciousness, is destined to cover with his black veil more selves than are given to others. In a sense, every man is in exile; in a sense John Donne was mistaken, every man is an island. But the Jew—American or Israeli or whatever—is the paradigm of the man in exile. The ambiguity of Jewish existence, the problem of Jewish identity, follows him wherever he goes or rests or is driven. He cannot ever be the sailor home from sea, or the hunter home from the hill.

13

Herman Melville Makes a Pilgrimage to the Holy Land

Shortly before the Civil War, Herman Melville took a seven-month journey abroad that included Palestine. He kept a journal, which he rewrote over a period of about fifteen years, and the pages that he devoted to the Holy Land became the basis for his long poem Clarel: A Poem and Pilgrimage in the Holy Land. *It is clear from all the years and hours that he spent on the journal and on the poem that his eighteen days in the Holy Land occupied his mind for countless days and nights. This essay was first published in December 1979 in* Midstream. *A Hebrew translation is a chapter in* America and the Holy Land, *published by the America–Holy Land Project of the Avraham Harman Institute of Contemporary Jewry, Hebrew University, Jerusalem—a project founded by Professor Moshe Davis.*

1

In January 1857 Herman Melville made a pilgrimage to the Holy Land. Although he spent there only eighteen days, his visit was no ordinary sightseeing tour. The trip was motivated by psychological and spiritual needs that were more deeply rooted than Melville himself realized at the time, and it led to consequences that loomed large in the following twenty years of his life.

At the age of twenty-seven Melville was catapulted into popularity with the publication of his first book, *Typee* (1846), followed the next year with *Omoo* (1847). *Mardi*, however, published only three years after *Typee*, lost him a large part of his readership, which he was never able fully to regain. When *Moby Dick* was published in 1851, its author's reputation and following seemed to have suffered irretrievably. As strange as the facts may be to us today, it is noteworthy that although two thousand copies of *Moby Dick* were sold in the first five months, the hostile reviews or critical indifference pushed Melville into virtual obscurity (although it should be added that he enjoyed a more understanding critical reception in England). Annual sales of *Moby Dick* over the next decade averaged only 123 copies, and during the next twenty-five years the average sale was only 22 copies per year. Between 1851 and 1887, a period of thirty-six years, fewer than 4,000 copies had been sold.[1] Raymond Weaver recalled that in 1918 he has able to buy a first edition of *Moby Dick* for less than one dollar.[2] We might recall the comparable case of Thoreau's *Walden:* published in 1854, the book sold only two thousand copies in the remaining eight years of its author's life.[3]

Melville did not stop writing and publishing. *Moby Dick* was followed by *Pierre, Israel Potter, The Piazza Tales,* and *The Confidence Man.* However, these works met either with hostility or with cold and even unfriendly indifference. By 1857 Melville was thirty-seven years of age and had a wife and four children. To make a living, he had tried to secure a post in the United States Treasury Department, and when he failed in this effort he tried to get into the consular service, again without success. Failing as an author, he found no solution to his desperate economic problem. His physical health was in a deplorable condition, for he suffered from sciatica, backache, rheumatism, eye trouble, and insomnia, and psychically he was on the verge of what they then called insanity but what we today would call a crack-up or a breakdown. After *The Confidence Man,* Melville would cease writing prose for years. Only at the end of 1888, at the age of almost seventy, would he start his last prose work, *Billy Budd,* which he finished in April 1891, five months before he died. *Billy Budd* would not be published until 1924.

Now, Melville's pilgrimage to the Holy Land took place just as he had finished writing *The Confidence Man* and had ended his career as an author of prose fiction. On September 1, 1856, Melville's father-in-law wrote to his own son:

> I suppose you have been informed by some of the family, how very ill Herman has been. It is manifest to me from [Melville's wife] Elizabeth's letters, that she has felt great anxiety about him. When he is deeply engaged in one of his literary works, he confines him[self] to his study many hours in the day, with little or no exercise, & this especially in winter for a great many days together. He probably thus overworks himself & brings on severe nervous affections. He has been advised strongly, to break off his labor for some time & take a voyage or a journey & endeavor to recuperate. No definite plan is arranged, but I think it may result in this, that in the autumn

he will go away for four or five months. . . . I think he needs such a change & that it would be highly beneficial to him & probably restore him.[4]

Melville's father-in-law loaned him fourteen or fifteen hundred dollars, and Melville left on what was to be his third trip to Europe and his first to the Holy Land. He sailed for Glasgow on October 11, 1856, He visited Hawthorne at Liverpool, where the latter held the post of American consul. Hawthorne and Melville had been neighbors near Lenox, Massachusetts, and *Moby Dick* was dedicated to Hawthorne. The two friends had long talks on this visit, which Hawthorne described in his *English Notebooks,* published posthumously. In a famous passage, Hawthorne wrote:

Melville, as he always does, began to reason of Providence and futurity, and of everything that lies beyond human ken, and informed me that he had "pretty much made up his mind to be annihilated"; but still he does not seem to rest in that anticipation; and, I think, will never rest until he gets hold of a definite belief. It is strange how he persists—and has persisted ever since I knew him, and probably long before—in wandering to-and-fro over these deserts. . . . He can neither believe, nor be comfortable in his unbelief; and he is too honest and courageous not to try to do one or the other.[5]

In all, Melville's journey took seven months. He kept a journal in which he made occasional entries, from the style of which it is clear that he had no intention to publish it—and indeed the journal was not published until 1935.[6] Much of it is only a record of where he was, what he did, what he saw—rather cold, lifeless facts as seen by the outer eye. This is not the case, however, with many of the entries that he made in Egypt and Palestine, which evidence

the peculiar urgency, the sharpness, vividness, and freshness of much of Melville's writing . . . when he has been particularly moved. Many passages, such as those on the Pyramids, or the descriptions of the Jerusalem scene and the Palestinian landscape, are in his finest rhetorical style; many of his comments on people, places, and things display the most cutting edge of his irony and satire, as in his accounts of the Church of the Holy Sepulchre and of the missionaries in the Near East. But of even more interest than these considerations is the display in this, one of the few extant Melville manuscripts, of his mind in the actual process of composition, of the setting down of ideas hot from the creative process.[7]

There is some evidence that Melville worked on and revised passages of his journal for a period of some fifteen years, and, as we will see, the pages devoted to the Holy Land became the foundation of the single long poetic work of his career.

2

First, however, let us take a closer look at what Melville wrote in his journal about the Holy Land and what thoughts and emotions it provoked.

Early in the morning of January 6, 1857, Melville landed in Jaffa. He hired a Jew as a dragoman to take him to Jerusalem, forty miles away, a journey that normally took twelve hours by horse. They broke up the journey by staying overnight at an Arab inn at Ramlah, where they had supper from broken crockery and were pestered by mosquitoes and fleas. "Dese Arab no know how to keep hotel," remarked the dragoman to Melville; "I fully assented," Melville added. After a horrible night, the travelers arose at 2 o'clock in the morning to continue on their journey. The ride was hot and wearisome over arid hills: "At day break found ourselves just entering the mountains. Pale olive of morning. Withered and desert country." They arrived in Jerusalem at 2 o'clock in the afternoon and took up quarters in one of the three principal hotels of the city, a hotel located near the Jaffa Gate and considered the least bad of the three. What was reputed to be the Pool of Hezekiah immediately adjoined it to the rear and caused the rooms to be damp; the charges were high and the food was bad. From a platform or balcony in front of his room, Melville had a view of the Church of the Holy Sepulchre and of the Mount of Olives. The landlord, who was a German and a converted Jew, pointed out to Melville the damaged dome of the Church of the Holy Sepulchre from the beginning of the Crimean War, the alleged cause of which was the asserted claims of the Russian Czar to the right to protect most of the Christian sites in the Holy Land on behalf of the Greek Orthodox Church, which claims were disputed by Louis Napoleon as self-appointed guardian of the Roman Catholic interests. Melville spent some ten or eleven days wandering about Jerusalem, accompanied by a Jewish or a Druze dragoman. Then, like nearly every other traveler to the Holy Land, Melville made a three-day circuit to Bethany, Jericho, the River Jordan, the Dead Sea, the Greek convent of Mar Saba, Bethlehem, and back to Jerusalem. Besides his Druze dragoman, Melville probably went with a party, which paid for protection. Robbery was a common occurrence; in one of the journal entries, made on his way to Jaffa, Melville wrote: "Rode from Ramlah to Lydda. A robbery of a village near by, by party of Arabs, alarms the whole country. People travel in bands. We rode to Lydda in train of the Governor's son. A mounted escort of some 30 men, all armed."[8]

One afternoon Melville called on Charles and Martha Saunders, who were sent to Palestine by the Seventh Day Baptist Church to teach modern agricultural methods to Jews and to Arabs and, incidentally, to try to redeem the latter's souls. The Saunderses maintained their mission outside the Jerusalem walls. Melville commented on their efforts: "Dismal story of their experiments. Might as well attempt to convert bricks into bride-cake as the Orientals into Christians. It is against the will of God that the East should be Christianized."[9]

The expression of contempt for missionary undertakings was typical of Melville. Indeed, one finds it even in his first book, *Typee,* which at once became popular except among persons committed to the missions. A review of *Typee* in 1846, immediately upon the book's publication, noted that Melville had a special abhorrence for missionaries and for missionary labor: "If he meets a native female Islander, she is a goddess;—if a missionary's wife, she is a blowzy looking, red-faced, fat oppressor of the poor native—reducing him [the native] to the station of drudge."[10]

With respect to the two objectives that the missionaries set for themselves to accomplish among the Jews of Palestine, Melville had rather firm views. As to conversions, his journal records that one of the missionaries under the Bishop of the English Episcopal Church in Jerusalem confessed to Mrs. Saunders "that out of all the Jew converts, but one he believed to be a true Christian. . . . The Jews would come, pretend to be touched & all that, get clothing & then—vanish. Mrs. S[aunders] said they were very 'deceitful.'"[11] As to making farmers of the Jews in Palestine, Melville noted different projects conducted under mission auspices to achieve this end, all unsuccessful. He gave four reasons for the failure:

> The idea of making farmers out of the Jews is vain. In the first place, Judea is a desert with few exceptions. In the second place, the Jews hate farming. All who cultivate the soil in Palestine are Arabs. [In the third place,] the Jews dare not live outside walled towns or villages for fear of the malicious persecution of the Arabs and Turks.— Besides [in the fourth place], the number of Jews in Palestine is comparatively small.

He then followed immediately with this afterthought: "And how are the hosts of them scattered in other lands to be brought here? Only by a miracle."[12]

However, in the middle of the nineteenth century, it was precisely the miraculous ingathering of the Jews—with some assistance from the Christian missionaries—that excited much interest and activity. It was a time when religious fervor and millenarianism swept America and Europe. Melville was aware of these movements and noted the fact in his journal:

> Be it said, that all these movements combining Agriculture & Religion in reference to Palestine, are based upon the impression . . . that the time for the prophetic return of the Jews to Judea is at hand, and therefore the way must be prepared for them by Christians, both in setting them right in their faith & their farming—in other words, preparing the soil literally and figuratively.[13]

The journal records a conversation that Melville had with Walter Dickson, who left Boston in 1853 with his wife, son, and three daughters to work as independent agricultural missionaries in Palestine. "Have you any Jews working with you?" Melville asked Dickson. "No. Can't afford to have them. Do my own work, with my son. Besides, the Jews are lazy & don't like work." Dickson went on to say that this fact is a hindrance to making farmers of the Jews, but the Christians must teach them better: "The fact is the fullness of Time has come. The Gentile Christians must prepare the way." He then asked Melville if in America people believed "[basically] in the restoration of the Jew?" Melville replied that he could not really answer that question.[14]

What mainly strikes the reader of Melville's journal, however, and the impression that he will retain most firmly in his memory, is the feeling of the land's utter destitution—its barrenness, its rockiness, its appearance of abandonment both by man and by God. Here is a characteristic passage:

> Whitish mildew pervading whole tracts of landscape—bleached— leprosy—encrustation of curses—old cheese—bones of rocks— crunched, gnawed, & mumbled—mere refuse & rubbish of creation—like that laying outside of Jaffa Gate—all Judea seems to have been accumulations of this rubbish.—You see the anatomy— compares with ordinary regions as skeleton with living and rosy man.—So rubbish, that no chiffonier could find any thing all over it.—*No moss as in other ruins—no grace of decay—no ivy—the un-leavened nakedness of desolation—*[15]

What Melville noted most often were the stones—stones everywhere in the Holy Land:

Judea is one accumulation of stones—Stony mountains & stony plains; stony torrents & stony roads; stony walls & stony fields, stony houses & stony tombs; stony eyes and stony hearts. Before you, & behind you are stones. Stones to right and stones to left. In many places laborious attempt has been made, to clear the surface of these stones. You see heaps of stones here & there; and stone walls of immense thickness are thrown together, less for boundaries than to get them out of the way. But in vain; the removal of one stone only serves to reveal there stones still larger, below it. . . . —The toes of every one['s] shoes are all stubbed to pieces with the stones. They are seldom a round [kind] of an [sic] stone; but sharp, flinty & scratchy.[16]

With tongue in cheek, Melville attempted to account for these stones: A long time ago, he wrote, some whimsical King of Judea took it into his head to pave the country and entered into contract to have this done; but the contractor became bankrupt midway in his work, the stones were all dumped on the ground, and there they lie to this day.[17] In another passage Melville described the hills as all made out of stone—they are "stones in the concrete. Regular layers of rock . . . . In some of the fields, like large grotesque rocks—all perforated and honey combed—like rotting bones of mastadons." Then he added: "Everything looks old. Compared with these rocks, those in Europe or America look juvenile."[18]

The view of Jerusalem as he looked back on his way to Bethlehem, six miles away, struck him forcibly. Unless he had known it was Jerusalem that he was seeing in the distance, he wrote, he would not have recognized it—"it looked exactly like arid rocks."[19]

Jerusalem made a devastating impression. At its entrance by way of the Jaffa Gate, in a part of the city strictly denominated Mt. Zion, Melville saw lepers, clustered by a dung-heap: "They sit by the gates asking alms,—then whine." One could only avoid them with a feeling of horror.[20] Further, Melville noted caves everywhere, and tombs wherever one looked: "The city besieged by army of the dead.—cemeteries all round."[21] He tried to sum up some of his impressions of Jerusalem as follows: "The mind cannot but be sadly & suggestively affected with the indifference of Nature & Man to all that makes the spot sacred to the Christian. Weeds grow upon Mount Zion; side by side in impartially [sic] equality appear the shadows of church & Mosque, and on Olivet every morning the sun indifferently ascends over the Chapel of the Ascension." He then noted ironically: "Mosque of Omar—Solomon's Temple. Here the wall of Omar rises upon the foundation stones of Solomon, triumphing over that which sustains it, an emblem of the relationship of the two faiths."[22] In another attempt at a summary impression, Melville wrote:

No country will more quickly dissipate romantic expectations than Palestine—particularly Jerusalem. To some the disappointment is heart sickening. &c. Is the desolation of the land the result of the fatal embrace of the Deity? Hapless are the favorites of heaven. In the emptiness of the lifeless antiquity of Jerusalem the emigrant Jews are like flies that have taken up their abode in a skull.[23]

Obsessed as he was with the omnipresence of rocks, Melville recalled the prophecy of Isaiah: "Go through, go through the gates; prepare ye the way of the people; cast up, cast up the highway; gather out the stones; lift up the standard of the people."[24] In this connection Melville noted that he heard that ministers of the Scottish Church who had gone to Palestine to investigate the possibility of missionary work among the Jews went to Sir Moses Montefiore with the proposal that Jews might be employed in building roads through the land, since stones were abundant, and that that might be the beginning of Isaiah's prophecy. Obviously the proposal did not attract Montefiore.[25]

Melville learned to have a strong distaste for the smell of Jerusalem. "There is at all times," he recorded, "a smell of burning rubbish in the air of Jerusalem."[26] He felt often that he simply had to escape from the pent-up air of the walled city; when he went outside the walls for walks and for a bit of fresh air, he found that there were always others, in groups, who similarly sought relief "from the insalubriousness of so small a city pent in by lofty walls obstructing ventilization."[27]

The Church of the Holy Sepulchre had a special fascination for Melville, and he visited the church many times. It was a morbid attraction that he felt, however, for the scenes that he faced there distressed and even disgusted him. One of his descriptions is as follows:

Smells like a dead-house. dingy light.—At the entrance, in a sort of grotto in the wall a divan for Turkish policemen, where they sit crosslegged & smoking, scornfully observing the continuous troops of pilgrims entering & prostrating themselves before the anointing-stone of Christ, which veined with streaks of a mouldy red looks like a butcher's slab. . . . The door of the church is like that of a jail—a grated window in it . . . a sort of plague-stricken splendor reigns in the painted and mildewed walls around. . . . In the midst of all stands the Sepulchre; a church in a church . . . you enter the tomb. It is like entering a lighted lanthorn. Wedged and half-dazzled, you stare for a moment on the ineloquence of the bedizened slab, and glad to come out, wipe your brow glad to escape as from the heat & jam of a show-box. All is glitter and nothing is gold. A sickening cheat.[28]

Melville refers to the competition among the various sects with their little chapels and to the fact that Jews were not allowed to enter the church. He noted that if one approached the church "from the squalid alley leading towards it from the Via Dolorosa," one comes to a main wall of the church, at the base of which there "lies in open exposure an accumulation of the last and least nameable filth of a barbarous city." When one passed this wall and entered the court of the church, one found a considerable area occupied by a multitude of "hawkers & peddlers of rosaries, crucifixes, toys of olive wood and Dead Sea stone, & (various) other amulets & charms."[29]

Indeed, wherever Melville turned in Jerusalem—or elsewhere in the Holy Land—he was taken aback by the sharp contrast between anticipation and realization, between ideal and fact. Typifying this contrast is the record he made of what he heard guides tell their touring clients: "'Here is the stone Christ leaned against, & here is the English Hotel.' Yonder is the arch where Christ was shown to the people, & just by that open window is sold the best coffee in Jerusalem."[30]

After Mark Twain made a similar pilgrimage to the Holy Land ten years after Melville's visit there, he wrote for a newspaper that Christ would never come to Palestine a second time—he had been there once. Melville would have agreed with and would have greatly enjoyed that remark.[31]

3

After Melville returned to America, his career as a prose writer was at an end. He turned to lecturing for several years, but in three years devoted to the lyceum circuit he grossed a little over twelve hundred dollars.[32] At the end of 1866 he finally was appointed an inspector of customs in New York at the wage of four dollars per day. He held this job for nineteen years, retiring from it at the age of sixty-six. His inspector's salary, supplemented by the modest inheritance that his wife had from her father, Chief Justice Shaw, when he died in 1861, made it possible for Melville to live quietly and with dignity at his home on East 26th Street in New York. He shunned social contacts and devoted his evenings and weekends to writing poems, especially *Clarel: A Poem and Pilgrimage in the Holy Land*, to a brief consideration of which we now turn.

Although his journey to Europe and to the Near East had taken seven months and Melville had traveled some fifteen thousand miles in nine different countries—and had spent only eighteen days in the Holy Land, of which he saw only a small part (he did not go to

Nazareth or to the Sea of Galilee)—yet his journey to the Holy Land seemed to have preoccupied his mind for almost twenty years. Although less than one-fourth of his journal was devoted to the days he spent in the Holy Land, he constantly worked and reworked these entries and made over a hundred borrowings from these journal entries for use in *Clarel*—borrowings that he blended with Biblical materials and with descriptions he found in the standard travel books of the time.[33]

Clarel consists of four parts with the following titles: I. Jerusalem. II. The Wilderness. III. Mar Saba. IV. Bethlehem. It has 150 cantos and consists of over 18,000 lines—a poem that is longer than the *Iliad* or the *Odyssey* and almost twice as long as the *Aeneid* of Virgil. It was first published in 1876 in two volumes at a cost of $1200, contributed by his favorite uncle.[34] Melville paid even for the review copies that were sent out to some periodicals. As Melville was getting the manuscript ready for the publisher, his wife wrote a confidential letter to a cousin in which she said: "If ever this dreadful incubus of a book (I call it so because it has undermined all our happiness) gets off Herman's shoulders I do hope he may be in better mental health—but at present I have reason to feel the gravest concern & anxiety about it—to put it in mild phrase—please do not speak of it."[35] The writing of the poem and the work of getting it at last ready for publication had evidently involved, as its most recent editor has said, a high psychic cost.[36]

One can hardly speak of the book being received by the American public. As one scholar has summarized the situation: "The pattern of American reception was to ignore *Clarel* completely, or dispense with it brusquely; no review indicates anything more than a hasty skimming of the poem."[37]

The poem has ten major and twenty-two minor characters, yet it has barely any plot. Clarel, a young divinity student torn between belief and unbelief, arrives in Jerusalem in the course of his travels. As he visits the holy places, he gets to know some people. He falls in love with a Jewish girl, Ruth, whose father, an American immigrant into Palestine, is murdered by Arabs. Unable to visit Ruth during her period of bereavement, Clarel sets out with a group of companions to see the land, and thus he gets to the Dead Sea, Mar Saba, and Bethlehem. On his return to Jerusalem, he finds that Ruth too has died. This is about the only action, if one can call it that, that takes place. Much of the rest of the poem—in iambic tetrameter lines, with rhymes at irregular intervals, written in language often archaic or misfittingly pompous—is devoted to talk, discussion, and argument by characters that bespeak different philosophies of life. Derwent, for example, is an Anglican clergyman who is firm in his belief that everything that happens must inevitably, or providentially, turn out for the best. Mortmain, on the contrary, tends to see only the evil, black side of things. Margoth, only nominally a Jew, is a geologist who views things and events only from the standpoint of a materialistic and all-enveloping science. The two most interesting characters are Vine, who is a projection of Hawthorne, and Rolfe, who is probably Melville himself. The pilgrimage of these and the other characters makes up no Chaucerian Holy Land Tales, for there is no intent to tell stories but rather to state points of view, to argue for positions relating to the moral and religious aspect of life. As Justice Holmes would say, they twist the tail of the cosmos.

According to Newton Arvin, the poem is a product of the mood of reaction, letdown, and anxiety into which Melville had fallen and is a full and rich expression of the author's later intellectual ife. Still, although disposed to look upon *Clarel* with favor, Arvin recognizes that the book was destined to have only few readers—if only for the reason that it is almost twice as long as *Paradise Lost*. More than the length stands in the way of the poem's popularity, however, for Arvin notes that much of the time the "tetrameters are painfully clogged and gnarled. . . . They force him back constantly on ugly ellipses and grotesque inversions. . . . The pages of the poem are strewn with archaisms of the wrong kind."[38] Nevertheless, Arvin rightly concludes that the stylistic crudities should not be allowed to stand in the way of our recognizing the greatness of Melville's achievement in *Clarel*, for it successfully conveys the sense of desolation that so deeply impressed and depressed Melville as he moved about in Jerusalem and in the other places he visited in Palestine—and, no less, the desolation of the inner spiritual world that this outer world so closely matched.[39]

It seems to me that Melville's approach in *Clarel* closely approximates that of the Preacher in Ecclesiastes. In chapter 1, the Preacher—who says that he had been king over Israel in Jerusalem—states that he has applied his mind to seek and to search out by wisdom all that was done under heaven, and in the following chapters and pages he proceeds to test different ways of life and different sets of values. His conclusion is as complex as it is simple: "The end of the matter; all has been heard. Fear God and keep his commandments; for this is the whole duty of man. For God will bring every deed into judgment, with every secret thing, whether good or evil."[40] This is precisely what Melville does in *Clarel:* he sets out to seek and to search out, by the light of his own mind, what meaning life could offer to one who takes life and its challenges and problems seriously. His characters, like those in a dialogue by Plato, represent different and conflicting approaches—but in *Clarel* there is no Socrates who knows the answers, no Preacher who knows the end of the matter. In *Clarel* all has been heard but the conclusion is no certainty; it is only a possibility, only a hope:

> Even death may prove unreal at the last,
> And stoics be astounded into heaven.
>
> Then keep thy heart, though yet but ill-resigned—
> Clarel, thy heart, the issues there but mind;
> That like the crocus budding through the snow—
> That like a swimmer rising from the deep—
> That like a burning secret which doth go
> Even from the bosom that would hoard and keep;
> Emerge thou mayest from the last whelming sea,
> And prove that death but routs life into victory.[41]

What we end up with, according to Arvin, is "an unillusioned humanism, a hopefulness within distrust, a skeptical theism, a spiritualism strongly biased toward the realistic." It is "a Yea-saying of the most reserved and melancholy sort. . . . The serene trust of a confident religious belief he [Melville] never achieved, and if he returned in these years to the conception of some transcendent, and not merely immanent, deity, which he was willing to call God, it was a God that he found in none of the creeds that were available to him. It was a God of the most impersonal, inscrutable, and even fearful sort."[42]

Indeed, one may say that the mood of Melville in the years between his pilgrimage to the Holy Land and the publication of *Clarel* nearly twenty years later was very much like that which one often detects in the Wisdom books of the Bible, which were Melville's favorites. Nathalia Wright has identified no less than fourteen hundred allusions to the Bible in Melville's works, and the number mounted as his career developed; they increased from a dozen in *Typee* to six hundred in *Clarel*. Of his Biblical allusions, two-thirds were to the Hebrew Scriptures, and the Scriptural books most extensively represented in his works are the Wisdom books: Job, Proverbs, and Ecclesiastes from the Hebrew Scriptures and Ecclesiasticus from the Apocrypha.[43] In a letter that Melville wrote to Hawthorne in 1851, he said: "I read Solomon more and more, and every time see deeper and deeper and unspeakable meanings in him."[44]

Strange, indeed, are the ways of the mind. As matters turned out, we see that Melville went to the Holy Land not as a mere tourist seeking diversion and the satisfaction of curiosity but because of a great inner compulsion that had been nurtured by the Bible and by his experience of life. He desperately wanted to become a reborn man, if not a reborn Christian. He failed in that quest, for everywhere in the Holy Land he found stones, stones, stones, and not that for which he yearned. What he had seen and felt, however, possessed his mind and soul like an obsession, and the arid atmosphere and scenery of Palestine pervades his poem just as the air of Jerusalem was pervaded by the smell of burning rubbish. Like the Preacher in Ecclesiastes, Melville sought meaning and God, sobriety and understanding.

In *Moby Dick*, published twenty-five years before *Clarel*, Melville wrote: "So, therefore, that mortal man who hath more of joy than sorrow in him, that mortal man cannot be true—not true, or undeveloped. With books the same. The truest of all men was the Man of Sorrows, and the truest of all books is Solomon's and Ecclesiastes is the fine hammered steel of woe."[45] Indeed, one might say that *Clarel* programmatically fulfills what he said in *Moby Dick* a man in his predicament ought to do: "But when a man's religion becomes really frantic; when it is a positive torment to him; and, in fine, makes this earth of ours an uncomfortable inn to lodge in; then I think it high time to take that individual aside and argue the point with him."[46] For in the poem, Melville does precisely that: he lets Rolfe, Derwent, Ungar, and other characters take him aside and argue with him the points that drive a man frantic, the points that torment him and that give him no rest. He tries and tests different and conflicting views of life and death, of good and evil. In *Moby Dick* he may have been reconciled with the idea that death annihilates life, as he seemed to have intimated to Hawthorne; for in that great book he said that he was quite willing to leave eternity to God, "for what is man that he should live out the lifetime of his God?"[47] In *Clarel*, however, in the Epilogue—which is attached to the poem as the Conclusion seems to be attached to Ecclesiastes[48]—he intimates that perhaps "death may prove unreal at the last," but what the reality may be he leaves unsaid except that death may rout life into victory. But what is that victory? That Melville leaves unsaid.

4

Given the task that Melville had set for himself, it is no wonder that he took as the locale for his poem the Holy Land. No other place on earth had promised so much, had given so much, and had lost so much. In 1857 the land had the same impact on Melville that it had on Maimonides and his predecessors among the sages of Israel centuries before. In his great redaction of the Code, Maimonides formulated the rule as follows:

> A person who beholds the ruined cities of Judea should say, *Thy holy cities are become a wilderness* (Isaiah 64:9), and should rend his garment. If he beholds the ruins of Jerusalem, he should say, *Jerusalem, a desolation* (ibid.) and likewise rend his garment. If he beholds the ruins of the Temple, he should say, *Our holy and our beautiful house, where our fathers praised Thee, is burned with fire* (Isaiah 64:10), and again rend his garment. . . . The rending of the garment . . . must in every case be done by hand, and while standing. Furthermore, one must rend every garment he is wearing, until his heart is laid bare. The rent may never be sewn up with regular stitching, but may be basted, hemmed, gathered, or sewn with a ladder-stitch.[49]

Melville's journal records the fact that he found the holy cities a wilderness and Jerusalem a desolation and that he rent his garments time and again. In his poem, and for almost twenty years before its publication, Melville tried to lay bare his heart that was exposed by the garments that he had rent, but he also tried desperately to sew up the rent with a ladder-stitch. He never quite succeeded in covering his nakedness. "There is," he had said in *Moby Dick*, "no steady unretracing progress in this life; we do not advance through fixed gradations, and at the last one pause:—through infancy's unconscious spell, boyhood's thoughtless faith, adolescence' doubt (the common doom), then skepticism, then disbelief, resting at last in manhood's pondering repose of If. But once gone through, we trace the round again; and are infants, boys, and men, and Ifs eternally."[50]

"To pray," wrote Ludwig Wittgenstein, "is to think about the meaning of life."[51] *Clarel*, from this point of view, may well be said to be one long prayer. However, it is not an exception among the works of Melville; his great novels (especially *Moby Dick*) and his great short stories (especially *Benito Cereno* and *Billy Budd*) bear ample testimony to this fact. Camus has noted that the best novelists do not merely tell stories but create their universes. Their novels have their logic, their reasonings, their intuitions, and their postulates, and they resemble a great philosophical work in being long and reasoned personal confessions. It is no wonder, then, that Camus rated Melville with Balzac, Stendahl, Dostoevsky, Malraux, and Kafka as a great novelist who was a philosophical novelist.[52]

After *Clarel* Melville wrote some short poems and finally, after the lapse of over thirty years, returned to prose fiction with the writing of *Billy Budd*, which (as we have noted) was not published until 1924, thirty-three years after Melville had died and had been practically forgotten. In *Billy Budd* Melville was still preoccupied with the problem of evil in the world, the problem of theodicy, the question whether it is possible to vindicate the justice of God if evil is permitted to exist in the world and seemingly to have its way.

Billy Budd was a handsome young sailor on a British warship in the time of the Napoleonic wars. He was falsely accused by Claggart, the Master-at-Arms, of plotting a mutiny. During moments of great emotional stress, Billy stammered or totally lost his power of speech; when Claggart made his outrageously false accusation in the presence of Captain Vere, Billy, unable to utter a sound, instinctively shot out his arm and struck Claggart a blow that proved to be fatal. Vere set up a court to hear the case, and because he alone (in the presence of Billy) had heard Claggart's accusation, he brought the charges and practically instructed the three-men court to bring in a judgment of guilt, for which the penalty was hanging. Such a judgment was returned, and Billy was executed.

Now there was no doubt that Billy Budd, though he struck the fatal blow, was morally innocent; nor was there any doubt that Claggart told brazen lies and had wholly contrived the story of Billy Budd as a fomenter of a mutiny; nor was there any doubt that the captain was a wholly honorable and decent man whose sympathies were entirely with the accused but who yet felt himself bound to follow the law relating to mutiny in time of war—and striking Claggart, regardless of the enormity of the provocation, was an act of mutiny, for which the penalty was death. Captain Vere himself observed that Claggart, the villain of the story, had been struck dead by an angel of God, and yet the angel, he added, must himself be struck dead. Billy, he said, will be acquitted at the last assizes, but here, in this world, we must proceed under the law of the Mutiny Act. When the time came for Captain Vere himself to die, he was heard to whisper, "Billy Budd, Billy Budd."

The story recalls the drama *Antigone* by Sophocles. Antigone, a young girl, tries to give decent burial to her brother, an act that was criminal under an order issued by Creon, ruler of the city. Antigone knew that she was violating the law, but she acted in accordance with tradition and with the law of nature, a law superior to an order or law issued by an earthly ruler. She told Creon that his order had not come from God:

> Justice,
> That dwells with the gods below, knows no such law,
> I did not think your edicts strong enough

> To overrule the unwritten unalterable laws
> Of God and heaven, you being only a man.[53]

Creon, however, kept his eye on the earthly law that he had issued. Antigone broke the law, and she could not flout that law with impunity. Creon was not vindictive or mean; Antigone was his sister's child; she was betrothed to his son. Like Captain Vere, Creon concentrated on what to him was fundamental: "He whom the state appoints must be obeyed / To the smallest matter, be it right—or wrong."[54] Creon ordered Antigone's execution by having her sealed in a cave, as if this form of death would somehow be "softer" than death at the hands of the executioner.

Some critics say that Creon is the hero of the drama, for he tried to vindicate law and order, stability and morality. Some argue that Antigone was right. Some, like Hegel, argue that the drama must be read on two levels, for (as in the case of Socrates) each side was right.[55] Anouilh, in his version of the drama, gives the Hegelian contrast by posing two equally headstrong, absolutist wills.[56] It is doubtful, however, as A. C. Bradley points out, that to Sophocles Creon and Antigone were equally right.[57] For throughout the play Creon's decree is spoken of as an affront to humanity. In Greek tragedy, when a character acts out of a fundamental necessity of human life or in response to basic, deep, and sacred instincts, he is said to be working with the gods and they with him. Thus a universal principle gets to be particularized.[58] Thus Antigone is shown to be working with the gods and Creon against them—just as Socrates claimed that he was only obeying God.

Hannah Arendt, in her book *On Revolution*, considers the case of Billy Budd and suggests provokingly that perhaps we have here an instance of the reversal of the case of Cain killing Abel; for in Melville's story, Abel kills Cain. The subject of Melville's story is "goodness beyond virtue and evil beyond vice, and the plot of the story consists in confronting these two." The greatness of the story, she says,

> lies in that goodness, because it is part of "nature," does not act meekly but asserts itself forcefully and, indeed, violently so that we are convinced: only the violent act with which Billy Budd strikes dead the man who bore false witness against him is adequate, it eliminates nature's "depravity." This, however, is not the end but the beginning of the story. The story unfolds after "nature" has run its course, with the result that the wicked man is dead and the good man has prevailed. The trouble now is that the good man, because

he encountered evil, has become a wrongdoer too. . . . It is at this point that "virtue" in the person of Captain Vere is introduced into the conflict between absolute good and absolute evil, and here the tragedy begins. . . . [V]irtue finally interferes not to prevent the crime of evil but to punish the violence of absolute innocence. Claggart was "struck by an angel of God! Yet the angel must hang!" Laws and "lasting institutions" break down not only under the onslaught of elemental evil but under the impact of absolute innocence as well.[59]

Nothing was resolved in *Clarel,* and nothing is resolved in *Billy Budd.* The mystery of life remains. God is in His heaven, but the world is full of moral cracks. It will be recalled that before he left for the Holy Land, Melville visited with Hawthorne in Liverpool, and after a long conversation between the two friends, Hawthorne reported that Melville "will never rest until he gets hold of a definite belief. . . . He can neither believe, nor be comfortable in his unbelief."[60] The visit to the Holy Land did not remove his predicament; *Clarel* and *Billy Budd* bear out this judgment. He remained fixed in and clinging onto the Solomonic wisdom of Ecclesiastes without the comfort of the "end of the matter," "that God will bring every deed into judgment, with every secret thing, whether good or evil."[61] To the end, Ecclesiastes—and perhaps life itself—remained for Melville "the fine hammered steel of woe."[62] He went to see the Holy Land. He never saw it. No one ever sees it. Not even Moses saw it, except what God chose to let him see from the top of Pisgah in the strange land of Moab. Melville, as he said of his friend Hawthorne, remained "a seeker, not a finder yet"—or ever;[63] and yet, at the end of *Clarel,* one hears again a faint echo of faith and trust such as he uttered in *Moby Dick,* a faith and trust that can be found even among stones, wild beasts, and graves, a faith and trust that he saw all about him in the Holy Land: "Faith, like a jackal, feeds among the tombs, and even from these dead doubts she gathers her most vital hope."[64]

Notes
Index

Notes

1. The Confluence of Torah and Constitution

1. Deuteronomy 5:13–14.
2. *Encyclopedia Judaica* 12:118.
3. Shabbat 88b.
4. Menachot 29b.
5. Roscoe Pound, *Introduction to the Philosophy of Law* (New Haven, 1922), 1.
6. Exodus 23:2.
7. Baba Mezia 59b.
8. *Authorized Daily Prayer Book,* trans. S. Singer, new ed. (London, 1962), 14.
9. Solomon B. Freehof, *Reform Judaism and the Law* (Cincinnati, 1967), 20–21.
10. *United States v. Butler,* 297 U.S. 1 (1936).
11. *Youngstown Sheet and Tube Co. v. Sawyer,* 343 U.S. 579, 610 (1952).
12. *Everson v. Board of Education,* 330 U.S. 1 (1947).
13. *Dred Scott Case,* 19 How. 393 (1857).
14. *Allied Stores v. Bowers,* 358 U.S. 522 (1959).
15. *Railway Express Agency v. New York,* 336 U.S. 106 (1949).
16. E.g., *Shapiro v. Thompson,* 394 U.S. 618, 638 (1969).
17. Edward S. Corwin, *The "Higher Law" Background of American Constitutional Law* (Ithaca, N.Y., 1928), 38–39.
18. Benjamin N. Cardozo, *The Nature of the Judicial Process* (New Haven, 1921), 141.
19. Genesis 9:11.
20. Exodus 19:5–8. Cf. Deuteronomy 29–31.
21. Perry Miller, *The New England Mind: The Seventeenth Century* (New York, 1939), 374.
22. Daniel J. Boorstin, *The Americans: The Colonial Experience* (New York, 1958), 17.
23. Edmund S. Morgan, ed., *Puritan Political Ideas* (Indianapolis, 1965), 75–93.
24. A. W. Plumstead, ed., *The Wall and the Garden* (Minneapolis, 1968), 197, 199, 203, 204, 208, 209.
25. Harry S. Stout, *The New England Soul* (Oxford, 1986), 173.
26. Ibid., 171.

2. Religious Liberty
The Congruence of Thomas Jefferson and Moses Mendelssohn

1. Thomas Jefferson, letter to James Madison, Feb. 17, 1826, in *Thomas Jefferson Writings* (New York, 1980), 1512, 1515.
2. Jefferson, 702. Cf. Dumas Malone, *Jefferson and His Time* (Boston, 1948), 116.
3. Malone, *Jefferson and His Time,* 115–16.
4. Ibid., 269–73.
5. Ibid., 251–57.
6. Ibid., 264.
7. Ibid., 269.
8. Ibid., 280.
9. Jefferson, 703.
10. Malone, *Jefferson and His Time,* 285.
11. Jefferson, 706.
12. Adrienne Koch, *The Philosophy of Thomas Jefferson* (New York, 1943), 47.
13. For the full text of the statute, see Jefferson, 346.
14. *Everson v. Board of Education.*
15. Jefferson, letter to Danbury Baptist Association, in Jefferson, 510.
16. Adrienne Koch, *Power, Morals, and the Founding Fathers* (Ithaca, N.Y., 1961), 29; Dumas Malone, *Jefferson and the Rights of Man* (Boston, 1951), 211, 287.
17. Koch, *Power, Morals, and the Founding Fathers,* 24.
18. *Everson v. Board of Education,* 1.
19. Jefferson, letter to Sam. Kercheval, July 12, 1816, in Jefferson, 1401–3.
20. Jefferson, letter to Jos. Priestley, Jan. 27, 1800, in Jefferson, 1073.
21. Jefferson, *Notes on Virginia* (1787), in Jefferson, 301; Jefferson, letter to John Jay, Aug. 23, 1785, in Jefferson, 818.
22. *Encyclopedia Judaica* 15:1210.
23. Moses Mendelssohn, *Jerusalem,* trans. Allan Arkush, introd. and commentary Alexander Altmann (Hanover, N.H., 1983), 126.
24. Ibid., 94.
25. Ibid., 70; cf. 61.
26. Ibid., 71.
27. Ibid., 139.

3. The Jewish Quest for Equality and the American Experience

1. John W. Warner, letter to the editor, *New York Times,* Jan. 11, 1976.
2. *New York Times,* Aug. 7, 1976.
3. Quotation in E. E. Urbach, *The Sages* (Jerusalem, 1975), 1:547.
4. Aviva Zuckoff, "For Making Bricks without Straw, Etc.," *Israel Horizon,* June 1969, 14.
5. See Bertram W. Korn, *American Jewry and the Civil War* (Philadelphia, 1951), ch. 6.
6. Henry L. Feingold, "The Condition of American Jewry in Historical Perspective: A Bicentennial Assessment," *American Jewish Year Book* 76 (1976): 3.
7. John Higham, *Send These to Me: Jews and Other Immigrants in Urban America* (New York, 1975), 182.
8. Feingold, "Condition of American Jewry," 28.
9. As one recalls the action of General Grant, one cannot help but compare it with the action of General George S. Brown, chief of staff, when he made his disparag-

ing remarks about Jewish influence before an audience at Duke University on October 10, 1974. This incident involved no action but only speech. Brown was called to the White House and rebuked by the president, and he was also severely criticized by members of the U.S. Senate and House of Representatives, by other prominent Americans, and by editorials in newspapers throughout the country. "The Brown Affair— Reactions and Aftermath," American Jewish Committee, Dec. 20, 1974; Hyman Bookbinder, Washington Letter, American Jewish Committee, Jan. 1, 1975.

10. Ralph R. Marcus, *Early American Jewry* (Philadelphia, 1951), vol. 1, ch. 2; A. V. Goodman, *American Overture* (Philadelphia, 1947), ch. 5.

11. Marcus, 31.

12. Ibid., 32.

13. Quoted in Urbach, 2:394, note 89.

14. Feingold, "Condition of American Jewry," 6.

15. Andrew M. Greeley, *Ethnicity, Denomination and Inequality—A Bicentennial Report to the Ford Foundation* (Center for the Study of American Pluralism, National Opinion Research Center, Chicago, Oct. 1975).

16. The Census Bureau survey was of 45,000 households in 50 states and the District of Columbia. Persons were asked to identify themselves as belonging to one or another of eight listed ethnic groups: English, German, Irish, Spanish, Italian, French, Polish, and Russian. Persons also identified themselves by their mother tongue. The Census Bureau listed only Yiddish as the original language of the Russian group. Almost all scholars in the field have correlated "Russian" with "Jewish." Greeley, in his report to the Ford Foundation, belittles ethnic surveys and rightly says: "It is possible that if a religious question is asked before an ethnic question, a Jewish respondent whose family came from Poland will not describe himself as Polish. If, on the other hand, an ethnic question is asked, and a Jewish answer rejected, a Jew with a Polish family background may have no choice but to answer 'Polish'" (*Ethnicity, Denomination and Inequality*, 14).

17. Greeley, *Ethnicity, Denomination and Inequality*, 58, table 4.

18. Ibid., 19; see table 6.

19. Ibid., 20–21; see tables 9, 10, and 11.

20. Ibid., 27, and tables 12, 13, and 38.

21. Ibid., 26, and table 18. Only about 40 percent of non-Jewish youth attended college at this time. *Newsweek*, Mar. 1, 1971, 63.

22. Andrew M. Greeley, *Ethnicity in the United States* (New York, 1974), 42–43, table 4.

23. Ibid., 112.

24. Nathan Glazer, *American Judaism*, 2nd ed. (Chicago, 1972), 108.

25. Nathan Glazer, "Social Characteristics of American Jews, 1654–1954," *American Jewish Year Book* 56 (1955): 12, 13.

26. Ibid., 17.

27. Ibid., 29.

28. Sidney Goldstein, "American Jewry, 1970: A Demographic Profile," *American Jewish Year Book* 72 (1971): 85.

29. The Carnegie study is summarized in detail by Seymour M. Lipset and Everett C. Ladd, "Jewish Academics in the United States," *American Jewish Year Book* 72 (1971): 89.

30. Before World War II, when one tried to think of Jews who were professors, one could recall the names of Morris R. Cohen, Harry A. Wolfson, Isaac Husik, Felix Frankfuter, Morris Jastrow, and Franz Boas.

31. See *American Jewish Year Book* 73 (1972): 570; " These Panthers Wear Yarmulkes," *New York Times*, May 31, 1971.

32. *New York Times*, Jan. 23, 1973; Jack S. Cohen, "Jewish Poverty and Welfare," *Congress Bi-Weekly*, May 24, 1974.

33. Bertram H. Gold, introduction to *The Other Jews: Portraits in Poverty*, by Dorothy Rabinowitz (New York, 1972), 7.

34. Ibid., 8.

35. *New York Times*, Sept. 14, 1971. For other materials on poverty among Jews, see *The Jewish Poor: A Brief Bibliography*, leaflet published by the American Jewish Committee, July 1973. For the special problem of old age among Jews, see "A Rationale for Synagogue Programming with the Jewish Aging," *Analysis* (Washington, D.C.) 50, Mar. 17, 1975.

36. According to the Bureau of Census figures, in 1971, 12.5 percent of Americans were poor; in 1974, 11.6 percent, or close to 25 million people, including 7,467,000 blacks—31.4 percent of the black population.

37. *New York Times*, Sept. 28, 1975. The per capita income for Sweden was the highest in the world—$5,596; the United States was a close second with $5,523. The countries with the lowest incomes were Mali, $50; Rwanda, $61; Upper Volta, $62; India, $93.

38. Greeley, *Ethnicity, Denomination and Inequality*, 44, and tables 38, 39, 40.

39. Ibid., 46.

40. Ibid., 51–52.

41. Ibid., 49.

42. Ibid., 46.

43. Glazer, "Social Characteristics," 30–33, What is set forth in the text is part quotation from and part paraphrase of Glazer's article.

44. Ibid., 32.

45. Ibid., 33.

46. Glazer, *American Judaism*, 80.

47. Joseph L. Blau, *Judaism in America* (Chicago, 1976), 113; cf. Blau, "The Spiritual Life of American Jewry, 1654–1954," *American Jewish Year Book* 55 (1956): 99ff.

48. Blau, *Judaism in America*, 114–15.

49. Ellis Rivkin, "A Decisive Pattern in American Jewish History," in *Essays in American Jewish History*, ed. Jacob R. Marcus (Cincinnati, 1958), 39–41.

50. A. J. Toynbee, *The Study of History* (London, 1934), 2:393.

51. Greeley, *Ethnicity in the United States*, 28.

52. John Clive, *Macaulay: The Shaping of the Historian* (New York, 1973), 117.

53. Isaac Herzog, *Judaism: Law and Ethics* (London, 1973), 148.

54. Cf. Oscar Handlin and Mary F. Handlin, "The Acquisition of Political and Social Rights by the Jews in the United States," *American Jewish Year Book* 56 (1955): 43, 48.

55. Mass Jewish immigration did not begin until towards the end of the nineteenth century. In 1880 there were 300,000 Jews in the United States. By the end of the century the Jewish population was about a half-million. From 1900 to 1914, the beginning of World War I, another 1,500,000 were added; from 1914 to 1924, another 350,000 came. From 1899 to 1914, Jewish immigration averaged 90,000 persons per year.

56. David M. Potter, *People of Plenty* (Chicago, 1954), 91–92.

57. Ibid., 95.

58. Glazer, "Social Characteristics," 17; Handlin and Handlin, 73.

59. See Jacob Katz, "Religion as a Uniting and Dividing Force in Modern Jewish History," in *The Role of Religion in Modern Jewish History*, ed. J. Katz (Cambridge, Mass., 1975).

60. See Daniel J. Elazar, *Community and Polity* (Philadelphia, 1976).

61. Blau, *Judaism in America*, 19–20.

62. See Will Herberg, *Protestant, Catholic, Jew* (New York, 1955).

63. Sanhedrin 44a. In the Brother Daniel case in 1966, however, the Supreme Court of Israel held that Brother Daniel, despite his valid Halakhic claim to being a Jew, had lost his Jewish status by having chosen to remove himself from the Jewish community by conversion to Christianity, and so did not quality under the Law of Return.

64. Cf. J. G. Herder, "Essay on the Origin of Language," in *J. G. Herder on Social and Political Culture*, ed. F. M. Barnard (Cambridge, 1969).

65. Deuteronomy 5:3.

66. See Milton R. Konvitz, *Fundamental Liberties of a Free People* (Ithaca, N.Y., 1957), 345–61.

67. Hugh Trevor-Roper, ed., *Critical and Historical Essays, Lord Macauley* (New York, 1965), 116, 127; John Clive and Thomas Pinney, eds., *Thomas Babbington Macauley, Selected Writings* (Chicago, 1972), 181, 187. Jews were barred from Parliament by an act of 1701 that required an oath "on the true faith of a Christian." *Statutes*, 13 Wm. III, c. 6, 1.

68. See Richard B. Morris, "Civil Liberties and the Jewish Tradition in Early America," in *The Jewish Experience in America*, ed. A. J. Karp (New York, 1969), 1:404, 417.

69. Konvitz, *Fundamental Liberties*, 346.

70. Morris, 423.

71. See Milton R. Konvitz, "Legislation Guaranteeing Equality of Access to Places of Public Accommodation," *Annals of the American Academy of Political and Social Science* 274 (1951): 47; Milton R. Konvitz and Theodore Leskes, *A Century of Civil Rights* (New York, 1961), 155 ff.; Thomas I. Emerson, David Haber, and Norman Dorsen, *Political and Civil Rights in the United States*, student ed. (Boston, 1967), 2:1407, 1512, 1618, 1673, 1680; Civil Rights Act, *U.S. Statutes* 78 (1964): 241; Fair Housing Law, Title 8 of Civil Rights Act, *U.S. Statutes* 82 (1968): 82; Equal Employment Opportunity Act, *U.S. Statutes* 86 (1972): 103; Equal Credit Opportunity Act, *U.S. Statutes* 90 (1976): 251.

72. *Brown v. Board of Education*, 347 U.S. 483 (1954).

73. Kiddushin 30b.

74. Konvitz, *Fundamental Liberties*, 346; cf. Saul K. Padover, ed., *The Complete Madison: His Basic Writings* (New York, 1953), 243.

75. *New York Times*, Aug. 20, 1976.

76. Potter, *People of Plenty*, 114.

4. Profane Religion and Sacred Law

1. Jeremiah 22:1, 13–16.

2. Jonah 1:2.

3. *New York Times*, Mar. 18, 1977. Cf. Leonid I. Brezhnev, *New York Times*, Mar. 22, 1977.

4. The book may have been written in the fourth century B.C.E. It would therefore have been written in Judah, centuries after the destruction of Nineveh in 612.

5. Archibald Cox was dismissed on October 20, 1973, after he threatened to secure a judicial ruling that Nixon was violating a court order to turn over the Watergate tapes to Judge Sirica.

6. Francis Bacon, *Novum Organum*, book 1, aphorisms 39 and 44.

7. Ralph Waldo Emerson, "Self-Reliance," *Ralph Waldo Emerson* (Oxford and New York, 1990), 141.

8. Ralph Waldo Emerson, "The Over-Soul," *Ralph Waldo Emerson* (Oxford and New York, 1990), 165.

9. 1 Kings 21.

10. *United States v. Nixon,* 418 U.S. 683 (1974).

11. 1 Kings 21:20.

12. John Macmurray, *Interpreting the Universe* (London, 1936), 137.

13. Genesis 1:26; Psalm 8:5 (Revised Standard Version).

14. Genesis 1:26–27. Italics supplied.

15. John Macmurray, *Persons in Relation* (London, 1961).

16. Luke 10:25–37.

17. Leo Baeck, *The Essence of Judaism* (New York, 1948), 193.

18. Søren Kierkegaard, *Works of Love,* trans. Howard and Edna Hong (London, 1962), 38.

19. Hermann Cohen, *Religion of Reason out of the Sources of Judaism* (New York, 1972), 114.

20. Ibid., 115.

21. Ibid., 114.

22. Luke 10:25–28.

23. Deuteronomy 6:5; Leviticus 19:18.

24. William Ernest Hocking, *The Meaning of God in Human Experience* (New Haven, 1912), 11.

25. Theodore Parker, "The Transient and the Permanent in Christianity," sermon delivered in Hawes Place Church, Boston, May 11, 1841; reprinted in *Three Prophets of Religious Liberalism: Channing—Emerson—Parker* (Boston, 1961).

26. Jeremiah 7:22–23.

27. Jeremiah 9:23–24.

28. Leviticus 19:2.

29. Matthew 5:48.

30. Parker, 140.

31. William Ellery Channing, "Unitarian Christianity," sermon delivered in Baltimore on May 5, 1819; reprinted in *Three Prophets of Religious Liberalism: Channing—Emerson—Parker* (Boston, 1961), 81.

32. Job 29:12–17.

33. Jeremiah 22:16.

34. Deuteronomy 25:13–16; cf. Leviticus 19:35–36.

35. Deuteronomy 20:19.

36. See Milton R. Konvitz, ed., *Judaism and Human Rights* (New York, 1972), 247ff.

37. Psalm 24:1–2.

38. United States Code, Title 16, secs. 1131ff.

39. Martin Buber, *Tales of the Hasidim* (New York, 1948), 2:89.

40. Nicolas Berdyaev, *The Fate of Man in the Modern World* (Ann Arbor, Mich., 1935), 124.

41. Psalm 36:9.

42. Acts 26:5; Galatians 1:13, 14; James 1:26, 27.

43. Avot 2:17.

44. Maimonides, *Mishneh Torah,* quoted in David Hartman, *Maimonides, Torah and Philosophic Quest* (Philadelphia, 1976), 231.

45. Maimonides, *Guide of the Perplexed,* trans. Shlomo Pines (Chicago, 1963), 263–64.

46. *Engel v. Vitale,* 370 U.S. 421 (1962).

47. See Milton R. Konvitz, *Expanding Liberaties* (New York, 1966), 44ff.

48. Numbers 11:29.

49. Jeremy Taylor, *Holy Living* (1650), in *Holy Living and Dying* (London, 1883), 4, 12.

5. Law and Morals in the Bible, Plato, and Aristotle

1. Ahad Ha-am, *Selected Essays*, trans. Leon Simon (Philadelphia, 1912), 130–32.

2. Leviticus 18:5, 19:2.

3. Babylonian Talmud, Baba Mezia 30b; *Mekilta de-Rabbi Ishmael*, ed. J. Z. Lauterbach (Philadelphia, 1933), 2:182. The present essay, as its title indicates, is concerned with the Bible; it does not explore the subject from the standpoint of the Talmud or of Jewish law generally. For the latter, see Haim H. Cohn, "Ancient Jewish Equity," in *Equity in the World's Legal Systems—A Comparative Study*, ed. Ralph A. Newman (Brussels, 1973); Adin Steinsaltz, "Ethics and *Halakhah*," ch. 24 of *The Essential Talmud* (London, 1976).

4. Leviticus 19:9–10; Deuteronomy 24:19–21.

5. Micah 6:8.

6. Isaiah 1:16–17.

7. Hosea 6:6.

8. Leviticus 19:19.

9. Deuteronomy 10:17–19.

10. Deuteronomy 30:4.

11. Proverbs 7:3.

12. Deuteronomy 5:14.

13. Deuteronomy 15:1.

14. Deuteronomy 22:8.

15. Leviticus 19:9.

16. See Samson Raphael Hirsch, commentary on Genesis 15:6, Deuteronomy 15:8, and Psalm 72:3.

17. Deuteronomy 15:9–11.

18. Deuteronomy 11:13–17.

19. Isaiah 10:5–6.

20. Isaiah 10:1–3.

21. Psalm 37:1–9.

22. Job 4:7–8.

23. Deuteronomy 32:4.

24. Isaiah 30:18.

25. Daniel 4:34.

26. Psalm 37:25.

27. Jeremiah 12:1.

28. Job 33:19–28.

29. Isaiah 52 and 53.

30. Psalm 73:23, 25, 28.

31. Job 19:25–27.

32. Matthew 22:21.

33. Jeremiah 29:1–7.

34. Babylonian Talmud, Sanhedrin 56a.

35. Aristotle, *Politics* 1252b.

36. Proverbs 3:18.

37. Deuteronomy 33:5.

38. Deuteronomy 30:15–16.

39. Plato, *Crito* 50a–51c.
40. Heraclitus, frag. 114 D–K.
41. Sophocles, *Antigone* 440–49.
42. Plato, *Laws* 875.
43. Plato, *Politicus* 294.
44. Ibid., 295.
45. Ibid., 300.
46. Plato, *Laws* 768.
47. Plato, *Politicus* 297.
48. Ibid., 299.
49. Aristotle, *Politics* 1287a.
50. Aristotle, *Nicomachean Ethics* 1134b.
51. Ibid.
52. Aristotle, *Rhetoric* 1373b.
53. Aristotle, *Nicomachean Ethics* 1110a.
54. Plato, *Apology* 28c–30a.
55. Aristotle, *Nicomachean Ethics* 1162b–63a.
56. Ernest Barker, *Politics of Aristotle* (Oxford, 1946), 366.
57. Aristotle, *Rhetoric* 1374a.
58. Aristotle, *Nicomachean Ethics* 1137a. See Milton R. Konvitz, "Equity in Law and Ethics," in *Dictionary of History of Ideas* (New York, 1973), 2:148–54.
59. Aristotle, *Rhetoric* 1374b.
60. Ibid., 1375a.
61. Leviticus 20:7.
62. Deuteronomy 6:6–7.
63. The Hebrew Bible itself has no word for "religion." The word implies that there may be a secular realm separate from the sacred or religious, and such a separation was foreign to the Hebraic mind. See chapter 4 in this volume.
64. Deuteronomy 4:8.
65. Psalm 19:7–9.
66. Psalm 119:62–64.
67. Isaiah 1:26–27.
68. Amos 2:6–7.
69. Amos 5:14–15.
70. Job 1:1.
71. Job 29:14.
72. Job 29:15–17.
73. Galatians 3:23–29.
74. Amos 5:24.
75. Plato, *Republic* 514a–17b.
76. Plato, *Laws* book 5.
77. Ibid., 726–34.
78. E.g., Ibid., 741, 772–73, 870.
79. Ibid., 857.
80. Ibid., 811.
81. Aristotle, *Nicomachean Ethics* 1179b–81a.
82. Ibid., 1180b.
83. Ibid., 1103b.
84. Aristotle, *Politics* 1280a.
85. Ibid., 1280b.
86. Ibid.; emphasis supplied.

87. Ibid., 1324a.
88. Plato, *Laws* 629.

6. Natural Law and Judaism
The Case of Maimonides

1. Sophocles, *Antigone*, 450.
2. Cicero, *De Republica* 3.xxii.33.
3. Cicero, *De Legibus* 1.x.29; 1.xii.33.
4. Frederick Pollock, *Essays in the Law* (London, 1922), 3.
5. George H. Sabine, *A History of Political Theory*, 3rd ed. (New York, 1961), 170, 180.
6. Grotius, *De jure belli ac pacis*, trans. F. W. Kelsey (Washington, 1913), bk. 1, ch. 1, sect. 10, 1, 5; quoted in Sabine, 424.
7. Sabine, 459.
8. Ibid., 424–25.
9. Julius Stone, *Human Law and Human Justice* (Stanford, Calif., 1965), 64–65.
10. H. M. Kallen, *Secularism Is the Will of God* (New York, 1954).
11. Maurice Cranston, "Are There Human Rights?" *Daedalus* 112 (fall 1983): 14.
12. *New York Times*, Apr. 21, 1994.
13. Cranston, 13.
14. Leo Strauss, *Natural Right and History* (Chicago, 1953), 81–86.
15. Ibid., 74.
16. Genesis 1:26, 27.
17. Genesis 9:5, 6.
18. Babylonian Talmud, Sanhedrin 56a–b.
19. J. H. Hertz, *The Pentateuch and Haftorahs* (London, 1938), 33.
20. Isadore Twersky, *A Maimonides Reader* (New York, 1972), 221. See M. Kellner, *Maimonides on Judaism and Jewish People* (Albany, 1991), 75, regarding the question of the correctness of the phrase "but one of their wise men."
21. Genesis 1:17. Regarding "feared God," see Hertz, 208.
22. Leviticus 18:5.
23. Babylonian Talmud, Baba Kamma 38a.
24. Marvin Fox, *Interpreting Maimonides* (Chicago, 1990), 127.
25. Ibid., 127. Quote from Babylonian Talmud, Yoma 67b.
26. *Art Scroll Siddur*, 102.
27. *Authorized Daily Prayer Book*. 48.
28. Exodus 15:26.
29. 1 John 5:11–12.
30. Matthew 7:13–14.
31. Sifra 36b, quoted in C. G. Montefiore and H. Loewe, *A Rabbinic Anthology* (London, 1938), 564.
32. Isadore Twersky, *Introduction to the Code of Maimonides (Mishneh Torah)* (New Haven, 1980), 458. There is another passage in *Mishneh Torah* that may be relevant although it does not concern itself with the Noahide laws. In the treatise on Sabbatical and Jubilee Years *(hilkot Shmittah ve-Yoval)*, Maimonides considers the status of the Levites with regard to shares in the land of Israel. At the end of his treatment of the subject, Maimonides explains why the tribe of Levi were granted no right to such shares, and then he states the following:

> Not only the Tribe of Levi, but also each and every individual of those who come into the world [not Israelites, but "each and every individual"] whose

spirit moves him and whose knowledge gives him understanding to set himself apart in order to stand before the Lord, to serve Him, to worship Him, and to know Him, who walks upright as God had made him to do, and releases his neck from the yoke of the many speculations that the children of man are wont to pursue—such an individual is consecrated to the Holy of Holies, and his portion and inheritance shall be in the Lord forever and evermore. The Lord will grant him in this world whatsoever is sufficient for him, the same as He had granted to the priests and the Levites. Thus indeed did David, upon whom be peace, say, "O Lord, the portion of mine inheritance and of my cup, Thou maintainest my lot" (Psalm 16:5). (*The Code of Maimonides—Book Seven—The Book of Agriculture,* trans. Isaac Klein [New Haven, 1979], 403.)

The passage in its context, and when read as against the passage in *Mishneh Torah* dealing with the heathen who observes the Noahide laws (*Kings and Wars,* ch. 8, sec. 11) raises questions that I cannot resolve. Perhaps, given that the passage quoted above speaks of priests and Levites, when Maimonides used the phrase "every individual" he meant Israelites as distinguished from priests and Levites, and did not mean non-Jews.

33. Haim Cohn, "Authority and Reason in Ancient Jewish Law," in *Selected Essays* (Tel Aviv, n.d.), 122–23.

34. Ibid., 158–59. In the Cohn statement of the position of Maimonides it is said that the gentile "is not deemed either righteous or wise." In other versions it is said that the gentile would not be considered righteous but that he would be considered as one of the wise men among gentiles. It depends on which of the ancient texts of Maimonides the scholar uses. Cf. ibid., 150–51; see also note 20 above.

35. Galatians 3:23–29.

36. Micah 6:6, 8.

37. Amos 5: 23–24.

38. Philo, *De Officio Mundi* ch. 61.

39. Louis Jacobs, *Principles of the Jewish Faith* (London, 1964), 9–10.

40. Ibid., 15.

41. What I have said should not be taken to mean that I hold the position that there are no dogmas in Judaism. There is a place in Judaism as a religion for dogma, ritual, and ethics; countless numbers of Jews have chosen martyrdom rather than avow what they considered heretical beliefs. Priority, however, is given to ethical conduct, not to beliefs or to ritual observance, and there is no consensus on fundamental beliefs, nor on their number or on their interpretation.

42. Aharon Lichtenstein, "Does Jewish Tradition Recognize an Ethic Independent of Halakha?" in *Modern Jewish Ethics,* ed. Marvin Fox (Columbus, Ohio, 1975), 63.

43. Erubin 100b.

44. Abot 3:17.

45. Lichtenstein, 63.

46. Ibid., 64.

47. Robert Gordis, *The Root and the Branch* (Chicago, 1962), 46. The quotation is from Jubilees 7:22.

48. Acts 15:20, 29.

49. Gordis, *Root and the Branch,* 47. The quotation within the passage is from *Yalkut Shimoni* on Judges, sec. 42.

50. The chapter is substantially reproduced in a later book by Gordis, *Judaic Ethics for a Lawless World* (New York, 1986), published twenty-four years later. In the latter work, the matter is presented in two chapters, "Natural Law for the Modern World" and "Jewish Sources for Natural Law." The paper is also published in a collection of

lectures and papers for the Center for the Study of Democratic Institutions, *Natural Law and Modern Society* (Cleveland, 1963), and as a chapter in *Ethics in an Age of Pervasive Technology*, ed. Melvin Kranzberg (Boulder, Colo., n. d.).

51. Gordis, *Root and the Branch*, 225.

52. Ibid., 213.

53. Ibid., 234.

54. Ibid., 215, 216.

55. Ibid., 219.

56. Ibid., 221.

57. Ibid., 222.

58. Ibid., 235.

59. Jeremiah 17:9.

60. Jacob Katz, *Exclusiveness and Tolerance* (Oxford, 1961), 176–77. See also 175 regarding the authority on which Maimonides relied for his formulation.

61. Ibid., 177.

62. Jacques Maritain, *The Rights of Man and Natural Law* (New York, 1943), 59–60.

63. Norman Lamm and Aaron Kirschenbaum, "Freedom and Constraint in the Jewish Judicial Process," *Cardozo Law Review* 1 (1979): 111, 116, 117, 118, 119. In a letter to the author, Rabbi Lamm identified the section beginning at p. 105 as having been written by him.

64. See also Steven S. Schwartzschild, "Do Noachides Have to Believe in Revelation?" *Jewish Quarterly Review* 57 (1962) and 58 (1962). This scholarly discussion supports my analysis and conclusions.

65. Eugene Korn, "Gentiles, the World to Come, and Judaism," *Modern Judaism* 14 (1994), 276, 277.

7. Many Are Called and Many Are Chosen

1. Amos 3:2.

2. Genesis 17:7.

3. A famous story named for Bontscha the silent one. See Maurice Samuel, *Prince of the Ghetto* (Philadelphia, 1948), 75–83.

4. *Authorized Daily Prayer Book*, 7.

5. Declaration of Independence. See Henry Alonzo Myers, *Are Men Equal?* (Ithaca, N.Y., 1945), 4.

6. Mishnah, Sanhedrin, 4, 5.

7. Romans 9:6.

8. The Second Vatican Council—for the first time in the history of ecumenical councils—in 1964, in its document *Constitutio Dogmatica de Ecclesia*, speaks of Jews and Moslems as being within "the plan of salvation," which encompasses also those who "through no fault of their own do not know the gospel of Christ or His Church, yet sincerely seek God and, moved by grace, strive by their deeds to do His will as it is known to them through the dictates of conscience. Nor does divine Providence deny the help necessary for salvation to those who, without blame on their part, have not yet arrived at an explicit knowledge of God, but who strive to live a good life, thanks to His grace." In a footnote, the council made reference to the letter of the Holy Office to Cardinal Cushing of Boston, 1949, which explained how it may be possible for non-Catholics to attain salvation according to the grace of God. See *Documents of Vatican II*, ed. Walter M. Abbott (New York, 1966), 34–35. Compare Babylonian Talmud, Baba Kamma 38a, Sanhedrin 59a, and Sifra 86b, on the teaching that a gentile who lives or acts according to the Torah, or studies Torah, is equal to the High Priest. The sages

cited Leviticus 18:5, which says "which if a man do," and emphasized that it does not say "which if an Israelite do"—"which if a man do, he shall live through them."

9. Pirke Aboth 4:15–17.

10. Isaiah 53:3.

11. Romans 8:31.

12. Deuteronomy 13:4.

13. Saadye Gaon, *The Book of Beliefs and Opinions*, trans. Samuel Rosenblatt (New Haven, 1948), 126.

14. Amos 9:7.

15. Exodus 15:1.

16. Amos 1:5.

17. Amos 1:6.

18. Ralph Waldo Emerson, "The Young American" (1844), in *Ralph Waldo Emerson: Representative Selections*, ed. F. I. Carpenter (New York, 1934), 167.

19. Hugh Lloyd-Jones, "Gladstone on Homer," *Times Literary Supplement*, Jan. 3, 1975.

20. Maimonides, *Mishneh Torah*, Kings, ch. 11, in Twersky, *A Maimonides Reader*, 226–27.

21. See Jacob B. Agus, *Modern Philosophies of Judaism* (New York, 1941), 191ff.

22. H. Wheeler Robinson, *Religious Ideas of Old Testament* (London, 1913), 221.

23. Babylonian Talmud, Shabbath 88b; cf. Exodus Rabbah 38.4; Tanhumah, Yitro, 2, f. 124.

24. Louis D. Brandeis, *The Words of Justice Brandeis*, ed. Solomon Goldman (New York, 1953), 51.

25. Ibid., 50n.

26. 1 Corinthians 12:4.

27. Walt Whitman, preface to *Leaves of Grass* (1855), in *Viking Portable Walt Whitman*, ed. Mark Van Doren (New York, 1945), 41.

28. Mishnah, Sanhedrin, 4:5.

29. Leo Baeck, *This People Israel* (Philadelphia, 1965), 402–3.

8. Tradition and Change in American Judaism
A Letter to David Daiches

1. Plato, *Laws* 7:798.

2. Plato, *Philebus* 58.

3. Ralph Waldo Emerson, *Ralph Waldo Emerson* (Oxford and New York, 1990), 140, 143.

4. Plato, *Philebus*.

5. T. S. Eliot, *Selected Essays*, 3rd ed. (London, 1951), 13–22; also in *Selected Prose*, ed. John Hayward (London, 1953), 21–30. Cf. Sean Lucy, *T. S. Eliot and the Idea of Tradition* (London, 1960).

6. *The Haggadah*, ed. Cecil Roth (London, 1934), 11–12, 36.

7. Babylonian Talmud, Menahot 29b.

8. Pirke Aboth, 5:25.

9. Martin Buber, "Der Preis," *Der Jude*, Oct. 1917.

10. Genesis Rabbah, Lek leka, 44:1; Leviticus Rabbah, Shemini, 13:3.

11. Jeremiah 7:4, 14.

12. Babylonian Talmud, Makkot 23b–24a.

13. Saadye Gaon, 395–97.

14. See Jacob B. Agus, *Banner of Jerusalem: Life, Times, and Thought of Abraham Isaac Kuk* (New York, 1946), 63, 82.

15. George Santayana, *The Life of Reason: Reason in Society* (New York, 1905), 174; "Apologia Pro Mente Sua," in *The Philosophy of George Santayana*, ed. P. A. Schilpp (Evanston, 1940), 572.

16. Genesis Rabbah, Bereshet, 24:7.

9. What Is Jewish Living?

1. Ezekiel 28:22.

2. Deuteronomy Rabbah, Re'eh 4:4.

3. Ralph Barton Perry, *Puritanism and Democracy* (New York, 1944), 38.

4. William James, *The Will to Believe* (New York, 1903), 61.

5. Ezekiel 36:23.

6. Martin Buber, *Hasidism* (New York, 1948), 32.

7. William James, *Memories and Studies* (New York, 1911), 204.

8. Jeremy Taylor, *The Rule and Exercise of Holy Living* (1650), ch. 1, sec. 2.

9. Quoted in Perry, *Puritanism*, 36.

10. Ibid., 60.

10. Chaim Grade's Quarrel

1. Chaim Grade, "My Quarrel with Hersh Rasseyner," trans. Milton Himmelfarb, in *A Treasury of Jewish Stories*, ed. Irving Howe and Eliezer Greenberg (New York, 1954), 579–606.

2. Erich Auerbach, *Mimesis* (New York, 1957), 3–5.

3. Eliot, *Selected Essays*, 13–22.

4. J. J. Weinberg, "The 'Mussar' Movement and Lithuanian Jewry," in *Men of the Spirit*, ed. Leo Jung (New York, 1964), 213ff. See also I. Etkes, *Rabbi Israel Salanter and the Mussar Movement* (Philadelphia, 1993).

5. Grade, "My Quarrel," 587.

6. Ibid., 587.

7. Plato, *Laws*, 942 A–B.

8. Maimonides, *Shemona Perakim*, ch. 8.

9. Babylonian Talmud, Yoma 67b.

10. Romans 2:13, 14.

11. Babylonian Talmud, Baba Bathra 16a.

12. Amos 9:17.

13. Genesis Rabbah 9:7.

11. Zionism
Homecoming or Homelessness?

1. Pirke Aboth 3:19.

2. Ibid., 1:14.

3. Genesis Rabbah 12:15.

4. Pirke Aboth 1:3.

5. Exodus 20:5; Ezekiel 18:4, 20.

6. Robert Louis Stevenson, "Requiem".

7. Tennyson, "The Lotus-Eaters."

8. Jeremiah 29:5–7.

12. Of Exile and Double Consciousness

1. John Woolman, *Journal*, ed. J. G. Whittier (London, 1871), 88.
2. Thomas Browne, quoted in Victor Gollancz, *Man and God* (Boston, 1951), 258–59.

13. Herman Melville Makes a Pilgrimage to the Holy Land

1. A. R. Humphreys, *Melville* (Edinburgh, 1962), 7.
2. Hershel Parker, ed., *The Recognition of Herman Melville* (Ann Arbor, Mich., 1967), viii.
3. Joseph Wood Krutch, *Thoreau* (New York, 1948), 103.
4. Quoted in Herman Melville, *Journal of a Visit to Europe and the Levant, October 11, 1856–May 6, 1857*, ed. Howard C. Horsford (Princeton, 1955), 6. Hereinafter this work will be referred to as *Journal*.
5. *Journal*, 23.
6. In 1935 Raymond Weaver edited Melville's journal for the first time, under the title *Journal up the Straits, October 11, 1856–May 5, 1857*; it was published by The Colophon in a limited edition and is difficult to obtain. The Horsford edition is the only one now used by Melville critics and scholars.
7. *Journal*, 16.
8. Ibid., 128.
9. Ibid., 130.
10. The review is reprinted in Parker, 4.
11. *Journal*, 156–57.
12. Ibid., 160–61.
13. Ibid., 158.
14. Ibid., 159.
15. Ibid., 137.
16. Ibid., 152.
17. Ibid., 153.
18. Ibid.
19. Ibid., 139.
20. Ibid., 140.
21. Ibid., 144.
22. Ibid., 142.
23. Ibid., 154.
24. Isaiah 62:10.
25. *Journal*, 154–55.
26. Ibid., 153.
27. Ibid., 145.
28. Ibid., 148–49.
29. Ibid., 150.
30. Ibid., 151.
31. Franklin Walker, *Irreverent Pilgrims: Melville, Browne, and Mark Twain in the Holy Land* (Seattle, 1974), 198. Other American literary men who were Melville's contemporaries and who toured Palestine and then published their accounts and impressions, besides Mark Twain, were Bayard Taylor, George William Curtis, William Cullen Bryant, J. W. DeForest, and Charles Dudley Warner. The most famous of the accounts is by Mark Twain, *Innocents Abroad* (1869). From 1850 to 1900 there were 131 American travelers to the Holy Land who published accounts of their experiences. See bibliogra-

phy by Y. Goell and M. B. Katz-Hyman in *With Eyes Toward Zion*, ed. Moshe Davis (New York, 1977), 100–125.

32. Walker, 133.

33. Herman Melville, *Clarel: A Poem and Pilgrimage in the Holy Land*, ed. Walter E. Bezanson (New York: 1960), xiii.

34. There was another edition published in England in 1924, also in two volumes. Both the first and the 1924 editions have long been out of print and copies are scarce.

35. Melville, *Clarel*, xxxviii.

36. Ibid.

37. Ibid., xli. For several reviews appearing in 1876, see Parker, 104–14.

38. Newton Arvin, *Herman Melville* (New York, 1950), 269, 271.

39. Ibid., 276.

40. Ecclesiastes 12:13, 14.

41. Melville, *Clarel*, end of Epilogue.

42. Arvin, 283–87.

43. Nathalia Wright, *Melville's Use of the Bible* (Durham, N.C., 1949), 8, 9, 10, 94.

44. Willard Thorp, *Herman Melville: Representative Selections* (New York, 1938), 389, 392.

45. Herman Melville, *Moby Dick*, (Norton Critical Edition,1967), ch. 96.

46. Ibid., ch. 17.

47. Ibid., ch. 9.

48. Robert Gordis, *Koheleth—The Man and His World* (New York, 1951), 118.

49. *The Code of Maimonides (Mishneh Torah), Book Three: The Book of Seasons*, trans. Solomon Gandz and Hyman Klein (New Haven, 1961), 452. Cf. Babylonian Talmud, Baba Bathra 60b.

50. Melville, *Moby Dick*, ch. 114; cf. *Pierre* (Signet Classic, 1964), bk. 4.

51. Cf. Samson Raphael Hirsch, *The Pentateuch: Deuteronomy* (London, 1962), 5:185, commentary on 11:13, concept of prayer.

52. Albert Camus, *The Myth of Sisyphus and Other Essays* (New York, 1959), 74–75.

53. Sophocles, *Antigone*, 450.

54. Ibid., 144.

55. Hegel, *On Tragedy*, ed. A. and H. Paolucci (New York, 1962), 73–74, 325.

56. Anouilh, *Antigone and Eurydice* (London, 1951), 58–59.

57. A. C. Bradley, "Hegel's Theory of Tragedy," *Oxford Lectures on Poetry* (London, 1950), reprinted in Hegel, 371.

58. H. D. F. Kitto, *Form and Meaning in Drama* (London, 1956), 155.

59. Hannah Arendt, *On Revolution* (New York, 1963), 78–79.

60. See note 5 above.

61. Ecclesiastes 12:13–14.

62. Melville, *Moby Dick*, ch. 96.

63. Herman Melville, *Hawthorne and His Mosses*, in *The Portable Melville*, ed. Jay Leyda (New York, 1952), 416.

64. Melville, *Moby Dick*, ch. 7. It was perhaps this faith, tenuously held, that motivated Melville to be a member or communicant of All Souls Unitarian Church in New York; but it was a faith grounded in doubt, yet maintained by hope. See W. D. Kring and J. S. Carey, "Two Discoveries Concerning Herman Melville," *Proceedings of the Massachusetts Historical Society* 87 (1976). I am grateful to my friend James Luther Adams for calling this article to my attention.

Index